TRANSNATIONAL KOREAN CINEMA

TRANSNATIONAL KOREAN CINEMA

Cultural Politics, Film Genres, and Digital Technologies

DAL YONG JIN

R

RUTGERS UNIVERSITY PRESS

New Brunswick, Camden, and Newark, New Jersey, and London

Library of Congress in Publication Control Number 2019006595
ISBN 978-1-9788-0789-1 (cloth)
ISBN 978-1-9788-0788-4 (paper)

A British Cataloging-in-Publication record for this book is available from the British Library.

∞ The paper used in this publication meets the requirements of the American National Standard for Information Sciences—Permanence of Paper for Printed Library Materials, ANSI Z39.48-1992.

www.rutgersuniversitypress.org

Manufactured in the United States of America

CONTENTS

PREFACE

Korean cinema has experienced a roller-coaster ride over the past several decades. Since the adoption of neoliberal cultural reforms by the military regimes of the 1980s, the Korean film industry's market share domestically and exports abroad have both plummeted. However, Korean cinema has recuperated since the mid-1990s. With the elimination of severe censorship and with financial support from democratic governments, Korean cinema has rapidly grown to become one of the most significant forms of culture in the early "Korean Wave"—the rapid growth of local cultural industries and sudden increase in the exportation of Korean popular culture that began in the late 1990s. It has since become the sixth-largest box office of the 2010s, and Hollywood continues to work with the Korean film industry and to invest in the Korean film market. These fluctuations have historically depended on shifting media environments surrounding the film industry, and several players have competed to control the domestic market—one that is seemingly small, yet significant.

As Korean cinema has rapidly changed, it is vital to learn about it. Several film scholars have produced interesting and valuable research, but in focusing on the analysis of film texts, they often only address the uniqueness of local films—which is commendable. However, these existing works somewhat miss several focal points. First, they do not concentrate on the history of Korean cinema, which is crucial to understanding the recent rise and fall of the Korean film industry. Second, there has been a lack of context in comprehending Korean cinema, meaning they did not emphasize the role of the socio-economic milieu surrounding the film industry. Third, they do not reflect on the significance of digital technologies and culture embedded in contemporary Korean cinema. Last but not least, as the majority of recently published books focus on the cultural aspects of domestic films, they do not emphasize the significance of the transnationalization of Korean cinema—in particular, in relation to Hollywood.

To fill the gap, I want to explore and historicize the major characteristics of Korean cinema in a socioeconomic and cultural politics context. Cultural policy and industry studies embrace broad areas embedded in cultural production and consumption; therefore, I do not want to treat them as isolated from cultural texts. Censorship, screen quotas, cultural diversity, and public funding have greatly shaped film content, encouraging me to look at Korean cinema from a historical, political-economy perspective. I also plan to map out the close interplay between local and global forces to analyze the power relationships between them, paying particular attention to the interactions at the nexus of the U.S. government, Hollywood studios, and local forces—which includes the complex relationship between the Korean government and the film industry. Since Korean cinema has been impacted by Hollywood, I analyze these transnational influences from the West in the production of local films, which have eventually resulted in the global sensation that is Korean film. However, I also attempt to determine whether Korean cinema stands as a meaningful cultural force in the global film market. Of course, I emphasize the historicization of Korean cinema by focusing on the analysis of film genres and the convergence of digital technologies and films through transnational storytelling.

This book is a continuation of my study on Korean cinema, which began in the early 2000s. The ideas in it originally appeared in a few academic publications, although I have extensively developed my ideas and debates to a new level in this book. This has been a long journey, and I really want to express my sincere gratitude to Rutgers University Press, who effectively dealt with the production process. My special thanks also go to a number of film scholars with whom I have talked about Korean cinema in this book, as well as their guidance, knowledge, and vision. Kyu Hyun Kim, Darcy Parquet, KwangWoo Noh, and Sangjoon Lee are some of the leaders in this field, and their insightful knowledge and thoughts have been very helpful.

TRANSNATIONAL KOREAN CINEMA

1 · THE EMERGENCE OF CONTEMPORARY KOREAN CINEMA

Korea has emerged as one of the major centers for the production of non-Western cinema since the mid-1990s. Korean cinema has rapidly become a global phenomenon among Western audiences as well as Asian ones in the early 21st century. Due to the swift growth of digital technologies, such as the internet and smartphones, as well as new platforms (e.g., Naver and Kakao), Korea's broadcasting industry has experienced a huge setback in terms of view rates and advertising revenue; however, Korean cinema has substantially risen in popularity as one of the oldest but most refreshing cultural activities.

Several dimensions, both national and global, point to the recent growth of Korean cinema. Domestically, the Korean film industry has achieved huge success in several fields, such as production and exhibition. The market share of domestic films was recorded at 63.8 percent in 2006—the highest in the modern era, compared to only 15.9 percent in 1993—and has continued to maintain at around 50 percent in the 2010s. The admission per capita in 2013 also reached 4.25, up from 1.1 in 1998 and 2.98 in 2005, surpassing the U.S.-Canada combined figure (4.0) for the first time in history to become the highest in the world (Korean Film Council 2008; 2014a; MPAA 2014). Based on the increasing numbers of moviegoers and domestic films produced, Korea has become one of the top film markets. It ranked 12th in 2001 when it reached $510 million in the box office, but in 2017, with its record high of $1.6 billion, it had risen to 6th, only beaten out by the U.S., China, Japan, the U.K., and India (PricewaterhouseCoopers 2006; MPAA 2017).

Globally, Korea started to play a discernable role in the film markets in the late 1990s. Korea has since continued to increase its export of domestic films to both Asian and Western countries, from only 208 films in 2006 to as many as 679 films in 2016 (Korean Film Council 2017a), especially after the regional success of the blockbuster film *Shiri* (1999), the first Korean movie to open nationwide in Japan in 2000, grossing almost $20 million. *Joint Security Area* (2000) also performed well and netted over $10 million in Japan (Schwarzacher 2002).

Later, some Korean films, such as Park Chan-wook's *Oldboy* (2004) and Kim Jee-woon's *A Tale of Two Sisters* (*Janghwa Honglyeon*, 2003), went on to achieve noticeable success in several countries, including the U.S. and France (S. Jung 2011). In 2014, *The Admiral: Roaring Currents*—the story of the real-life 1597 battle of Myeongnyang, when the Japanese invaded Korea—became the fastest-growing local film ever in the country (Busch 2014). The movie has been exported to several countries, including the U.S., Indonesia, Vietnam, and Thailand. A few major global cities—including New York, Paris, London, and Vancouver—screen Korean films regularly, which suggests the growth of Korean cinema in the global markets. Some international airlines, including Air Canada, also regularly select Korean movies like *The Admiral*, *Luck-Key* (2016), and *The Age of Shadows* (2016) as some of the highest-rated international films for the passengers.

Meanwhile, Korean cinema has achieved global fame at various film festivals. Several directors and actors have frequently received major awards from international festivals like the Cannes Film Festival and the Venice Film Festival. For example, Jeon Do-yeon received the award for best leading actress for her role in *Secret Sunshine*, directed by Lee Chang-dong, at Cannes in 2007 (Festival De Cannes 2007). *Thirst* (2009), directed by Park Chan-wook, won the Jury Prize at the 2009 Cannes Film Festival, and director Kim Ki-duk's *Pieta* won the Golden Lion at the 69th Venice Film Festival in 2012 (Shim 2012). More recently, actress Kim Min Hee received the Silver Bear for Best Actress at the 67th Berlin International Film Festival in February 2017 for her leading role in director Hong Sang Soo's *On the Beach at Night Alone*. Bong Joon-ho finally won the Palme d'Or at the Cannes film festival for his black comic–thriller *Parasite* in 2019. Director Gina Kim also won the Best VR Story Award for *Bloodless* at the 74th Venice International Film Festival in 2017.

KEY FEATURES IN KOREAN CINEMA

There are several key dimensions that have characterized contemporary Korean cinema: cultural policy, infrastructural growth, digital technologies, and changing consumption patterns of audiences, as well as transnational influences, including those of Hollywood.

To begin with, the Korean government has maintained policies in line with neoliberal globalization since the late 1980s, and its cultural policies have substantially changed the nature of Korean cinema. Instead of reducing its role, the Korean government has interestingly initiated development in the domestic film industry over the past two decades, resulting in swift and steady growth. Of course, some cultural policies have negatively influenced the Korean film industry. For example, the Korean government changed the screen quota system to facilitate a free trade agreement (FTA) with the U.S. government–supported Hollywood majors in 2006, which triggered a setback for local films in the latter part of the 2000s. Thus the Korean government has sometimes developed policy measures to boost up the Korean film industry but at other times has taken a neoliberal turn that inconvenienced the film sector, which shows the contradictory nature of the role of the nation-state.

Second, Korean cinema has experienced a surge in the popularity of domestic films, marked by a significant increase in audience viewership figures, because of screen monopoly and oligopoly (hereafter *screen oligopoly*; see chapter 4, note 1). These are phenomena in which a few powerful film distributors influence overall box-office outcomes by screening a few commercial films on the majority of screens so that other films cannot find screens or are screened in a limited number of places. Several blockbuster movies—such as *The Host* (2006), *Masquerade* (2012), and *The Thieves* (2012)—recorded huge successes, with 10 million viewers each, partially because of screen oligopoly. When the 2014 movie *The Admiral: Roaring Currents* was released, Koreans rushed headlong into theaters, resulting in an all-time high audience of 17.6 million—35.1 percent of Koreans (Korean Film Council 2014b). In one of the more recent examples, during the release of *The Battleship Island* (2017)—a Japanese occupation–era historical action movie based on the true story of when, toward the end of World War II, hundreds of Koreans attempted to escape forced labor on the Japanese island of Hashima—it screened on more than 2,000 of the 2,575 screens nationwide. Hollywood films have also strongly occupied Korean theaters in the 2010s due to loosened screen quotas, and in April 2018, *Avengers: Infinity War* was shown on a record-breaking 2,553 screens (Korean Film Council 2018a)

This new trend has been controversial, however. As selected blockbuster movies are being shown on the majority of screens and attract moviegoers, low-budget movies created by independent filmmakers cannot establish a tangible presence. While some blockbuster movies have been shown on more than 1,500 screens all over the country, low-budget movies, including art house films, have difficulty finding screens, resulting in dismal failures. This is to be expected, as a handful of large, vertically integrated film distributors control the entire Korean film industry, from production to exhibition.

Third, the Korean film industry has developed new production models in the era of digital media. They are not only utilizing digital technologies, such as cameras and audio systems adapted from Hollywood's—for example, Korea's first-ever 3D film (*The Song of the String*, 2010) employed the U.S. photography system of 3ality (A. Park 2010). They are also developing new forms of film through the convergence of movies with webtoons (web comics) and mobile and digital games. Many film producers have created films based on these kinds of digital content, and therefore, many screenwriters are using transmedia storytelling, "a process where integral elements of a fiction get dispersed systematically across multiple delivery channels for the purpose of creating a unified and coordinated entertainment experience" (Jenkins 2011). These shifts show that the historical evolution of the Korean film industry must be understood based on the characteristics it developed in the early 21st century.

Last but not least, the Korean film market has been transformed by its relationship with transnational forces, including Hollywood. Two contrasting opinions have emerged regarding the transnationalization of Korean cinema in recent years. Some scholars, including Jimmyn Parc (2016) and Patrick Messerlin with Parc (2017a; 2017b), argue that Korean cinema has effectively resisted transnational influences, and they claim that screen quotas and subsidies have not tangibly contributed to the growth of Korean cinema. For example, Parc (2016, 13) argues, "The core element of Korea's success is the role of business in the dynamic business environment. Large enterprises, such as chaebols, are particularly interesting since their activities affect the final result of policies regardless of the initial aims. These large companies brought huge investment into the Korean film industry and have successfully challenged the Hollywood blockbusters, despite the screen quota cut and other changes in the business environment. Their proactive responses to maximize benefits in a context of domestic and international changes have tended to deliver competitive cultural products in the end." Kyung Hyun Kim (2017, 207) also claims that the Korean film industry "protects its domestic production with an overwhelming majority of the audiences voluntarily choosing to watch local products over Hollywood's" while exporting its films throughout the world. Even popular magazines like *Newsweek* have reported that, based on the growth of the Korean film industry between the late 1990s and the early 21st century, "Hollywood no longer rules South Korean cinema, which is breaking out all over" (Russell and Wehrfritz 2004).

However, Hollywood has maintained global dominance around the world, and in particular, it has deeply influenced Korean cinema in several ways. As Korea rapidly adopted neoliberal globalization policies, Hollywood penetrated the Korean film market through direct distribution rights, the reduction of screen quotas, and screen oligopoly. Since the late 1980s, Hollywood has not only impacted the Korean film market but also lived in Korea as part of its local scene, as its genres and themes have been embedded in contemporary domestic films. As foreign exports for local films have shifted so that profits are not guaranteed, foreign films, including commercial movies from Hollywood majors, are again becoming a major part of Korean cinema. A collapse in export revenues (rather than the number of films exported), along with "widespread losses at the box office, and the bursting of a film financing bubble" led many in the domestic film industry to "declare a crisis" (Paquet 2011, 18). At the height of Korean films' global popularity, local film producers and distribution companies were optimistic that they would become a stable icon of a non-Western film industry with worldwide reach (D. Y. Jin 2016, 71). However, this has not come to pass. In recent years, Korean cinema has been giving rise to several "cycles of downturn and recovery . . . creating a degree of uncertainty and instability" (Yecies and Shim 2016, 4).

The Korean film industry has always fluctuated whenever foreign forces, including Hollywood, expand their control of Korean cinema. This means that its rise and fall has closely, but in a complex way, related to transnational forces, including also Japan and China. The nature of Korean cinema—in particular, its relationship with Hollywood—asks us to carefully review and analyze the Korean film industry from various diverse perspectives.

MAJOR GOALS OF THE BOOK

The major goal of this book is to investigate the contemporary Korean film industry. It explores and historicizes the contemporary characteristics of Korean cinema in a socioeconomic and cultural politics context. It begins with the analysis of state cultural policy and its impact on Korean films within the broader social structure of society, as "cultural policy embraces that broad field of public processes involved in formulating, implementing, and contesting governmental intervention in, and support of, cultural activity" (Cunningham 2008, 14).

This book does not treat cultural policy as an isolated element. Instead, it mainly investigates the close interplay between local forces, such as the Korean government and film industry, and global forces, including the U.S. government and Hollywood, and therefore the power relationships between them. It asks what the roles of national politics and policy formulation are in the structure of the relationship between foreign forces and domestic forces in the growth of a national film industry. Given that changing cultural policies in conjunction with the economic and historical particularities of the region have played a pivotal role in Korean cinema, I attempt to examine the most significant yet least discussed factor in the development of the Korean film industry and film culture: the role of the Korean government.

This book also examines the rapidly changing domestic film industry and the roles played by the government and domestic producers. The political-economic approach to the study of films focuses on analyzing cultural industries, so I especially address the economic and industrial aspects of the story, explore questions related to the interaction of politics and economics, and articulate the relations among film industries, global markets, and governments to provide a better view of the big picture. In addition, the political economy approach encourages concentrating on technology, given technology is imperative to all stages of marketing culture, and so I emphasize the role of digital media—in particular, transmedia storytelling. This book critically and historically contextualizes the nascent development of Korean cinema as influenced by both neoliberal globalization and new digital technologies.

Most of all, since cultural policies in the era of transnationalism have significantly influenced the local film industry, I look at the operations and globalization strategies of the Korean film industry alongside changing cultural politics. *Cultural politics* in this book refers to the way that cultural policies, including censorship, screen quotas, cultural diversity, and public funding shape film content. The term also implies the interplay between Korean cinema and transnational forces, as conflicts embedded in these two forces have greatly influenced the transformation of both the film industry and content. As cultural politics is the political ramification of local cultural production and consumption in tandem with transnational forces, including Hollywood's continued influence, it is critical to comprehend these power relations, both national and global.

In other words, the book not only emphasizes the role of Korean cultural politics, emphasizing domestic socioeconomic milieu, but also pays attention to the interaction between global forces (mostly the U.S. government and Hollywood studios, which have fervently worked to expand their global hegemony) and local forces (the complex relationship of the Korean government with the film industry), which not only resist but also accommodate foreign expansionism and commercialism. Furthermore, since several neighboring countries—in particular, China—have closely worked with Korean cinema, this book attempts to understand the increasing role of the Chinese film market (e.g., through coproduction) as one of the most recent and potentially most forceful transnational forces.

Lastly, in the context of growing global interest in local popular culture—the *Hallyu*, or "Korean Wave," phenomenon—I interrogate the transnational globalization of domestic cinema not only through its export but also through its utilization of Western culture in its production. Since many Koreans and cultural producers have been influenced by Hollywood, it is logical to analyze this influence, which eventually resulted in the global sensation of Korean films. However, my goal is not only to analyze Korean cinema, which has been influenced by Hollywood, but also to attempt to understanding whether Korean cinema is able to play as a meaningful transnational culture force in the global film markets.

A TRANSNATIONAL CULTURAL RETURN IN KOREAN CINEMA

The rise and fall of Korean cinema in recent decades has been in large part due to neoliberal globalization imposed by the U.S. government and Hollywood major studios. The domestic cultural system in many countries, as part of the global communication system, has become increasingly transnational, as several media scholars (McChesney and Schiller 2002; Miller and Maxwell 2006; Pendakur 2013) have argued.

In the field of culture, neoliberal globalization emphasizes a reduction in government intervention in cultural production, which opens domestic cultural markets and privatizes public sectors, such as the telecommunications and broadcasting industries. This has resulted in the transnationalization of domestic industries, including the film industry. Starting in the late 1980s, transnational cultural industries—in particular, Hollywood majors—penetrated Korean cultural markets with their capital and cultural products and become prominent players in the country.

Transnationalization is closely related to globalization; it refers to "a condition by which people, commodities, and ideas cross national boundaries and are not identified with a single place of origin" (Watson 1997, 11). With the rapid growth of new media technologies, the notion of transnationalism draws attention to the ways in which "the intensifying scale and speed of the transnational flow of people, capital, and media has disregarded, though not entirely, the efficacy of demarcated national boundaries and ideologies" (Iwabuchi 2002, 52). Therefore, transnational globalization can be identified as a set of systems that are not shaped by specific national interests and standards and that operate globally, and it especially "pressures nation states to adapt to the expectations and requirements of transnational actors and systems" (Schirm 1996, 12–13).

Limiting our discussion to film studies, the transnational designates "spaces and practices acted upon by border-crossing agents, be they dominant or marginal" (Lionner and Shih 2005, 5); it indicates cross-cultural cinematic connections (Chan 2009; Kokas 2017). Of course, the transnational flow of films and connections in cinema is nothing new, which means that "the movement of films and filmmakers across national borders and the reception of films by local audiences outside of their indigenous sites of production" have been common since the 1990s—and even earlier (Higbee and Lim 2010, 9). Due to diasporas of filmmakers, actors, and moviegoers—mainly from the local to the global (e.g., Hollywood) but also vice versa—transnationalism has become one of the major topics in film studies in the early 21st century.

As a reflection of these developments, several previous works in transnationalism studies have emphasized two distinctive perspectives. One viewpoint is focused on the celebratory achievement of local films in global markets through the migration of domestic players to the Western film industry (e.g., local directors and actors like Ang Lee, Jackie Chan, and Lee Byung-hun) and through Hollywood remakes of local films (e.g., Shall We Dance, The Ring, and My Sassy Girl). The other perspective studies mutual interactions between local and global forces through coproductions and collaborations. As Dong Hoon Kim (2009, 5–6) points out, Hollywood remakes of East Asian films, global film coproductions, and the popularity of Korean cultural products, including films, have received considerable attention from film scholars who triumph the trend because it "represent[s] not only the intensified travels of East Asian films across the globe but also a reversal of the presumed flow of influence from Hollywood to other national cinemas."

What is significant, however, is that the transnational globalization process is not politically, economically, culturally, and technologically equal, and the issue of imbalances of power in production, distribution, and exhibition between the local and the global needs to be carefully analyzed. The transnational cannot be simply used to indicate international coproduction or collaboration, as well as flow of films, without any real consideration of what the political, economic, and cultural implications of such transnational alliance might mean (Higbee and Lim 2010). The perspectives mentioned above in the East Asian cinema context "is problematic as it disregards the complex histories of the transnational dissemination of cultural across nations, regions, and empires" (D. H. Kim 2005, 6). In the study of films, a critical transnationalism should interrogate "how filmmaking activities negotiate with the national on all levels from cultural policy to financial sources, from multiculturalism of difference to how it reconfigures the nation's image of itself." In theory, "it scrutinizes the tensions and dialogic relationship between national and transnational, rather than simply negating one in favor of the other" (Higbee and Lim 2010, 18).

Therefore, it is crucial to comprehend and analyze the historical influences of transnational forces, particularly that of Hollywood in the local film industry and film genres. Since examining all forms of cross-border filmmaking activities asks us to focus on not only cultural flows but also politics and power, and because of the ways in which these dimensions uncover new forms of imperialist practices in the guise of film genres and themes, we need to examine the tensions and power relationships between national and transnational forces within the broader context of global cultural scenes. This means that it is critical to historically determine the role of local-based transnational forces—both the government and the film industry—as well as global forces.

On the one hand, the Korean film industry has been substantially influenced by the U.S. government and Hollywood majors in production, distribution, and exhibition. Neoliberalism picked up momentum in the 1990s, and it has become "a powerful storm reshaping the global political economy" in the interest of capital and culture (Pendakur 2013, 125). Korea witnessed massive foreign inroads at this time (in particular, from Hollywood) and, thereafter, the transnationalization of the film industry. As the BBC reported in 2014,

Hollywood is like an octopus with tentacles extending across the globe. For decades, most of its sustenance came from domestic ticket sales within the United States but in recent years, overseas markets, particularly China and Russia, have become increasingly important. . . . Almost 70% of the studios' annual revenue from box office now comes from international markets. Speak to anyone in the film industry in Los Angeles and they will tell you that the growth in global box office is bringing about fundamental change in Hollywood. . . . In fact, the Hollywood studio staple has for a while been the big budget extravaganza that will sell overseas. Content has been shaped accordingly. . . . They're making films that have fairly universal ideas and themes, they're not really culturally specific. A good example might be the recently released action film "Fast & Furious 6" which has already hauled in almost twice as much revenue overseas as it has in the U.S. (Brook 2014)

On the other hand, domestic forces such as the Korean government and domestic film producers still play significant roles in both the formation of cultural policy and the film business, including production and exhibition, to (even just partially) protect cultural sovereignty. The Korean government in particular has developed mechanisms to support Korean cinema even though it has continued to pursue neoliberal cultural reforms. While the consecutive administrations since the late 1980s embraced the neoliberal globalization trend, they also developed cultural policy measures to resuscitate the dying film industry. Korea's cultural policy makers applied globalization logic to the film industry not only by opening up the market but also by integrating the film business into the global film markets (G. J. Han 1994, 156–157). Although transnational cultural industries, including the Hollywood majors, have provided investments and films for the Korean film market, "national and regional processes have also substantially influenced cultural policies. The government can block, mediate and, in some cases, even reverse neoliberal tendencies. That is, in the era of neoliberal globalization, characterized by market deregulation and reduced state intervention in economic and cultural affairs, the Korean government pursued a proactive cultural policy" (D. Y. Jin 2006, 18–19).

What we have to emphasize is that the transnationalization of Korean cinema—mainly transnational influences on the local film industry but also, increasingly, the role of Korean cinema in global markets as a local-based transnational force (compared to one that is Hollywood based)—should be understood by focusing on the interactions between foreign- and domestic-based transnational forces. Since the growth of local popular culture in the forms of cultural texts, capital, and industrial systems (e.g., coproduction) is the result of the interplay between the national and the transnational, it is necessary to interpret the transnationality of the Korean film industry in the realm of local films.

METHODOLOGICAL FRAMEWORKS OF THE BOOK

This book analyzes contemporary Korean cinema by employing a critical political economy perspective as an analytical strategy and conceptual framework to evaluate the consequences of increasing cooperation between Hollywood film studios and the Korean film industry. The primary objective of the movie industry under capitalism is market dominance through cooperation and concentration; therefore, it is important to investigate the political and economic repercussions of the interplays between these global entertainment industries (Rasul and Proffitt 2012).

The critical political economy of communication examines the nature of the relationship between media/communication systems and the broader social structure of society. As Dan Schiller (1996, vii) points out, the study of communication is not only concerned with the contributions of a restricted set of media: "The potential of communication study, in short, has converged directly and at many points with analysis and critique of existing society across its span." Robert McChesney (2000, 110) emphasizes that "the political economy of communication looks at how ownership, support mechanisms such as advertising, and government policies influence media behavior and content." Meanwhile, Vincent Mosco (1996, 25) defines the political economy of communication as "the study of the social relations that mutually constitute the production, distribution, and consumption of communication resources, such as newspapers, videos, films, and audiences."

In regard to the film sector, Janet Wasko (2004) argues that political economy facilitates the understanding of production, distribution, and consumption patterns of media products. In comparing political economy with media economics, Wasko et al. (2011, 3–4) point out, "Media economics avoids political and historical analysis, both fundamental components of the critical study of political economy. Importantly, media economics mostly accepts the status quo, whereas political economy represents a critical orientation to the study of the media, challenging unjust and inequitable systems of power." In film studies, therefore, political economy research has been crucial, mainly because "the interaction of political and economic considerations is pivotal not only in giving cultural and economic regulation of the cinema its characteristic shape in film classification and urban zoning of cinema, but also in informing cultural and industry policies such as incentives for the production of films and even the building of cinemas. The combination of politics and economics is also writ large in the actions of media corporations and industry associations and agencies—especially Hollywood majors and the MPAA—in securing friendly operating conditions both at home and abroad for their operations" (O'Regan 2008, 244; see also Guback 1969; Miller et al. 2005; Pendakur 1990).

Meanwhile, in terms of methodological frameworks, much previous scholarly analysis and discourse about Korean cinema (e.g., Hyangjin Lee 2000; Shin and Stringer 2005; Kyu Hyun Kim 2011; Chung and Diffrient 2015; An 2018) has focused on the cultural aspects of local popular culture, such as identities among audiences and changing lifestyles, by employing either textual analysis or audience studies. As one of the most recent books on Korean cinema, for example, Hye Seung Chung and David Diffrient (2015) examine global genre transformation and the concept of cross-cultural intertextuality through analyses of Korean melodramas, literary adaptations comedies, and westerns. After textually and historically analyzing domestic films, Youngmin Choe (2016) also identifies several key characteristics and delves into the ways in which Hallyu cinema inspired both domestic and global tourists to visit movie sets, filming sites, and theme parks developed for and inspired by these motion pictures. In fact, the majority of studies on Korean cinema have been rooted in cultural studies and cultural anthropology and have taken to textual analysis with a focus on case studies and a strong tendency to prioritize analysis of textual content and images used in domestic films (see Abelmann 2003).

Of course, there have been a few attempts (J. H. Choi 2010; Yecies and Shim 2016) to explore the emergence of Korean cinema from industrial and historical perspectives. Jinhee Choi (2010) provides both an industrial and an aesthetic account of how the Korean film industry managed to turn an economic crisis into a fiscal and cultural boom. She examines how Korean film production companies, backed by affluent corporations and venture capitalists, concocted a variety of winning production trends. Through close analyses of key films, she demonstrates how contemporary Korean cinema portrays issues immediate to its own Korean audiences while incorporating the transnational aesthetics of Hollywood and other national cinemas. By utilizing various approaches, including archival research and historical and textual analyses, Brian Yecies and Aegyung Shim (2016) examine the dynamic ways in which Korean cinema has undergone a transformation between 1960 and 2015. As these works exemplify, many film scholars have analyzed the specificities of Korean cinema drawing upon major paradigms of film theory and criticism, including film genres, aesthetics, postcolonialism, and migration. However, none of them have focused on the local film industry and policy through the lens of critical political economy.

What is crucial in this regard is that we should understand that popular culture is no longer a discrete and distinct sector. All its circuits, technology, texts, and cultural policy have become intertwined with the wider orbits of digital networks, becoming critical zones for growth and profits (Kline et al. 2003). Cultural products, including films, must be defined based on specific combinations of sociocultural, political, and economic as well as technical characteristics, not exclusively on any of these ones (D. Y. Jin 2016, 11). Unlike previous works that primarily examined film texts and directors from cultural studies perspectives, this book focuses on not only the celebratory achievement of local film culture through the analysis of film texts but also the significance of social milieu in the growth of Korean cinema. It therefore examines the Korean film industry through the convergence of two methodological frameworks: political economy and textural analysis, differentiating this book from previous works that have been mainly focused on various cultural studies approaches.

On the one hand, I utilize political economy by means of historical and institutional analyses, which are useful to ascertain the causes and major players behind the changing process of the Korean film business. While emphasizing the historical documentation of the growth of Korean cinema, I examine the roles that are played by national politics and policy formulation and the structure of the relationship between foreign forces and domestic forces in the growth of the Korean film industry. On the other hand, I analyze film texts produced in Korea between 1971 and 2016 by selecting the 10 highest-grossing films of each year and interpreting film genres and themes as two of the most important features for determining the major characteristics of films. In other words, I evaluate 460 films, from the dark age of Korean film to the recent boom period, bye textually analyzing some exemplary films from the same period. I historically investigate not only the major characteristics of Korean cinema but also Hollywood's influence over local film content. In addition, I conducted a number of intensive interviews with film experts—including film directors, film scholars, and film critics—between the fall of 2017 and the spring of 2018. Although the number of interviewees is not high, they are people who have for a long time witnessed the rise and fall of contemporary Korean cinema, and their expertise certainly provides meaningful perspectives that we can rely on.

To summarize, I employ political economy methods in combination with partial textual analysis and interviews to strengthen the book's analytical framework. This converging approach allows for an in-depth examination that does not lean on a limited interpretation of Korean cinema. In other words, through the examination of the local film industry in light of its sociocultural elements and political-economic contingencies, I hope to illuminate some of the underexamined complexities inherent in the development, implementation, and reception of Korean cinema in a global arena.

ORGANIZATION OF THE STUDY

The study is organized as follows. In chapter 2, I investigate the changing role of the nation-state in the context of the broader social structure of society amid neoliberal globalization with a case of the film industry. It attempts to clarify the cause of the changes and goes on to discuss the Korean film industry with a special focus on state cultural policy. It discusses how neoliberal ideologies embedded in the influence of Hollywood, the most significant and largest foreign force in the Korean film market, have not completely altered the leading role of the nation-state in Korean cinema (despite the dominance of neoliberal turns emphasizing a small government in economy and culture). It also addresses the major characteristics of censorship in contemporary Korean cinema.

Chapter 3 explores the contextualization between the film industry and government cultural policies in association with screen quotas in the era of FTAs. It examines the historical set of social relations and the balance of power between the U.S. and Korea, as well as between the commercial interests of Hollywood and the critical political ideology of the Korean film industry. It analyses whether the U.S., supporting and lobbying for Hollywood, has hampered cultural diversity and sovereignty in Korea, given that a prerequisite of the Korea-U.S. FTA was that Korea change its screen quotas. It articulates the consequences of FTAs in the realm of culture in Korea in order to determine their crucial influence on domestic film and cultural markets.

In chapter 4, I investigate the structural change in contemporary Korean cinema, with a special focus on market structure. I discuss the recent growth of the monopolistic market structure, with not only local films but also Hollywood films, in order to determine the increasing role of foreign forces in the exhibition sector as well. I examine the causes of the structural turn toward screen oligopoly as well as the oligopolistic distribution system in the Korean film industry in order to investigate the major reasons for the monopolistic market structure in Korean cinema and its impact on cultural diversity.

Chapter 5 investigates the Korean film industry with a special focus on the state public film fund. It explores the major reasons for the development of the public film fund and its impacts on Korean cinema. It in particular maps out the ways in which the Korean government has developed the public film fund in the era of neoliberal globalization to offset the effects of the 2006 screen quota reduction. It finally discusses the impact of these changing policies on the film business by examining the influx of foreign capital—a strategic form of transnationalization in the realm of culture—especially from Hollywood and China.

In chapter 6, I analyze the several major reasons the Korean film industry has pursued coproduction. This chapter examines coproduction as one of the most important transnational strategies in Korean cinema. It articulates why Korean cinema has started to pursue coproductions not only with other countries in the same region but also with those in the West—in particular, with U.S. corporations.

Chapter 7 examines Korean films between 1971 and 2016 in terms of movie genres. By analyzing 460 movies, it examines the swift changes experienced by the Korean film industry, the fluctuating patterns of film genres, and the major reasons for these shifts (particularly cultural policies and Hollywood's influence). It analyzes the nature of hybridity in terms of genre-bending by investigating whether such fusions have created new cultures, distinct from that of Hollywood. It also discusses whether such genre-bending has been uniquely developed by local films or influenced by Hollywood formulas.

Chapter 8 historicizes the evolution of Korean film in relation to the surrounding digital media ecology, which has driven change and continuity in the *manhwa* (comic book), and now webtoon, industries over the past 15 years. By employing as a theoretical framework the concept of media convergence, supported by transmedia storytelling, it analyzes the crucial elements that have characterized the emergence of the contemporary film industry and the ways in which film has managed to become one of Korea's signature forms of popular culture. It then maps out whether films utilizing transmedia storytelling are the primary products in global cultural markets in the 2010s.

In Chapter 9, after summarizing the major characteristics of Korean cinema, I discuss what Korean cinema needs to develop as a localized film industry, even as the industry itself is rapidly becoming part of the transnational global film market.

2 · STATE FILM POLICY AND THE POLITICIZATION OF CENSORSHIP

Korean cinema has undergone tumultuous changes over the past several decades. Since the inception of the Korean film industry in the early 20th century, the Korean government has shifted its cultural policies, resulting in both continuity and change for the local film industry. Korean cinema has been closely influenced by each administration's political direction: sometimes the government—in particular, the authoritarian regimes—introduced measures to control Korean cinema through severe censorship and regulations (as in other cultural and media sectors, such as television and newspapers); at other times, the government encouraged growth by providing financial subsidies for the film industry.

Korean cinema has especially changed its structure and content since the late 1980s, when the government adopted neoliberal cultural reforms both proactively and under U.S. coercion. The Park Chung Hee regime (1961–1979) had already introduced a Hollywood studio system. However, in the late 1980s, the Korean government and the film industry began to develop unique relationships with the U.S. government and Hollywood. After the Korean government enacted neoliberal cultural reforms, emphasizing market deregulation and reduced state intervention into cultural affairs, the Korean film industry lost ground while Hollywood majors became primary actors in Korean cinema. These Hollywood studios and distributors have continued to play significant roles in developing the complex terrain on which the Korean film industry advances.

Of course, the Korean government has not entirely given up its role in the film sector, as it feels a need to protect Korean cinema from Hollywood. The Korean government has resisted Hollywood's hegemony and sustained control of the Korean film market through film policies, including both subsidies and legal forces (e.g., screen quotas). Therefore, while acknowledging the significant role of Hollywood in the local film industry, it is critical to recognize the increasing intervention and substantial influence of the Korean government in the growth of Korean cinema.

This chapter investigates the changing role of the nation-state in the context of the broader social structure of society amid neoliberal globalization, using the film industry as a case study. It documents several major policy shifts in the government's treatment of the film industry between the authoritarian regimes and the democratic governments of the early 1990s. I will discuss the ways in which Hollywood's cultural politics has affected local film policies and industries while analyzing the impact of neoliberal cultural policies on the transnationalization of the Korean film industry. Finally, I will map shifts in film censorship, one of the major cultural policy issues that will determine whether contemporary Korean cinema achieves freedom of expression and diversity.

HOLLYWOOD'S EARLY PRESENCE IN KOREAN CINEMA, 1945 TO THE 1960S

The Korean film industry has had a long history. Its first movie, *Fight for Justice* (*Uilijeog guto*) screened at Dansungsa, Korea's first theater, on October 27, 1919 (KMPPC 1977; Ho 2003).[1] This film was "a hybrid film used as a short vignette for backstage imagery in theatrical stage productions. Then, in 1922, Korea witnessed the release of the first commercial feature film, *Ch'unhyangjŏn*, which was based on popular folklore" (An 2018, 5). Hollywood's impact on Korean cinema goes back to 1945, when American influence replaced Japan's after the liberation of Korea from Japanese occupation.[2] This initial guidance from 1945 through the 1960s came with several major shifts, including cultural policies and broadcasting programs, as well as growing film sales.

To begin with, the U.S. government controlled Korean cinema through the United States Information Service (USIS), which was responsible for the planning and implementation of propaganda and cultural activities. Several local film directors and producers learned necessary film skills from the USIS film division, which also equipped them with cutting-edge equipment (Mee Hyun Kim 2014).[3] American films distributed by the Central Motion Picture Exchange (CMPE), located in Japan, indeed dominated Korean cinema after liberation. The CMPE had "a monopoly on exporting and distributing American films from the eight major U.S. film companies" (Kim and An 2010, 107). Hollywood started to impact Korean cinema in all areas—production, distribution, and exhibition, one after another.

With more than 100 American films being screened annually in Korean movie theaters, American films had more than 50 percent of the local film market. This was unavoidable given that there were only 61 Korean films made in the first five years after the liberation—4 in 1946, 13 in 1947, 22 in 1948, 20 in 1949, and 2 in the first half of 1950 (KMPPC 1977). Box-office revenues generated by domestic films were increasingly undermined by the rising popularity of foreign films—predominantly from Hollywood (Yecies and Shim 2016, 108). As Miller et al. (2005, 296) point out, "Hollywood realized early on that its dominance of the world market depended on owning the means of distribution," and Hollywood's hegemony in Korea started with distribution rights, as can be seen in the role of the USIS, the CMPE, and later, direct distribution by Hollywood studios. From this early stage in the 1940s, the U.S. began to strongly influence Korean cinema, while Hollywood was developing its unique form of dominance.

American movies in Korea also directly related to the growth of the broadcasting system in the 1950s and the 1960s. The broadcasting system in Korea in the 1950s was in its infancy. The first and only private television broadcasting company, HLKZ-TV was established as a commercial television station in Seoul on May 12, 1956, and came on the air with the aid of an equipment contract with the Radio Corporation of America (RCA; Kang and Kim 1994, 109–110). The second television broadcasting network in Korea, the American Forces Korea Network, was established by the U.S. in 1957. AFKN was an affiliate of the American Forces Radio and Television Service, with a target audience of 60,000 U.S. military personnel, civilian employees, and their dependents (Kim et al. 1994, 49). The U.S. military television network became the only television center for a brief period of time, between the late 1950s and the early 1960s, until Korean television broadcasting took root. The U.S. Army network played a key role as an outlet for releasing U.S. television programs and films to Korean broadcasters in the 1960s. At that time, AFKN had fully utilized an American film package prepared in the United States and programs from various networks. AFKN then sold those films and programs to one of the two Korean networks, KBS and TBC, which were established in 1964 (Markey 1965, 39, 49; D. Y. Jin 2011a).

Throughout the early 1960s, Korea's television program production capabilities were underdeveloped, and "a number of programs were imported from foreign countries, mostly the U.S. Foreign programs, including programs bought from AFKN, accounted for about 30% of all programming in KBS, and they were mainly foreign movie and drama series" (Nam 1978, 44). American films were the most popular, especially westerns and situation comedies. Handout films from American embassies, including propaganda films, were also used (Markey 1965).

As such, in the initial stage of the development of Korean communication industries, American cultural industries, both broadcasting and film, greatly influenced local activity through several institutional channels. Hollywood films were among the most influential due in large part to America's political dominance over Korea from 1945 to the early 1960s. In this initial stage of Korean cinema,

Hollywood was already leaving deep footprints in Korea with its commercial model, which guided the future of the Korean film industry. Consequently, the Korean film industry had to develop its films amid interplay with the U.S. government and Hollywood over the next several decades.

THE GOLDEN AGE OF KOREAN CINEMA AND HOLLYWOOD'S STUDIO SYSTEM

The Korean film industry enjoyed its golden age, in terms of the number of films domestically produced, between the late 1950s and the late 1960s. Immediately after the Korean War (1950–1953), the country produced few films of its own; as explained above, Korea had to import American films for its broadcasting system. Korean cinema gradually developed a local film industry starting in the mid-1950s. During this period, the number of annual productions increased from 15 in 1955, to 111 in 1959, to 229 in 1969. The market share of domestic films was also stable, in the upper 40 percent to the lower 50 percent range each year (KMPPC 1977; Korean Film Commission Research Report 2001, 11–12). When Korea produced 229 films in 1969, it was already the second largest industry in Asia, only behind Japan. Among these, "Korean cinema created melodramas—70–80% each year—which have been the most significant film genre since then. In the 1960s, the major movie audiences were women in their 30s and 40s" (Ho 2003, 184). This was a high point for Korean cinema, "with theater attendance peaking at 173 million in 1969" (Mee Hyun Kim 2013, 78).

The golden era of Korean cinema was made possible partially due to oppressive government film policy, which ironically also caused the demise of the local film industry in the 1970s. In 1961, the Korean government asked the film industry to voluntarily integrate to reduce the number of production companies from 71 to 16, and in 1962, the Park Chung Hee regime enacted the Motion Picture Law (MPL), which allowed fewer than 20 registered film producers to produce motion pictures (until 1984; Korean Film Commission Research Report 2001, 11; Mee Hyun Kim 2013). It also allowed only motion picture producers to import foreign films, which meant that only about 20 registered film producers could do so. The government considered the film business an industry due to its popularity as an entertainment tool, and it wanted to put the business under the government's control while reducing the number of small- to medium-sized film producers (Korean Film Commission Research Report 2001, 11; D. Y. Jin 2011a). The MPL also introduced a registration system for film producers (the Producer Registration System) as well as one for importers and exporters.

The first revision to the MPL in 1963 required all film producers with 35-millimeter movie cameras and more than 661 square meters of studio space to register as film producers, and it explicitly required those who made over 15 motion pictures every year to maintain their companies' statuses as film producers (article 3). Since the majority of film producers could not make 15 movies per year, the Park regime changed it to 2 films per year in the second revision of the same law in 1966. Nevertheless, annual production reached 14.7 films on average per company in 1964 (J. Y. Park 2005).

Though the MPL supported the film industry, resulting in the golden period of Korean cinema, the government's control over the film business gradually became a hurdle, impeding the industry's development (Rousse-Marquet 2013). Because local film productions were controlled by around 20 registered producers until the early 1980s, many film producers—in particular, independent producers—did not thrive; their creativity could not develop under this oppressive cultural policy.

In particular, in 1972, the Park Chung Hee regime revised the MLP a fourth time, making the registration system a permissions system (article 4). Thus only several companies permitted by the government could produce films. The Park regime's industrialization agenda in the film industry also implied the adaptation of the Hollywood studio system: only a few film companies registered as producers, attempting to replicate Hollywood's vertical integration system (Byon, cited in Yecies and Shim 2016). In addition, "the Park government executed severe censorship on films by censoring films twice before and after production" (Mee Hyun Kim 2013, 16). Consequently, the golden era of Korean cinema eventually ended.

Furthermore, the Park regime enacted the Yusin Constitution (adopted in October 1972), which monopolized all government power under him and his Democratic Republican Party through the highly centralized, authoritarian Yusin System. The Yusin System also severely controlled the entertainment industries, including the film industry, to block any criticism of the Yusin System. Under these circumstances, Korean cinema experienced a deterioration of quality in both its films and film industries.

Interestingly, under Park Chung Hee's direction, Hollywood continued to influence Korean cinema through the construction of the local studio system as discussed thus far: the array of controls developed by Park's administration suggests that "the government's ultimate intention was to construct a studio system that operated in similar ways to Hollywood studios, but with an authoritarian twist" (Yecies and Shim 2016, 21). In its early history, the Hollywood film industry was run on the economic model of the studio system— "a pure example of a Fordist mode of production and a classic oligopoly" (Veron, cited in K. Lee 2008, 373): "Under the studio system, a film studio controlled all stages of a movie's economic life, from the birth of the screenplay written by a studio-employed writer to film production to final distribution in a studio-owned theater" (K. V. Lee 2008, 373). However, the studio system under the Park regime also strengthened the government's control over the film industry because those few studios had to adhere to its policy directives in order to stay in business at all (Yecies and Shim 2016).

The movies produced in the early 1970s had no choice but to portray government-directed themes—such as anticommunism, the establishment of national identity, and the rationalization of the Yusin System—in return for government subsidies. Korean cinema consequently dropped into a deep valley, where it remained until the early 1990s.

KOREAN CINEMA UNDER THE AUTHORITARIAN REGIMES

Korean cinema plunged into a deep slump in the early 1970s, and its popularity kept dropping until the early 1990s. After enjoying a period of fame and prosperity during the late 1950s and 1960s, it experienced a more than two-decade-long recession. The total number of admissions continued to decrease from 166 million in 1970 to 65 million in 1976 and then to 47 million in 1986 (Ho 2003). The market share of domestic films was as low as 15.9 percent in 1993. The lowest point in the industry in terms of foreign export was in 1985, when Korea exported only two films and generated $20,000, down from $406,683 in 1982 (Ministry of Culture and Tourism 2001; KOFIC 2003; Mee Hyun Kim 2013).

The major reasons for the demise of Korean cinema were thought to be the rapid growth of television, both black-and-white in the 1970s and color in the 1980s; the impact of neoliberal cultural policies; and the increasing role of Hollywood films in the Korean cultural market. Among these, the emergence of the television era in particular played a key role. As table 2.1 shows, as the number of television sets soared from only 43,684 in 1966 to 2.8 million in 1976, the number of movie attendees significantly dropped, from 156 million in 1966 to 65 million in 1976 (KMPPC 1977). Many moviegoers—in particular, those in their 30s and 40s, most of whom were women—turned their attention to television dramas, and many film actors and actresses moved to television. Another significant reasons for the recession in Korean cinema was the lack of variety. Melodrama continued to attract audiences; however, Korean cinema did not develop various movie genres, other than classics and movies aimed at older teens, in the 1970s (KMPPC 1977).

The government's neoliberal cultural policies, forced upon it by the U.S. government and Hollywood, also deeply affected the film business beginning in the 1980s. The Motion Picture Export Association of America (MPEAA), which changed its name to the Motion Picture Association of America (MPAA) in 1994, had been "lobbying for the opening of the Korean film market since the 1970s" (Paquet 2009, 50). The MPEAA acknowledged that

TABLE 2.1.   Number of movie attendees, 1966–1976

	Number of television sets	Number of movie attendees
1966	43,684	156,336,340
1967	73,224	164,077,224
1968	118,262	171,341,354
1969	223,695	173,043,273
1970	379,564	166,349,541
1971	616,392	146,303,355
1972	905,365	118,723,789
1973	1,282,122	114,625,241
1974	1,618,617	97,375,813
1975	2,014,927	75,597,977
1976	2,809,131	65,700,738

SOURCE: KMPPC (1977, 156).

Korean cinema would be a big market for Hollywood, because Korean audiences already liked Hollywood movies more than local films. Even during the recession in the domestic film industry, Koreans still went to theaters to watch Hollywood films: the number of attendees for Hollywood films in 1974 was 94,910 per film, compared to 21,920 for local films (KMPPC 1977, 160). This trend continued into the 1980s, which provided a good incentive for Hollywood studios who wanted to penetrate the Korean film market. The popularity of American films during the 1970s and 1980s also implies that Hollywood, even without the help of any particular policy measures, played a key role as a major cultural product provider.

In 1985, the MPEAA contacted the U.S. Trade Representative (USTR) "to report Korea's unfair import restrictions on foreign films." Taking up the complaint, the U.S. government pushed for "the liberalization of the Korean film market as a central issue in its trade negotiations with Korea. The Korean government succumbed to U.S. pressure, and the first Korea-U.S. film agreement was reached in late 1985." The agreement allowed for the local operation of foreign film companies and reduced import quotas, started in 1958 as mandatory upper limits on prices paid for imports. After this first agreement, negotiations between Korea and the U.S. concerning the film trade did not resume until 1988 (J. Y. Shin 2008, 49–50; Messerlin and Parc 2017b).

The second Korea-U.S. film agreement allowed for a gradual increase in the number of film prints imported of each film until 1994, when any limit was to be altogether abolished. It also simplified the process of censoring imported films (An, cited in J. Y. Shin 2008). What is more significant is that the 1988 agreement also let Hollywood studios begin setting up "branch offices in Korea to distribute their films directly" (J. Y. Shin 2008, 50); the Roh Tae Woo regime

(1988–1993) permitted this as part of its plan to liberalize the market for foreign players. Domestic films seemed to be ignored in policy considerations.

Consequently, the Korean film industry became a target for transnational cultural industries. Major Hollywood studios rushed into the Korean market: UIP and 20th Century Fox established their branches in 1988, followed by Warner Bros. (1989), Columbia TriStar (1990), and Buena Vista (1993). Together, they imported a total of 818 foreign films between 1988 and 2001 (Ministry of Culture and Tourism 2002). While the number of domestic films decreased from 229 in 1969, to 83 in 1975, and to 64 in 1993, imports of foreign films increased from only 24 in 1983, to 321 in 1989, and again to 483 in 1996 as these Hollywood majors directly distributed their films in the Korean film market (see table 2.2).

As these data prove, until the early 1990s, Korean cinema barely maintained its existence, while Hollywood majors played a large role in the local film market. As a result of these neoliberal cultural reforms, demanded of Korea by the U.S., Korean cinema became a new sector Hollywood majors could cross into with their capital and films. As will be discussed later, Hollywood majors in the 2010s directly produced Korean films while investing in the exhibition sector, resulting in yet another increase in Hollywood's influence on Korean cinema.

TRANSNATIONAL CAPITALS IN THE ERA OF GLOBALIZATION

The government's neoliberal cultural policies have deeply affected the film industry since the 1980s, but they picked up speed during the early 1990s. The rapid pursuit of neoliberal globalization by the Kim Young Sam administration (1993–1998) fundamentally influenced Korean cinema because its cultural policies substantially changed the structure of the film industry. The Kim government continued to develop neoliberal cultural policies as part of its economic reforms; however, neoliberal reforms in the cultural sector were not the same as they had been under the authoritarian regimes. Unlike the previous military administrations, which opened the cultural markets to foreign forces, the Kim government adopted these reforms actively to boost the national economy through the cultural industries. Kim's original declaration stated that the globalization policies would brace the nation for cascading developments and sweeping changes in the world; they would build the country into "a first-rate nation in the coming century by opening Korea to the world in all fields" (J. K. Oh 1999, 147).

Interestingly, the Kim government initiated the resuscitation of the film business while applying the logic of globalization to the cultural industries. Instead of reducing its role in the cultural industries, the Kim government developed

TABLE 2.2.   Historical development in Korean cinema, 1985–2017

Year	Number of imports	Total amount imported ($1,000)	Number of exports	Total amount exported ($1,000)	Number of screens
1985	30	5,879	2	20	561
1986	50	7,735	9	127	640
1987	100	15,418	29	425	673
1988	248	26,034	34	589	696
1989	321	26,581	23	365	772
1990	309	27,100	13	1,579	789
1991	309	31,993	17	472	762
1992	360	41,418	14	195	712
1993	420	60,228	14	173	669
1994	381	57,034	14	620	629
1995	378	67,862	15	208	577
1996	483	88,660	30	404	511
1997	431	69,270	36	492	497
1998	296	35,109	33	3,073	507
1999	348	26,664	75	5,969	588
2000	427	46,559	38	7,053	720
2001	355	48,470	102	11,249	818
2002	266	50,267	133	14,952	977
2003	271	58,865	162	30,979	1,132
2004	285	68,183	194	58,284	1,451
2005	253	48,813	202	75,994	1,648
2006	289	45,813	208	24,514	1,880
2007	404	67,526	321	24,396	1,975
2008	360	78,775	361	21,036	2,044
2009	311	73,645	251	14,122	2,055
2010	383	53,373	276	14,135	2,003
2011	508	46,356	366	15,886	1,974
2012	721	52,607	331	20,174	2,081
2013	844	50,339	403	37,071	2,184
2014	1,031	50,157	529	26,380	2,281
2015	1,262	61,542	650	29,374	2,424
2016	1,526	44,838	679	43,893	2,575
2017	1,437	*	802	40,726	2766

* Data unknown

SOURCE: MCST (2014a); KOFIC (2013, 143); MCST (2015, 65); KOFIC (2016a, 112–116); MCST (2016, 68); KOFIC (2017a); KOFIC (2018b); Korea Statistical Information Service (2018).

new policies to support the domestic film industry by introducing several mea-sures designed to promote the cultural industries. First, in 1994, it created the Cultural Industry Bureau within the Ministry of Culture and Sports. Then, in 1995, the Kim government enacted the Motion Picture Promotion Law, replac-ing the existing Motion Picture Law. In fact, one major element of the new law concerned the reintroduction of the Film Promotion Fund. In the older Motion

Picture Law, film importers were required to contribute to the Film Promotion Fund, but this stipulation was eliminated during the market liberalization of the late 1980s. In the new Motion Picture Promotion Law (as fully discussed in chapter 5), the government pledged to set up the Film Promotion Fund as a public fund, with a plan to contribute ₩10 billion (about $9 million in 1995 dollars) to it by 1996 (D. H. Kim 2005, 309). The Kim Young Sam government continued to develop several financial supports to the film production sector throughout the 1990s.

Then, in 2000, the Kim Dae-jung government expanded the budget of the Ministry of Culture to 1 percent of the national budget (Y. W. Kim 2012). The Kim Dae-jung government therefore planned to secure ₩1,700 million for promoting Korean cinema between 1999 and 2003 (H. S. Kang 2008). Amid this pursuit of globalization and government support, many domestic players—in particular, several chaebol (large, family-owned conglomerates)— invested capital in the film business (D. Y. Jin 2006). By the mid-2000s, this political-economic milieu surrounding the local film industry had caused fundamentally shifts within Korean cinema itself.

Chaebol's Involvement in Film Production

The Korean government's neoliberal cultural policies brought about massive investment by both domestic and foreign-based transnational capital in the domestic film industry, resulting in a boom in Korean cinema between the mid-1990s and the early 2000s. Korean domestic films indeed swiftly transformed, becoming like blockbusters in their content and budget. Several of these were funded or produced by chaebol and achieved huge commercial successes. Of course, several chaebol—such as Samsung, LG, and Daewoo—had been paying attention to the entertainment sector since the video market started to grow in the late 1980s—especially during the 1988 Summer Olympics in Seoul. Early on, Samsung purchased the video sale rights to *Marriage Story* (1992), which became an enormous success, triggering several conglomerates' entries into the film market and, in particular, film production.

In 1995, their manner of investment changed: they either funded 100 percent of production costs for film production or formed their own production companies (D. M. Hwang 2001, 25–26). They utilized a star system as well as marketing and public relations techniques learned from Hollywood (Mee Hyun Kim 2013, 70). Samsung launched Samsung Entertainment Group in 1995 as a new company, incorporating the previously dispersed film, home video, music, and cable TV divisions (Myung-Hwan Kim 1995; *Variety* 1997). The 22 feature films partly or entirely backed by Samsung—in particular, Samsung Entertainment Group—between 1992 and 1997 included *To the Starry Island* (1993), *Cinema of the Road* (1995), *A Hot Roof* (1995), and *Three Friends* (1996). Several other conglomerates also jumped into the film business, and as of December 1993, Hyundai, Daewoo, Lucky Gumsung (now LG), SK, Lotte, Donga, Doosan, and Buksan also had investments in film production and the purchase of sale rights of films. These chaebol expanded their existing home electronics companies to invest in the film business due in part to Kim's 1994 push for globalization (*JoongAng Ilbo* 1993; D. Y. Jin 2006).

The Samsung-funded film *Shiri* (1999), for example, was known as the country's first blockbuster movie in scale of budget and action and grossed $5.8 million. *Shiri* portrayed the confrontation between North Korean soldiers who were dispatched to South Korea as sleeper agents and South Korean antiterrorist agents and thus succeeded in reflecting two cultural tendencies: Korean history and Hollywood-style narratives. Although *Shiri* was acclaimed as one of the most successful local films, both financially and culturally, in most cases, for chaebol, cultural identity and sovereignty were not major considerations. Many film critics believe that due to their emphasis on commercial imperatives, the concentration of production in a handful of chaebol resulted in the consequent standardization of cultural expression (D. Y. Jin 2006). In the midst of critiques from several parts of Korean society alongside the 1997 financial crisis, many films produced by chaebol did not make enough profits. Therefore, several conglomerates retreated from the film industry. Samsung, for example, disbanded its Samsung Entertainment Group in 1999, and SK and Daewoo also gave up their film businesses.

Chaebol's involvement in the film sector did not last long primarily due to the financial crisis of 1997. In the midst of the worst economic recession in recent Korean history, several chaebol had to restructure their business plans and left noncore areas, including the film sector. After SK left the entertainment business in 1998, Daewoo and Samsung also shut down theirs and left the film sector (Mee Hyun Kim 2013). Of course, as is detailed later, chaebol investment in the film sector continued in the early 2000s when several conglomerates started to develop their businesses in the exhibition industry.[4]

Meanwhile, another major change in Korean cinema began in the neoliberal globalization era: several chaebol started to build especially close relationships with Hollywood studios in both production and distribution in the Korean film market (and of course later, in exhibition). Samsung Entertainment Group had a partnership with New Regency, and Cheil Jedang Entertainment (now CJ E&M) partnered with DreamWorks. Other chaebol also talked with Hollywood studios, although their negotiations were not successful. For example, Hyundai and Paramount, as well as Daewoo and Universal, negotiated to work together in the Korean market; however, for several reasons, including the financial crisis of 1997, no deals were ultimately made (Groves 1997). Nevertheless, what these attempts and actual partnerships indicate was that both domestic transnational corporations and Hollywood majors valued the Korean film sector as one of the most significant emerging markets.

More recently, as Chinese cultural industries have increased their investments in the Korean entertainment industry, a Chinese consortium signed a contract to purchase the country's third-biggest multiplex cinema operator, Megabox, in 2014: "Korea Multiplex Investment and other stake holders signed a stock purchase agreement (SPA) with a Chinese investment fund consortium, Oriental Star Capital, to sell their entire stake in Megabox for 570 billion won ($517.1 million)" (J. W. Park 2014).

Thus between the late 1990s and the early 2000s, Korean cinema was transnationalized by both domestic and foreign corporations. It achieved a noticeable commercial success based on both favorable film policies and transnational corporations' active involvement in the industry, resulting in the expedition of the commercialization of Korean cinema.

Chaebol's Dominance in Film Exhibition

Since chaebol left the production industry, the major sources of film investment have been venture capital companies and investment associations, crowdsourcing, and film exhibitors who are also owned by chaebol. Such resources have tended to pool their money into film investment funds that finance a broad slate of films. Most funds have an operating term of five to six years and devote 50–70 percent of their capital to film financing, with the remainder placed in stocks or other investments (Paquet 2008). For the purpose of providing a stable source of capital for venture investment, the Korean government established the Korea Fund of Funds based on the Special Measures for the Promotion of Venture Businesses Act. The government provided the capital, and by 2015, the Korea Fund of Funds, managed by Korea Venture Investment Corp (KVIC), had invested ₩5,017 million in several investment associations (instead of directly providing money to film corporations). In other words, in many cases, the Korea Fund of Funds, strategic investors—who are chaebol—and venture capitalists together invest in film production, which is a unique form of financing cinema (*Weekly Chosun* 2014). Since 2000, when film investment associations came into play, 125 film investment associations have invested in domestic film production (Korean Film Council 2016a, 200). For example, Union Investment Partners (2016), which was established in 2000, has created 14 investment associations to invest into several movies, such as *All about My Wife* (2013), *Snowpiercer* (2013), *The Admiral: Roaring Currents* (2014), and *Ode to My Father* (2014).[5]

Likewise, crowdfunding has become one of the most interesting forms of film production in the 2010s (Kil 2016b). Crowdfunding is a means to collect funds from the public, and in this format, artists and social activists can post their projects on the internet to raise money from a group of sponsors (S. J. Song 2014).

The Korean film industry is no stranger to crowdfunding; one of Korea's biggest hits of 2016, *Operation Chromite*, utilized it. Made with a budget of $12 million, including $448,000 raised through the Industrial Bank of Korea's stock-like crowdfunding campaign, *Operation Chromite* sold a total of 6.9 million tickets, so each crowdfunding investor received a 5.6 percent rate of return. The Korean nuclear disaster movie *Pandora* also raised ₩530 million through crowdfunding in 2016.

Some early Korean films that used crowdfunding were *26 Years* (2012) and *Another Family* (2014). In particular, 2012's *26 Years* hinted toward the future of crowdfunding in Korean cinema. Taking inspiration from a popular webtoon released in 2006, the action thriller blends fiction and recent Korean history, as its protagonists try to assassinate former strongman Chun Doo-hwan, who took power through a coup against a rival military faction in 1979. In less than three months, more than 12,000 people gave nearly ₩450 million in exchange for movie tickets and small gifts. The donations continued to grow as momentum built through word of mouth and social media. The crowdfunding project created enough buzz to lure some deep-pocketed individuals to take part, until nearly 90 percent of the entire budget had been secured (*Korea Herald* 2012). Later, a social drama about Samsung semiconductor factory workers who developed blood cancer, *Family*, was financed solely by crowdfunding from more than 7,000 individuals (Kil 2016b). While the majority of the crowdfunded films were indie productions, crowdfunding has gained momentum; several big-budget movies have used it as part of their marketing strategy recently.

Finally (as will be fully discussed in chapter 4), chaebol's involvement in the Korean film industry has expanded to other areas—in particular, the exhibition sector. This second wave of chaebol involvement in the film industry, has seen conglomerates such as the CJ Group (CJ E&M and CJ CGV), the Orion Group (Showbox), and the Lotte Group (Lotte Entertainment) take ownership of multiplex cinemas, becoming some of the biggest players in the industry: "[The current] chaebol's film divisions are particularly influential because they are vertically integrated like the Hollywood studios of old, with investment, production, distribution, exhibition and also international sales all falling under the same corporate umbrella. The fact that these companies operate major theater chains make them especially powerful" (Paquet 2008). Lotte Entertainment, one of Korea's largest film companies, teamed up with the city of Busan to launch the $17.3 million Busan-Lotte Creative Film Fund in March 2016. The fund is part of former president of Korea Park Geun-hye's Creative Economy Action Plan and is made possible because the Lotte Group supported the Busan Center for Creative Economy and Innovation, just as other groups supported similar centers built during the same period. Interestingly, half of the fund was to go toward commercial film production, while the other half would be dedicated to low-budget indie films or Busan Projects, which are produced or postproduced by Busan-based companies (Kil 2016a).

The corporate-oriented system engenders simmering frustration in an industry where a handful of conglomerates control investment, distribution, and exhibition. A growing number of directors and film critics as well as some actors have warned that the vertically integrated system is weighed against low-budget independent films, stifling diversity and creativity. Although many argue that the chaebol-driven market system is able to use resources effectively, "it is hard to deny that Korean cinema has become less an art form and more a commodity" (E. J. Park 2012). In this regard, Wasko (1981, 135) already has pointed out,

> film in a capitalist economy is a commodity—a rather special commodity because it is also an art form, a communications medium, and an ideological tool. Nevertheless, it is still a commodity, produced, distributed and exhibited under market conditions that must in some way affect what types of films are made, who makes them, and how they are distributed and exhibited to the public. The industry is capital-intensive by nature in that there is a continuing need for capital to cover costs of production and distribution, which must be expended long before revenue begins rolling in—if, indeed, it ever does.

As these chaebol have become major players, the investment structure of the Korean film industry has substantially changed. Several chaebol—both theater chain owners like CJ E&M, Showbox, and Lotte Entertainment and telecommunications corporations such as KT and SKT—are strategic investors and thus acquire the publication rights to movies. They also arrange for subinvestors, known as financial investors, including venture capitalists. Once they produce films, theaters and investors share the revenues by evenly distributing them. The investors then divide the profits, after eliminating total production costs and distribution fees, between the investors (60 percent) and the producers (40 percent; *Weekly Chosun* 2014; Export-Import Bank of Korea 2014).

POLITICIZATION OF CENSORSHIP IN CONTEMPORARY KOREAN CINEMA

The Korean government's control over the film industry through censorship has been one of the most significant cultural policies hurting Korean cinema. The Korean government had severely regulated the film industry through harsh censorship between the early 1960s and the late 1980s. As is well-documented, the successive military regimes headed by two autocrats—Park Chung Hee and Chun Doo-hwan—put the film business under government control (D. Y. Jin 2011a; J. H. Choe 2014; Chung and Diffrient 2015; Yecies and Shim 2016).

These military regimes decreased the capacity for cinematic expression that would be offensive or detrimental to the regimes.

After the May 16 coup d'état in 1961, the Park Chung Hee regime immediately took direct control of film production, regulation, and exhibition with the enactment of the Korean Motion Picture Law of 1962, as previously discussed. Under the new law, the military regime "centralized the film industry and enforced stringent double censorship rules (pre- and postproduction)" (Chung and Diffrient 2015, 85). Censorship authorities also "sought to eliminate films that might violate good taste or customs, that might hurt the interests and dignity of the country, or that were thought to praise North Korea and the communist state" (S. H. Park 2002, 123). The Park and Chun regimes wanted to control any negative form of expression toward the authoritarian regimes and enforce their national anticommunist agendas, which had the greatest impact on domestic film production (Yecies and Shim 2016), although the 1980s witnessed the relaxation of this censorship (James 2001).

In June 1987, antigovernment protests before the presidential election strongly challenged authoritarian rule, and consequently, freedom of expression increased and political authorities (the Roh Tae Woo regime, 1988–1993) lost control over mass media and culture. Film censorship laws became more lenient than ever as the censorship of scripts in preproduction was abolished (S. H. Park 2002). However, it was during the Kim Dae-jung administration (1998–2003) that government support for the cultural industries began in a real sense (Joo 2007). The Kim Dae-jung government's slogan for cultural policies was "provide support, but do not interfere." Accordingly, "controls such as film censorship disappeared and support for investment, production and distribution increased markedly. President Kim pledged that he would abolish censorship during his campaign in 1997, and censorship was abolished in January 2001. President Kim was able to keep his pledge only after four years with the 4th revision of the Motion Picture Promotion Law, because the opposition party insisted on controls over films and delayed reform" (H. J. Kim 2006, 352).

Contemporary Korean cinema, however, has not been entirely free from censorship and regulation in a broad sense. There are some major forms of control, which can be identified as new types of censorship: film classification, the control of movie production through the public film fund, artist blacklists, and political retaliation. Some of these measures are not based on written documents; however, the conservative governments certainly have utilized their political power to reign over the film industry.

To begin with, the Korean government has a new regulation arm to utilize in controlling movie content. Prior to the mid-1990s, there was a tremendous degree of direct governmental interference in the film industry, but since 1995, when the Kim Young Sam government initiated the growth of the Korean film industry, most censorship issues have been linked with the practice of classifying films. In 1995, government censorship of films was ruled unconstitutional and so the former governmental censorship board was disbanded—the Constitutional Court of Korea ruled that the censorship was unconstitutional, and therefore, the movie laws had to be changed. Consequently, the less powerful Korea Media Rating Board (KMRB) was founded, and it classifies films, videos, and other motion pictures, giving them age-based ratings (Korea Media Rating Board 2017). The KMRB does not technically have the power to cut or ban films on its own; however, "it frequently uses its influence to pressure film companies to cut or modify scenes which it feels to be inappropriate" (Paquet 2002). The KMRB has been criticized for utilizing this power to effectively ban some films.

The KMRB had five different levels of ratings in 1996. They were G, PG-12, PG-15, PG-18, and "reservation rate" (which means that rating would be delayed). The first movie that was given the reservation rating was *Yellow Hair*, directed by Kim Yu-min and starring former child actress Lee Jae-eun. The film was rejected once in early 1999 before being granted an 18+ rating on its second application, as the film caused controversy for its strong sexual content. The KMRB also banned *Lies* before it received an invitation to compete at the 1999 Venice Film Festival, after which the director still had to cut some scenes and lewd language between two high school girls. Another movie, *Yellow Flower* (1998), directed by Lee Ji-sang, received the reservation rating because the rating board claimed that the movie contained "inappropriate" scenes (full nudity and drug use). The production company sued the KMRB to the Constitutional Court, and the court ruled that the KMRB's practice of delaying the issuance of a rating for these movies infringed on freedom of expression (J. H. Park 2001). According to the court decision, made in August 2001, because KMRB members were nominated by the president and the KMRB received government subsidies, it could be categorized as a censorship agency.

The court decided that delaying the rating of some movies, including *Yellow Flower*, was nothing but prescreen censorship, which is unconstitutional. The KMRB has since changed "reservation rate" to "Restricted Rate," which officially, but not practically, ended film censorship. It is official in that film content can now only be regulated by criminal and youth protection laws; however, the government still utilizes several measures to regulate movies. As Darcy Paquet (2002) points out, "From a historic point of view, Korea has made great strides in reducing the level of government censorship in filmmaking. This has largely been a reflection of the political changes that have transformed Korea over the past decade from a military dictatorship into a lively democracy." However, the Korean government has continued to check and regulate film content through the rating board. For example, *Moebius*—a 2013 film directed by Kim Ki-duk—was also initially banned in Korea before the KMRB reviewed the film again and changed the rating. The Media Rating Board (2017) cited incest, violence and the need to protect youth as its reasoning behind the ban. Kim Ki-duk cut the film twice before it was allowed to be released in Korea. As an example of a recent case, the KMRB also banned the American action comedy *The Interview* (2014) in the Korean market because it depicts criticizing and killing the North Korean leader Kim Jong-un.

Instead of classifying films as part of regulation, the conservative governments have massively utilized their political discretion to control film content. Both the Lee Myung-bak (2008–2013) and Park Geun-hye (2013–2017) administrations attempted to control freedom of expression in the realm of film through several measures. While official censorship ended with the military regime, these conservative administrations still aimed to control the film industry and even made plans to restitute the old form of oppression.

Most of all, as a new form of censorship, "artist blacklisting," which began in the Lee Myung-bak era, has negatively influenced the film industry. In September 2017, the reform committee of the National Intelligence Service (Korea's spy agency) found that there was an unofficial blacklist of artists and cultural figures during the Lee Myung-bak administration from the years 2008 to 2013. According to the National Intelligence Service committee's investigative findings released during the same time, there were some 82 artists blacklisted across the cultural arts, and in the film, broadcast, and music industries (KBS World Radio 2017). Among these, 60 were either movie directors or actors, including Park Chan-wook (director, *Oldboy*), Lee Chang-dong (director, *Secret Sunshine*), and Moon Sung-geun (award-winning actor in 1996's *A Petal*).

This is just the tip of the iceberg; the Park Geun-hye government created an even more systematic blacklist of artists. President Park's office developed a list of people who were denied government support, and the document listed a total of 9,473 artists, including (again) Cannes-awarded director Park Chan-wook and leading actors, such as Song Kang-ho (*Snowpiercer*; T. S. Cho 2016). The president's office reportedly sent the list to the Ministry of Culture, Sports and Tourism in May 2015, "requesting that the artists should be denied financial and logistical support" (John Noh 2016). The artists in the blacklist either supported the opposing political party or protested against the government's handling of the 2014 Sewol ferry disaster (see below).

Both Lee Myung-bak and Park Geun-hye officially promised that they would work on expanding the national budget for cultural projects and investments as they planned to develop Hallyu (the Korean Wave) as a symbol of soft power. The Park Geun-hye government even sought measures to allocate 2 percent of the national budget to culture (up from 0.9 percent in 2010), which would be comparable to Organisation for Economic Co-operation and Development (OECD) countries, whose cultural budgets averaged 1.9 percent of their national budgets during the same period (Presidential Transition Team 2013). However, these two administrations created measures that were some of the worst in terms of violating freedom of expression. Park Geun-hye's political actions could be interpreted as a movement to revive practices of past military dictators like her father (the autocrat Park Chung Hee) and, in so doing, seriously undermined freedom of thought and expression (S. H. Choe 2016). As can be easily imagined, "the government blacklist was aimed at starving artists of official subsidies and private funding and placing them under state surveillance" (Agence France-Presse 2017).[6]

As mentioned, one of the primary reasons for the creation of the artist blacklist was related to the Sewol ferry disaster, in which 304 passengers, mostly students and crew, died in April 2014. The discussion around freedom of expression in Korean cinema erupted when a documentary film about the sinking of the ferry directed by Lee Sang-ho and Ahn Hae-ryong and called *Diving Bell* (or, in the English release, *The Truth Shall Not Sink with Sewol*) was planned to be screened at the 2014 Busan International Film Festival (BIFF)—Asia's biggest movie event. When BIFF selected *Diving Bell*, several groups opposed, which eventually became a huge controversy.

In particular, conservative Busan city mayor Seo Byeong-soo requested that the film's screenings be canceled, as the film criticized the Park Geun-hye government's rescue efforts in the aftermath of the disaster. BIFF believed it was very important for the film festival to guarantee the diversity and autonomy of its exhibition films, and so it was not willing to lose its own identity by succumbing to politically driven external pressures.

Since then, BIFF has been confronted with a series of challenges, including audits carried out by the city and cuts to its budget by the Korean Film Council (KOFIC; Kil 2016c). In 2015, one year after the *Diving Bell* turmoil, KOFIC drastically reduced its budget to BIFF by about 41 percent, from ₩14.6 million in 2014 to ₩8 million in 2015 while increasing its support to other local film festivals (KOFIC 2015a). These movements were certainly considered political retaliation against BIFF and a new measure to impose censorship on the local film industry. The budget to BIFF increased to ₩9.5 million in 2016 but decreased to ₩7.6 million in 2017. Luckily for filmmakers, President Moon Jae-in (2017–now) visited the 2017 Busan Film Festival held in October to express his support to the festival, emphasizing the significance of its independence and autonomy. This implies that, in opposition to the conservative administrations before it, the new liberal government wants to seek a very simple principle: "government support without interfering" in the festival's decision-making (Kil 2017).

Finally, the Korean government has also practically censored movies through its own financial arm. As was touched on above and will be detailed in chapter 5, the Korean government established the Korea Fund of Funds based on the Special Measures for the Promotion of Venture Businesses Act for the purpose of providing a stable capital source for venture investment. About 40 percent of Korean films have been financially supported by the fund; however, several movies, including *The Attorney* (2013), *Pandora* (2016), and *A Taxi Driver* (2017) were rejected by the fund, as these movies criticized conservative regimes; instead, the Korea Fund of Funds intentionally supported movies portraying anticommunism and driving patriotism (Yoo 2017). The outcome has been dire, as many film creators cannot focus on their creative works. As Ju Oak Kim (2018, 88) correctly observes, "At a certain level, the exclusion of financial support has caused Korean artists and cultural practitioners to have fewer opportunities in the production and circulation of their creative products and practices. Moreover, the recognition of being under surveillance has made it difficult for these artists to further their aesthetic and creative performances without self-censorship."

As such, censorship in the Korean film industry has been characterized by different political features. Film censorship in the conservative administrations between 2008 and 2017 was not the same as it was during the military regimes before 1988. While the military regimes sought to eliminate films that might hurt the dignity of the state, the conservative administrations attempted to control Korean cinema in order to prevent them from criticizing presidents' images rather than the state. In other words, the conservative administrations developed all kinds of measures to protect presidents, which is unconstitutional. In the previous decades, under the military regimes, censorship was predictable as "they used censorship to make their power seem legitimate" (S. H. Park 2002, 133). However, in contemporary Korean cinema, censorship could not be predictable because the government abused their authority through diverse means, which made the situations worse; the two consecutive conservative administrations developed more canny forms of censorship than ever, and the impacts were enormous and deeply hurt the film world. While official censorship, which had also hurt the growth of Korean cinema, seemingly disappeared, the Korean government continued to regulate the film industry through its political power, and in this sense, censorship in contemporary Korean cinema became politicized in the early 21st century. The specter of censorship still haunts Korean cinema.

CONCLUSION

Over the past several decades, cinema in Korea has changed based on the political economy of its society. The shifting cultural policies of its government, including those relating to censorship, have also been some of the major reasons for transformation in the local film industry.

Contemporary Korean cinema has risen against the background of the triumph of neoliberalism, as forced upon it by the U.S. government and Hollywood studios. As the Korean government has continued to develop neoliberal cultural reforms, foreign-based transnational corporations, mostly Hollywood studios, have expanded their investment in the Korean film business. The Korean government seemed to take a neoliberal turn in opening the film market to foreign players, and the film market certainly has moved in that direction. In particular, the Korean film industry has been closely related to transnational forces, including the U.S. government and Hollywood studios; key policies—such as changing screen quotas, providing direct film distribution rights to Hollywood studios, and permitting them to open branches in Korea—have been the outcomes of the interplay between local and global forces.

This does not mean the total elimination of the state's role in the film sector. Since the 1990s, instead, "most of the Korean governments have followed an active cinema policy in order to promote and protect its culture—a line not much different from the one adopted in certain European countries, such as France" (Parc 2016, 2). The Korean government has, either directly or indirectly, supported the film industry. Although the authoritarian regimes that held power until the early 1990s permitted Hollywood studios to have direct distribution rights and the Roh Moo-hyun government scrapped the screen quota in return for the Korea-U.S. FTA as part of its neoliberal globalization strategies, the Korean government also protected the film industry from Western forces and even reversed some neoliberal directions. At a time when official U.S. policies are moving toward the dismantling of regulatory restrictions in favor of free-market competition and deregulation, Korea is still relying on government regulations (Servaes 1989). Therefore, it is important to emphasize that Korean cinema has shifted and advanced through sometimes cooperative and at other times conflicting relationships among three major players: the Korean government, domestic-based transnational capitals (e.g., chaebol and venture capitals), and foreign forces.

What must be emphasized, though, is that the main goal of the government in supporting Korean cinema was not to safeguard cultural identity and uniqueness but to find a new economic source to help revive the Korean economy. As can be seen in the discussion of film censorship, the Korean government has not developed any countermeasures to unconstitutional censorship, as recent conservative administrations have been able to vehemently utilize their political power to reign over Korean cinema. In the early 21st century, film policy makers have not contemplated the ways in which they develop the unique character of domestic films into the logic of the economic imperatives.

3 · SCREEN QUOTAS IN THE ERA OF THE U.S.-KOREA FTA

While several liberalization measures in international treaty negotiations, such as the General Agreement on Tariffs and Trade (GATT) and the
entry into the World Trade Organization (WTO), characterized the 1990s.
Such bilateral investment treaties (BITs) between two countries symbolize
21st-century capitalism around the world. FTAs (free trade agreements) are
especially significant in the cultural industries, because many countries have
developed their neoliberal cultural and media policies by taking the clear stance
that cultural areas, including film, are best left in the hands of free-market forces.
Therefore, the issue of setting up a proper relationship between trade and culture
flared up in the Korea-U.S. FTA negotiations, which changed the existing screen
quota system in Korea (W. M. Choi 2007).

In the realm of culture, Korea and the U.S. have developed their convoluted
interplays by focusing on the change in Korea's screen quota system. The shift in
screen quotas is related to not only neoliberal reform in the form of deregulation
but also, accordingly, capital accumulation in the hands of Hollywood major
studios. Korea, like other national governments, had no choice but to open
its cultural market to global forces in the name of progress, mainly because of
U.S. pressure in the negotiation of FTAs (D. Y. Jin 2011b). As the U.S. has pursued its FTA strategy in the cultural sector as part of its overall liberalization
scheme, Korea and several other countries have had to adopt this form of global
trade negotiation, which has subsequently impacted the domestic film industry.

Korea was one of the first major countries that signed an FTA with the U.S.
Consequently, Korean cinema, as a major part of the national economy, has
experienced several significant tumultuous events since the Korean government
changed the screen quota system, a prerequisite for the Korea-U.S. FTA in 2006
(USTR 2017).[1] Any account seeking to understand what is currently unfolding
in Korean film policy therefore needs to engage with contemporary issues contextualized historically in relation to FTAs. This means that one must admit that

the FTA, as part of a new foreign and trade policy, has substantially changed the landscape of the Korean film market.

Protecting cultural industries from global forces, including Hollywood, has been the subject of multilateral negotiations around the world, including WTO negotiations and the UNESCO Convention on the Protection and Promotion of the Diversity of Cultural Expressions in 2005 (Kokas 2017). However, the Korea-U.S. FTA has suddenly—although not entirely—eliminated a cultural exception to protect domestic cultural industries.

About ten years after the reduction of screen quotas, opinions are split as to the results of the new system under the FTA regime. Some argue that the changed screen quota system has had no particular influence on the Korean film industry, while others claim that it has negatively impacted the Korean film market. By emphasizing the context of Korean cinema and cultural policies in association with the FTA, this chapter historicizes Korea's changing film policy on screen quotas. It especially analyzes the ways in which the Korean government has shifted its screen quota system in relation to pressures from both the U.S. government and Hollywood. It then articulates the processes and consequences of the FTA in Korean cinema in order to determine the crucial influence of the FTA on the domestic film market. Admitting that the FTA is not the sole reason for the decline in the Korean film market in the early 21st century, it investigates the causal relationships between the Korea-U.S. FTA in the realm of culture. Finally, it discusses whether Korean cinema has developed cultural diversity in the FTA era.

U.S. CULTURAL POLICIES ON SCREEN QUOTAS IN KOREAN CINEMA

The global box office has soared from $23.1 billion in 2005 to $40.6 billion in 2017 (MPAA 2007; 2017), and Hollywood has continued to dominate, taking a more than 60 percent share of the international film market in the 2000s and 70 percent in the early 2010s. Hollywood has also increased its presence in several countries, including Korea and China (Pfanner 2009; MPAA 2009; Breen 2010; Brook 2014). Given that much of the enormous revenue generated by U.S. cultural industries has come from foreign markets, the liberalization of the global cultural markets is very significant for the U.S. (Magder 2004). Therefore, it has always been a battleground between nation-states, mainly between the U.S. government and governments in Asia, Europe, and Latin America.

The U.S. government has long acknowledged that the American motion picture industry has been important for the national economy (Miller et al. 2001); however, it has gained even more importance due to the increasing role of emerging box offices, including China, in the early 21st century. The U.S. government—backed by Hollywood, the Motion Picture Association of

America, and neoliberal cultural policy practitioners—takes a clear position that culture, including television and film, is best left in the hands of free-market forces (Ouellette and Lewis 2004). In fact, cultural policy in the U.S. is an important dimension in the global dominance of the American film industry. It is not surprising to learn that one of the major goals of the U.S. government's film policy is to "eliminate film quotas in other countries so as to ensure that their film markets are open to American films" (Crane 2014, 372).

In the 21st century, U.S. cultural policies became particularly embedded in relation to FTAs after UNESCO confirmed that cultural expression and support for cultural diversity were no longer optional extras for rich societies and could not be contained by existing definitions of art or of entertainment; rather they involve "an ethical imperative, inseparable from respect for human dignity," as clarified in its Declaration on Cultural Diversity (article 4). As Irina Bokova (2014), the director-general of UNESCO, stated in her circular letter in celebrating the 10th anniversary of the UNESCO convention, "The convention affirms the right parties to adopt cultural policies and measures aimed at protecting and promoting the diversity of cultural expressions within their territory, and it opens access to and encourages dialogue with cultural expressions from around the world." By March 2016, 144 national governments had raised barriers against Hollywood's penetration by signing onto the UNESCO convention, while the U.S. government has continued emphasizing the need for the establishment of FTAs with individual countries (UNESCO 2017).

The U.S. State Department and the U.S. Trade Representative (USTR) have imposed pressure in support of increased corporate freedoms as part of bilateral talks in the negotiation of FTAs. Hollywood and private trade associations, including the MPAA have been beneficiaries of this advocacy (D. Y. Jin 2011b). Korea has become a major target due to the robust growth of its national economy, including the domestic film market. As noted, the Korean film market ranked sixth in the global box-office markets in the early 21st century; therefore, it was significant for Hollywood majors to furthermore penetrate the market. For example, due to the increasing significance of the Korean film market, Hollywood star Tom Cruise made his ninth visit to Korea in July 2018 to promote his latest movie *Mission: Impossible—Fallout*. Seoul was the first stop on his Asian promotional tour for this sixth installment of the franchise, as the film had its worldwide premiere in Korea on July 25 (A. Y. Kang 2018). The Korean government had remained the strongest supporter for the cultural industries; however, it lost this foothold when the Korean government took one of its most drastic neoliberal measures by reducing screen quotas—a move that had been vehemently required by the U.S. government, the Motion Picture Association of America, and Hollywood majors—in the very early part of its FTA negotiation with the U.S. (D. Y. Jin 2011b).

While policy makers and film corporations (in particular, multiplex cinema chains) as well as Hollywood welcomed the new screen quota system, film critics and movie actors have seen it as diminishing Korea's cultural sovereignty and "the rights of their citizens to enjoy locally created culture and employment in the industries that produce them" (Breen 2010, 673). In other words, "the FTA was driven not by human rights but by a powerful commitment from the U.S. political apparatus and the U.S. entertainment industry to take care of their own interests," resulting in unfettered access to the Korean market (Breen 2010, 673). Therefore, this careful investigation of the Korea-U.S. FTA in regard to Korean cinema will shed light on current debates on cultural diversity/protection versus neoliberal reform.

THE SCREEN QUOTA SYSTEM BEFORE THE KOREA-U.S. FTA

Public discussion about the impact of the FTA on the film industry began with a defense of Korea's long-standing commitment to cultural policies that supported local screen quotas for film. Until 2006, Korea had maintained the fundamental structure of the screen quota system, which arguably contributed to the development of the Korean film industry. However, the Korean government unexpectedly changed this crucial cultural policy. The policy change in the screen quota system supposedly came about as a result of outside pressure in the context of bilateral trade negotiations, whose negotiators made cutting the quota a precondition for starting talks for the Korea-U.S. FTA (D. Y. Jin 2008). Of course, one must admit that foreign pressure is not the sole factor, because several parts of Korean society, including film exhibitors and some ministries in the field of economy, also wanted to change the screen quota system. Thus one must critically consider not only the Korean context but also the interplay between the U.S. and Korea.

The Formation of the Screen Quota System and Early Changes

The screen quota system in Korea goes back to the enactment of formal film regulation through the Motion Picture Law (MPL) in 1962. As discussed in chapter 2, this was Korea's first real film policy and the true beginning of "a strong proclivity toward state protection of Korean culture as a national treasure. During President Park Chung Hee's military dictatorship (1961–79), the MPL systematized policies for all film producers, distributors and exhibitors, showcasing the government's preferred direction for the domestic film industry and the country—namely that of industrialization and modernization" (Yecies 2007, 4). Later in January 1965, the Korean government announced Public Notice No. 3297, "regulating the importation of foreign films, among other commodities. Foreign film rentals were limited to a total of $75,000 U.S. dollars per fiscal quarter" (U.S. Department of State, cited in Yecies 2007, 4).

Since then, there have been six major revisions that have fundamentally changed screen quotas and consequently Korean cinema (see table 3.1). There were two major protection measures. In the second revision of the MPL, conducted in 1966, the MPL protected the distribution and exhibition of Korean films by establishing an annual quota, often referred to as an embargo, on imported films. Import quotas were established at the onset of each year, limiting the number of foreign films screened annually to about one-third the level of domestic films (article 19). The same revision also clearly indicated that film exhibitors must not exceed the proportion of foreign films permitted by law (article 19). Based on that, in December 1966 the Enforcement Decree of the Motion Picture Law (article 25) asked film exhibitors to screen domestic films for a minimum of 90 days each year—guaranteeing screen time but not box-office performance. The screen quota system had been enforced in Korea since 1967 under the Promotion of the Motion Pictures and Video Products Act (National Archives of Korea 2007).

The screen quota was originally promulgated to filter out Western influences (Song, cited in C. H. K. Kim 2000), which means that the changes to screen quotas over the following decades have definitely been related to foreign forces—in particular, Hollywood films. In this way, the Park Chung Hee regime supported the development of the Korean film industry. Since then, the screen quota has been one of the most significant protective measures for Korean cinema, and the local film industry has considered it the key film policy for the survival of local films amid the onslaught of Hollywood movies.

The screen quota has subsequently changed several times in Korea, primarily due to the evolving political-economic situation. Between 1970 and 1972, the screen quota was reduced from 90 days to 30 days each year. In Korea, the early 1970s was the starting point of the spread of television sets. The Korean

TABLE 3.1.   History of the screen quota system in Korea's Motion Picture Law, 1966–2016

Enactment	1962	Motion Picture Law enacted
1st revision	1966–1971	Every cinema must exhibit domestic films for 90 days Cinemas need to screen at least 6 Korean films
2nd revision	1972–1974	Every cinema must exhibit domestic films for 30 days Cinemas need to screen at least 3 Korean films
3rd revision	1973–1984	Every cinema must exhibit domestic films for 126 days; this was increased again to 165 in 1981.
4th revision	1985–1996	Every cinema must exhibit domestic films for 146 days
5th revision	1996–2006	Local governments are allowed to have up to 40 days' discretion
6th revision	2006–present	Every cinema must exhibit domestic films for 73 days

government did not have any reason to continue this rigorous screen quota, which was enacted during the 1960s, because Korean cinema was booming, which made the change. However, with the rapid growth of television sets in Korean households in the early 1970s, Korean cinema experienced a huge setback, and the industry asked the government to revise the screen quota system. Therefore, the government required every cinema to exhibit domestic films for a minimum of 126 days each year starting in 1973 (J. B. Ha 2003).

With the adaptation of neoliberal cultural and economic policies starting in the early 1980s, during General Chun Doo-hwan's presidency (1980–1988), "Korea's cultural approach to film reached new heights as the government ironically attempted to uplift and protect the arts, and to forge a new cultural identity" (Yim 2002, 40). In 1981, the number of required screening days for domestic films was raised to a minimum of 165 days, the highest quota yet. In November 1985, the Ministry of Culture and Information proposed to reduce the minimum number of screening days for domestic films from the all-time high of 165 to 146 and to provide an additional 28-day reduction of the screen quota system on a special-needs basis (Yecies 2007). In this way, the screen quota system prevents theaters from concentrating on well-received foreign movies and squeezing out Korean films, even under the military regimes.

The Increasing Role of the Motion Picture Association of America in the Screen Quota System

The screen quota system underwent further changes in the middle of BIT talks between the Korean and U.S. governments. The relationship between the U.S. government and Hollywood had intensified during these talks, as "the U.S. government ha[d] actively advocated Hollywood's interests" in bilateral trade agreements "because of Hollywood's importance to the U.S. economy and the MPAA's influential lobbying efforts" (K. V. Lee 2008, 372). The U.S. government and the MPAA considered movies in global trade solely in "economic terms as commercial products that should be subject to market forces," while many countries, most notably France and Canada, "ha[d] traditionally tied movies to national identity and argue[d] that cultural works deserve a special status." In fact, "these conflicting views have been the source of disagreements over the propriety of quotas and subsidies as applied to the global movie trade" (K. V. Lee 2008, 373). For example, to uphold cultural diversity—referring to how different groups like ethnocultural minorities, Aboriginal peoples, and persons with disabilities are represented in culture—the Canadian Radio-Television and Telecommunications Commission uses two main approaches to ensure that Canada's multicultural nature is reflected in the broadcasting system. First, it supports programming by and for specific groups, and second, it reflects diversity (e.g., the linguistic duality and multicultural nature of Canadian society) in all broadcast services (CRTC 2016).

As briefly discussed in the previous chapter, the first film negotiation between Korea and the U.S. was held in October 1985. American attempts to eliminate or to reduce the obligatory days of screening domestic films began when the MPEAA filed a trade complaint with the USTR over Korea's allegedly unfair trade practices in the film market. The MPEAA sought a special investigation officially with a prompt corrective action by invoking a clause of section 301 of the Trade Act of 1974. The first trade complaints over the Korean film market, albeit eventually withdrawn, impelled domestic bureaucrats to head to the negotiating table (Chang 2014).

The pressure to change or remove screen quotas came from various levels, including the U.S. government to the MPAA. As Kevin Lee (2008, 397) aptly puts it, "In recent years, the MPAA has lived up to its reputation as 'The Little State Department' by successfully acting on its own in establishing independent bilateral agreements with foreign governments and enforcing its IP (intellectual property) rights abroad. This effective combination of close cooperation with Washington and independent action indicates that Hollywood will be able to maintain its dominant economic position in the international film trade in the decades ahead."

In the period from 1985 to 1998, the vast majority of official announcements by the U.S. came mainly from MPAA chairman Jack Valenti. He demanded that Korea opened the film market to Hollywood, harshly castigating Korea's protectionist film policy for functioning as a trade barrier at the entry of bilateral trade. The Korean government had to initiate a negotiation with the U.S. Owing to two months of intense negotiations for a consultation, the U.S. officially withdrew its trade complaint in December 1985. Even though Korea preserved "its screen quota regulation on its domestic movies, the rest of the conflicting points were modified according to the U.S. demands as a result of the bilateral negotiations. For instance, Hollywood major studios could gain the right to establish their own branch offices in Korea" (Chang 2014, 11). Both countries agreed that the current screen quota system would remain intact, which means that the U.S. was not serious about screen quotas at this stage; both the U.S. government and Hollywood had utilized screen quotas as a bargaining tool to get other significant and profitable measures, including direct distribution rights for Hollywood majors.

The Korean government continued to maintain screen quotas in May 1996, when the government established the Motion Picture Promotion Law, allowing local governments to have up to 40 days' discretion regarding the mandated quotas. This meant that local governments could allow theaters to play Korean films for 126 days in large cities and 106 days in small cities instead of a fixed 146 days (E. J. Oh 1998, 35). The Kim Young Sam government consistently expressed the opinion that the screen quota system was essential for maintaining cultural sovereignty (*Dong-A Ilbo* 2002). That is, the government did not want to change the screen quota system on the grounds that films should be excluded from free trade principles because protecting the Korean film industry was tantamount to maintaining Korea's cultural identity. Strong protests by the Korean film industry and the public, who also feared that the abandonment of the quota system would eventually lead to a total loss of Korean film and its cultural specificity, were one of the main reasons the government maintained the screen quota system (*JoongAng Ilbo* 2002; D. Y. Jin 2011a).

In the Korea-U.S. bilateral trade negotiations in the latter part of the 1990s, U.S. trade negotiators insisted on the abolishment or modification of the Korean screen quota system. Hollywood took the opportunity to utilize these talks, which had been stalled until 1998 with screen quotas being one of the major stumbling blocks. Hollywood clearly understood that the talks had resumed in 1998 because the Korean government wanted to negotiate in order to attract foreign investment under the International Monetary Fund (IMF) era right after the 1997 financial crisis. Hollywood leaders and majors vehemently lobbied the U.S. government to demand that Korea change screen quotas while also directly asking the Korean government and film industry to eliminate the screen quota system. During the negotiations, "on the ground that the screen quota is incompatible with the standard model of the BIT by imposing on theater owners an obligation to screen local films, the U.S. argued that the screen quota should be abolished" (B. I. Choi 2002, 76).

After a visit to Korea in spring 1999 by U.S. negotiators (again including MPAA chairman Jack Valenti) to get the talks back on track (Rosenberg 2000), "mass mobilization against American free-trade pressure erupted." The anti-free-trade screen quota movement catapulted many Koreans to defend Korean film "against a perceived Hollywood invasion" (Y. A. Park 2014, 78). In July 1999, at the Puchon International Fantasy Film Festival, the Seoul-based Coalition for Cultural Diversity in Moving Images began an international movement, calling for all countries entering into multilateral agreements, including with the World Trade Organization, to recognize cultural exceptions in moving images (Rosenberg 2000, 49).

William Baker, president and chief operating officer of the MPAA, also pressed for the quota's removal when he met with Korean government officials in May 1998. As explained previously, when the two countries discussed the liberalization of the local film industry for Hollywood studios, they agreed to keep the screen quota system intact while allowing for direct distribution rights; however, once they were on track to obtain those distribution rights, the U.S. government and Hollywood changed their minds about not wanting to abolish screen quotas, which proves how much U.S. forces wanted to control the Korean film market. They acknowledged that Korean cinema was growing, and as an incentive, Baker even suggested that $500 million in foreign investment be channeled into building 20 multiplexes in Korea if the quota were abolished (Hanna Lee 1998, 16). When he visited Korea with U.S. commerce secretary William Daley in March 1999, Jack Valenti suggested that "American filmmakers [were] ready to open a series of training for Korean filmmakers, as well as to dispatch experts to help enhance the infrastructure of the Korean film industry" (J. J. Hwang 1999). The U.S. government and the MPAA had teamed up to expand Hollywood's influence in the Korean film market, which clearly indicated the increasing role of U.S. forces in the local film market.[2]

The Destiny of the Screen Quota System after the Korea-U.S. FTA

In 2003, the U.S. government demanded that Korea reduce the quota from 40 percent (146 days) to 20 percent (73 days) of annual screenings before the two sides could sit at the negotiation table again. The U.S. ambassador to Korea Christopher Hill claimed that "Korea could not have the screen quota and a free trade agreement with the U.S. at the same time." Hill stated the Korean government needed to "devise other methods for helping its film industry hone its competitiveness rather than the screen quota system. . . . The global competitiveness of the Korean film industry could be further improved through full-scale competition with foreign films" (Korea Times 2005).

Before 2000, when the Korean film industry was in recession, it was deemed necessary to protect the screen quota system. However, in the early 21st century, with the renaissance of Korean film, the question of whether this mechanism continued to be needed had become more controversial (Korea Herald 2004; J. Y. Kim 2007, 178–180). With local films holding a market share of 48.7 percent in 2013, many theaters were regularly exceeding their quota requirements (KOFIC 2007a). Thus the need to protect them through a quota system had arguably diminished. For example, early on, Carolyn Hyun Kyung Kim (2000, 378) was already arguing that "Korea's screen quota should be repealed because it encourages the Korean film industry to produce films of poor quality that are not commercially viable. Moreover, the quota only requires that Korean companies make the films, not that the films reflect Korean culture. As a result, despite the fact that the screen quota has been in existence for more than thirty years, the Korean domestic film industry continues to be dominated by foreign films."

Some ministries of the Korean government also claimed that it was time to repeal or reduce screen quotas. This certainly reflected its confidence that the thriving Korean film industry of the early 21st century had become strong enough to compete with Hollywood and to survive neoliberal cultural reform. In fact, the market share for domestic films was recorded at 63.8 percent in 2006 (KOFIC 2007c); therefore, many people, including government policy makers and theater chains, argued that the reduction of screen quotas would not negatively influence Korean cinema.

In this context, in 2003, President Roh Moo-hyun tried to persuade people in the cultural industries to come to an agreement on the screen quota issue in order to avoid upsetting foreign investors (B. K. Sohn 2003). He indicated that achieving an FTA was a top policy goal during the remainder of his term in office (Gross 2006). The change of the Roh regime's position regarding screen quotas, from state-led protection to neoliberal deregulation, was mainly due to economic interests—in particular, in relation to the FTA with the U.S., which, according to some experts, could "bring some $4 billion in foreign investment to Korea" (J. Y. Kim 2007, 178–180). Korea has traditionally developed an export-driven economy (Oh and Larson 2011); in particular, the auto industry, which accounted for some 12 percent of total exports in 2003, had been a major driving force behind Korea's export market for a long time. The U.S. had been Korea's largest car export market, accounting for 48 percent of the country's auto exports in 2003 (*Korea Times* 2004), and the Korean government could not risk losing access to the U.S. auto market (J. Y. Kim 2007).

American forces certainly took advantage of this. Bonnie Richardson, vice president for trade and federal affairs at the Motion Picture Association of America, claimed that "screen quotas harm local cinema owners by forcing them to play to empty theaters without helping local film producers, since no quota can force audiences to buy tickets to films they do not find attractive" (Salmon 2004). The MPAA wanted the quota reduced and had been lobbying U.S. Congress, the U.S. Trade Representative, and the U.S. state and commerce departments to that effect since 1996. Hollywood had made little progress. When Christopher Hill became U.S. ambassador to Korea in August 2004, however, trade issues came to the fore, and the U.S. side insisted that the screen quota issue be resolved before free trade negotiations could begin in earnest. Tami Overby, executive vice president of the American Chamber of Commerce in Korea, said, "I know President Roh has said the quota must go, key ministers are in favor, and the polls I have seen suggest 60 % of the public are in favor of its reduction or elimination" (Salmon 2004).

Consequently, regardless of the cultural sovereignty or cultural diversity imperatives, the Korean government had to use the screen quota system as a sacrificial lamb "in order to facilitate the [Korea-U.S.] FTA" (D. Y. Jin 2011b, 657–658). As Jong-Honn Kim, chief delegate for Korea-U.S. FTA negotiations, expressed in a press conference held in July 2006, "The reduction of the screen quota is to create favorable conditions for FTA; the only thing to help the negotiations between the two countries is reducing the screen quota" (Hong 2006).

For decades, the Korean government had successfully protected the screen quota system regardless of the fierce opposition by the U.S. government and Hollywood majors; however, the Korean government was finally forced by the U.S. to reduce the screen quota in the interests of the national economy in July 2006.

Just as the UNESCO convention on cultural diversity was adopted with approval of 148 countries (except for the U.S. and Israel) at the UNESCO congress at the end of 2005, USTR president Robert Portman expressed his desire to begin the FTA negotiation with Korea on the precondition of the quota reduction. Portman remarked that "the FTA would be the reward for Korean economic reform which had been carried out since 1997" (Jin Hyuk Lee 2006, 11).

In the interest of the nation's economic development, the film industry was suddenly opened up without any preparation. Korean cinema experienced a severe setback for several years after the change, while Hollywood subsequently boosted its presence and revenue in the world's seventh largest film market throughout the world.

Interestingly enough, the U.S. had already substantially increased its exports of Hollywood films to Korea since 1996, when the Korean government had allowed 40 days' discretion to local governments. It did so again after 2006's fundamental change to the screen quota system. The U.S. exported only $24 million worth of films and television programs to Korea in 1992, but that increased to $88 million in 1996, and when Korea reduced its screen quotas in July 2006, the exports of American films to Korea soared from $65 million in 2005 to $148 million in 2006, and then to $250 million in 2007 (U.S. Department of Commerce 2016; see table 3.2). These data prove that the U.S. benefited from reduced screen quotas, as expected.

THE SCREEN QUOTA SYSTEM IN THE FTA ERA

The U.S. has intensified FTA negotiations with many other countries as well (USTR 2015a). There are no major economies—like the U.K., France, Japan, and China—among the countries that have signed the FTA with the U.S. because they, unlike Korea, have not rushed. However, countries such as Australia, Mexico, Canada, and Korea have lost power in their domestic markets after signing these FTAs, just as the U.S. government and the MPAA had planned and expected.

The potential consequences of the reduction of the screen quota in Korea were controversial, because Korean film corporations had developed their domestic market in terms of the numbers of films produced and screens. In fact, when the Korean government pursued the FTA, many people, including local filmmakers, worried about a potentially dire situation for Korean cinema in the FTA era. However, some parts of Korean society argued that the film market would be stable even with the reduction of the screen quota, because Korean cinema has achieved huge success in terms of the market share of domestic films as well as the foreign export of Korean films.

At a glance, there have been several significant positive developments in Korean cinema in the FTA era. Film has continuously grown as the dominant

TABLE 3.2.   Trade in films and television programs

Year	Number of films and television tapes distributed	Revenue from films and television tapes distributed ($1 million)
1992	24	*
1993	31	0
1994	31	*
1995	48	5
1996	88	2
1997	118	*
1998	80	*
1999	79	1
2000	102	1
2001	77	0
2002	78	1
2003	72	1
2004	80	0
2005	65	4
2006	148	*
2007	250	*
2008	196	7
2009	155	4
2010	181	*
2011	156	2
2012	208	1
2013	274	15
2014	285	No disclosure
2015	407	42

* Less than $500,000

SOURCE: Compiled from the annual survey of current business published by the Department of Commerce of the U.S. between 1992 and 2016.

leisure activity among Koreans during the early 21st century. Admissions per capita for Korean cinema has increased from 1.9 in 2001, to 3.0 in 2005, and again to 4.19 in 2014, which is the highest in the world. As explained in chapter 1 as well, during the same period, admissions per capita in the U.S./Canada film market had experienced a decreasing trend, from 4.4 in 2005 to 3.6 in 2017 (MPAA 2015; 2017; KOFIC 2015a). Additionally, box-office revenue has rapidly increased consequently, from around $898 million in 2005 to $1.6 billion in 2014. In terms of film production, the Korean film industry increased the number of films that it has domestically produced from 110 in 2006 to 248 in 2014. The Korean film industry has achieved substantial growth in the FTA era without much support from the screen quota system.

Of course, in return for sacrificing the screen quota system, the government has increased its financial support of the Korean film industry. The government needed to soothe the film industry, which was concerned about the negative impact of the reduction in screen quotas. It quickly developed its slate of contingency plans to placate the local film industry, including some new cultural policies and, most importantly, the Korean Film Council (KOFIC).[3] Right after the reduction of the screen quota, this self-administering body was created to raise and manage the Film Development Fund, approximately $430 million in total at the time, to promote and support the Korean film industry in the local and international markets (Rousse-Marquet 2013). The fund was financed by $172 million from the government, another $172 million from a 3 percent surcharge placed on every cinema ticket sold in Korea, and $86 million from leftover funds from previous years. The allotment from ticket sales was initially only temporarily applied from July 1, 2007, to the end of 2014 (KOFIC n.d.), but Korea's National Assembly subsequently passed a law that continued the 3 percent Film Development Fund, for at least another seven years (Ma 2014).

In order to stimulate original and innovate production, KOFIC additionally provides support programs for Korean producers, such as the independent film support program, the labor costs support program, and accumulative support for Korean films as they are being released. The independent film support program provides the production cost for independent feature films, short films, and documentary films with a certain budget[4] (KOFIC n.d.). Consequently, the Korean Film Council has increased its annual financial support to the film industry from approximately $30.7 million in 2006 to $52.6 million in 2014 (KOFIC 2007a; 2015a).

Nevertheless, Korean cinema also experienced several serious setbacks, which might be even more significant, demonstrating that a smaller quota would eventually lead to the downfall of the local film industry. First of all, the most noticeable consequence was the increase in the number of foreign films in the Korean film market. As expected, the U.S. rapidly increased its exports to Korea; in March 2015, U.S. trade representative Michael Froman stated, "After battling economic headwinds, our trade with Korea is expanding, American industries are gaining market-share across the range of sectors from autos and chemicals to film and telecom. The office of the trade representative said that trade in U.S.-Korea goods and services rose from $126.5 billion in 2011 to a record $145.2 billion in 2014" (USTR 2015b). U.S. influence since the FTA has been substantial. For comparison, there was an increase of 140 percent in American cars imported into the Korean auto market between 2011 and 2014; however, foreign film imports into Korea are up from 289 films in 2006 to 1036 films in 2014—a 258 percent increase—and the majority are Hollywood-made (KOFIC 2015a).

Second, the market share of domestic films, which is another critical standard in analyzing the health of the domestic film industry, has also confirmed the negative impact of the Korea-U.S. FTA. The market share of domestic films as a portion of local box-office sales has plunged from 63.8 percent in 2006 to 42 percent in 2008, although it bounced back to 51 percent in 2014 (KOFIC 2015a)—whereas Japan's market share of domestic films continued its rise to 58.3 percent during the same year (Gerow 2015)—however, it is not comparable to that of 2006.

Due to this bounce-back trend, several film experts believe that the reduction of the screen quota has not seriously harmed Korean cinema. During my interviews with them, KwangWoo Noh, Shin Dong Kim, and Junhyoung Cho argued that there is no clear evidence that the screen quota in the FTA era negatively influenced the contemporary film industry, because the number of moviegoers, the number of films produced per year, and the market size based on the local box office are similar. Chung-kang Kim also claims that "contemporary Korean cinema cannot be influenced by the abolishment of screen quotas due to its size. Instead, it is desirable for the local film industry to secure several supportive measures for independent movies and low-budget movies. The government needs to establish a new form of screen quota that protects these movies, instead of commercial movies." However, Chul Huh, the movie director of *The Return* (2017) argues, "The current screen quota has been executed in a strange [way] because theaters try to screen Korean movies in November and December while screening popular foreign movies until October. Therefore, many local films [in particular, low-budget movies] have no opportunity to be screened during the first 10 months, which makes the situation worse. This trend has been made possible because of the reduction of screen quotas. When Korea kept the screen quota at 40 percent [before] 2006, theaters could not meet the quota [if] they screened domestic films at the end of the year."

Regardless of this controversy, what is certain is that the current situation is not promising compared to the record of 63.8 percent in 2006. When we compare it to the Japanese film industry, where there is no FTA with the U.S., the problem becomes clearer. The Korean film market, in terms of the market share of domestic films, was relatively weak compared to others in East Asia, because the Japanese film industry has managed to claw back more and more of the audience share in recent years, from only 27.1 percent in 2002 to 65.7 percent in 2012 (Schilling 2013).

Revenues from the box office also clearly prove that mainly Hollywood has gained in the new screen quota system. The revenues of foreign (mostly Hollywood) movies at the box office soared by as much as 152 percent between 2006 and 2014, from ₩3,340 million in 2006 to ₩8,435 million in 2014. During the same period, Korean movies achieved a rise of only 38.5 percent, from ₩5,917 million in 2006 to ₩8,206 million in 2014 (KOFIC 2016a). As the market share of domestic films in the Korean film market in the 2010s was also lower than its peak year in 2006 (63.8 percent), Hollywood films have certainly replaced local films to garner greater revenues in Korea.

More important, it is critical to understand that Korea is able to meet the current screen quota primarily due to the oligopoly in the exhibition sector. As will be detailed in chapter 4, Korean cinema has one of the highest degrees of screen oligopoly. Only a handful of multiplex chains like CJ CGV, Lotte Cinema, and Megabox have dominated the Korean exhibition market. As of December 2013, CJ CGV held 901 screens, and it accounted for 43.3 percent of screens in multiplex theaters for the year. Lotte Cinema, as the second largest chain, had 657, followed by Megabox, which had 438 (KOFIC 2014b). In this regard, KwangWoo Noh clearly explains that "a few chaebol have started to control the film industries since the early 2000s, and the involvement of these chaebol has guaranteed the current status and/or growth of Korean cinema because the screen oligopoly initiated by several chaebol provides room for Korean films to be screened." The thing is that when these chain theaters screen the same Korean movie or only a few movies on more than several hundred screens, or even more than a thousand screens, it simply fulfills the screen quota given to domestic films. Since a few chains that also control distribution have intensified their market power, the Korean film industry in the FTA era has not been healthy economically or culturally. In other words, the smaller number of Korean films in these multiplex cinemas means that more of them are profitable at the expense of diversity. Previously, during the pre-FTA era with the strong screen quota system, diversity could also not be guaranteed, but it was due to the lack of Korean films that theaters wanted to screen. In the FTA era, with reduced screen quotas, a handful of multiplex chains alongside a few foreign distributors control the local film market, and therefore, regardless of the increase in the number of local films, only a few blockbuster films can find screens and the lack of diversity continues.

Additionally, although the Korean film industry has built up its own film production sector, producing a number of films, the change in the screen quota system has influenced production and therefore exports of Korean films. Korea exported as much as $75.9 million a year before the reduction of the screen quota in 2005; however, the exports of Korean films have plummeted to only $13.5 million in 2010, with some recovery to $29.3 million in 2015 (KOFIC 2009; 2016a). The Korean film industry has recently been able to again increase its export of domestic films, partially because of the diversification of outlets. Unlike previous years, it has exported some films like *The Handmaiden* (2016), an erotic psychological thriller directed by Park Chan-wook, and *Pandora* (2016), a disaster film directed by Park Jung-woo, to digital platforms—Netflix and Amazon Studio, respectively (KOFIC 2017a). As many people watch movies through these digital platforms instead of going to theaters, this new trend may substantially help local film producers in the future.

Of course, there are several elements contributing to the recent setback of the traditional export of Korean films other than the reduction of screen quotas.

For example, another major reason was the decreasing role of the Japanese film market. In 2005, Japan imported $60 million worth of Korean films in the midst of the soaring popularity of the Korean Wave in Japan; however, it significantly reduced its import to $10.3 million in 2006—an 82.8 percent decrease from the previous year (KOFIC 2007c, 11). In addition, the price per film also plummeted, from $376,211 in 2005 to only $25,882 in 2015 (KOFIC 2007c; 2016a).

What is significant behind these data is that the already deteriorating milieu surrounding the Korean film industry worsened with the new screen quota system, expediting the dismal situation of Korean cinema in all fields, including production, market share of domestic films, and foreign export. On the one hand, local producers had also experienced difficulties in competing with foreign films; therefore, the production values in many domestic films were lower than they had previously been (D. Y. Jin 2011a). On the other hand, the Korean film industry had not developed unique films representing Korean specificities. In Japan, movie audiences did not like Korean movies mainly because they were Korean; the popularity of such films continuously relied on a few Hallyu stars rather than unique or diverse aspects of the films' genres and themes (U. J. Seo 2007). In Europe, people used to enjoy art movies and films focusing on diverse issues; however, Korean movie directors and producers could not meet those needs because even famous Korean movie directors had to produce commercial movies to succeed at all in the Korean market (KOFIC 2007c, 11).

In contrast to this, the U.S. cultural industries, including Hollywood, are among the largest beneficiaries of the global capitalist economy, since they have utilized the WTO and now the FTA to liberalize trade, increasing their sales and activities abroad (McChesney 2008). Regardless of the other elements at blame for the recent setbacks in Korean cinema, discussed above, one must acknowledge the effect of Hollywood, backed by the U.S. government, which has rapidly increased its influence thanks to the reduction of screen quotas in the Korean film market.

Last but not least, Korean cinema has experienced difficulties in finding financing, regardless of increasing government funding. As a reflection of the growth of Korean cinema, mainly starting in the mid-1990s, the average production cost had increased, from only ₩10 million in 1996 to ₩41.6 million in 2006; however, it plummeted to ₩19.9 million in 2015. One year after the reduction of the screen quota in 2005, only 30 percent of films were categorized as low budget (less than ₩10 million); however, in 2015, as many as 70.3 percent of domestic films were (KOFIC 2007b; 2015a).[5] This implies that while there have been several Korean blockbusters, the majority of the movies in these years have not secured funds or theaters because they are either low-budget movies or screened on fewer than 100 screens at the same time (KOFIC 2015a). Since the production costs of Korean films excluding low-budget movies were not much different between 2006 (₩52.1 million) and 2015 (₩56.1 million), it is not difficult to tell that this was not a healthy situation for the industry (see table 3.3). The U.S. enjoyed most of the resultant benefits of the changes to the film quotas. The FTA and other market liberalization policies forced on certain nation-states by the U.S. government have played a crucial role in deteriorating the development and/or growth of the domestic film market in many countries—particularly in Korea in the realm of cinema.

In sum, discussion surrounding the screen quota system in the Korean context proves the intensifying interplay between local and global forces. As the screen quota started to minimize Hollywood hegemony, the continuity and change in screen quotas certainly reflected conflicts between these two forces at some times and, at other times, mutual consensuses. During the process, however, it is certain that both the U.S. government and Hollywood teamed up to maximize their benefits in this major film market. The story of the reductions of Korea's screen quotas shows how Hollywood utilizes its state machinery to control the local markets

TABLE 3.3.   Production cost in Korean cinema

	Overall (₩1 million)	Commercial movies (₩1 million)
1996	10	
1997	13	
1998	15	
1999	19	
2000	21.5	
2001	25.5	
2002	37.2	
2003	41.6	
2004	41.6	43.3
2005	39.9	47.2
2006	40.2	51.1
2007	37.2	52.1
2008	30.1	45.2
2009	23.1	51.3
2010	21.6	41.9
2011	22.7	49.1
2012	20.3	46.8
2013	21.4	57.4
2014	20.1	51.5
2015	19.9	56.1
2016	24.0	45.5
2017	26.3	52.9

SOURCE: Compiled from KOFIC annual film industry white papers between 1997 and 2017.

through diverse strategies and how the U.S. government's cheerleading for neo-liberal globalization emphasizing small government substantially helps the U.S. film industry. Against this backdrop, Korean cinema, left with limited options, has continued to open its market in the realms of distribution, exhibition, and pro-duction to foreign forces—in particular, Hollywood studios.

CONCLUSION

This chapter has analyzed Korea's cultural policies regarding screen quotas, focusing on the effects of the FTA between the U.S. and Korea since 2006. It discussed whether the Korean government's decision to sign the FTA with the U.S. has directly impacted Korean cinema and how the U.S. government has expanded its role in liberalizing the global cultural market with bilateral talks, often resulting in free trade agreements, between it and other countries. The major goal of the FTAs is seemingly fair competition in global trade; however, the U.S. government has insisted that governments like Korea's and Australia's adopt nondiscriminatory regulations in several areas, including the elimination of content quotas in the cultural sector (USTR 2009). While emphasizing open-ness and deregulation in other domestic markets in the name of neoliberal glob-alization, the U.S. as a nation-state alongside transnational film corporations and the MPAA has intensified its support of Hollywood through such FTAs.

In contrast to this, the Korean government has sacrificed the domestic film industry for the sake of the Korea-U.S. FTA in order to support other industries—in particular, the auto industry. The reduction of the screen quota has negatively influenced Korean cinema. Many countries, including France and Canada, have initiated efforts to develop their cultural markets through the UNESCO convention on cultural diversity; however, Korea abruptly gave up its cultural sovereignty along with the screen quota system that had supported it. The outcomes of the neoliberal policies that the Korean government has implemented have not seemed to favor the development of national cinema. In the neoliberal globalization era, the Korean government has developed a few measures to support the Korean film industry; however, the change in screen quotas has been recorded as one of the most significant neoliberal reforms.

Over the 10 years following the reduction of the screen quota in 2006, Korean cinema experienced ups and downs in its domestic film market. The Korean film industry recuperated from the early setback soon after the new screen quota sys-tem was implemented; however, the situation was not healthy because only a few local films achieved significant profiles, showing the skewed market situation. With the increasing level of globalization and commercialization, an enhanced degree of respect for cultural values, which can be maintained through various cultural policies, ought to keep pace with increasing trade among nations.

4 · CONGLOMERATION, SCREEN OLIGOPOLY, AND CULTURAL DIVERSITY

The Korean film industry has been undergoing significant changes in the early 21st century. After a downward trend in terms of the market share of domestic films and their export of in the late 2000s, Korean cinema has experienced another surge in the popularity of domestic films, marked by a large increase in audience viewership figures. Several movies—such as *The Host* (2006), *Masquerade* (2012), *Ode to My Father* (2014), *The Admiral: Roaring Currents* (2014), *A Taxi Driver* (2017), and *Along with the Gods: The Last 49 Days* (2018)—recorded noticeable success with more than 10 million viewers each, which is a milestone indicating blockbuster-level success. Arguably, the crisis in Korean cinema hovering over the latter part of the 2000s has disappeared—at least ostensibly, if not fully.

The contemporary accomplishments of the Korean film industry, however, raise several significant questions, primarily because only a few blockbuster movies are financial successes in the monopolistic and/or oligopolistic market structure of the film industry. The downside of the recent resuscitation of Korean cinema is that the majority of films cannot make profits. In 2013, only 19 movies passed the break-even point (BEP), which is when the total production cost is equal to the total sales revenue; that so few movies do pass is partially because of both the change in screen quotas and screen oligopoly[1] (KOFIC 2014b). The situation did not disappear; in 2016, only 19 out of 82 commercial movies (23 percent) passed the BEP (KOFIC 2017a). As only a few blockbuster movies focusing on commercial genres—such as action, comedy, and science fiction—make profits, the Korean film industry cannot sustain a healthy production environment for content nor develop diversity in content.

As selected blockbuster movies are being shown on the majority of screens, low-budget movies created by independent filmmakers cannot gain a tangible presence. In other words, while some blockbuster movies have been shown on more than 1,000 screens all over the country, low budget movies, including art house films, have difficulty finding places to play, resulting in dismal failures. Only a handful of film distributors, including CJ E&M and Lotte Entertainment, vertically control the local film industry (KOFIC 2014b, 23). These mega giants, both domestic and foreign, establish a corporate sphere, emphasizing the prioritization of capital gains instead of pursuing cultural diversity, through screen oligopoly. While Korean cinema has escaped from its worst recession during the early 1990s and a temporary setback right after the reduction of screen quotas in 2006, its recent success is far from stable in all three areas—production, distribution, and exhibition.

Political economy, as applied to cultural industries, stresses the particular nature of the economic structures and the dynamics of the cultural sector. This chapter investigates such a structural change in contemporary Korean cinema through that lens. It discusses the recent growth of the oligopolistic market structures in the film industry, and it examines the emergence of transnational corporate spheres embedded in those systems. It addresses the ways in which Hollywood films are gaining more capital than local films through screen oligopoly in the exhibition sector. Finally, it maps out the influence of screen oligopoly in the local film industry by investigating its impact on cultural diversity and identity.

VERTICAL INTEGRATION TOWARD OLIGOPOLY IN THE DISTRIBUTION INDUSTRY

While there are several reasons for monopoly and oligopoly in the film industry, one of the major drivers is vertical integration. *Vertical integration* means bringing the whole movie process, from production to exhibition, under a singular entity's control. It enables a film company to increase its market power by cross-promoting or cross-selling a show as part of its neoliberal direction, meaning the film industry does not need to be regulated much (McChesney 1999). Vertical integration was a key component of the Hollywood studio system during the 1920s–1940s and beyond (D. Y. Jin 2012).[2]

This vertical integration in Korean cinema, which was learned from Hollywood, has supposedly improved efficiency, "channeled more investments into local films and helped bring larger audiences to cinemas" (Ahn 2014a). Before 2000, roles were clearly divided in the film market: film companies produced the movies, distribution companies sold them, and cinemas screened them. However, transnational corporations (TNCs), both domestic and foreign, began to enter the cinema market in the late 1990s. Many blockbuster-style movies were produced. For heavily invested movies by mega TNCs, "a secure number of screens must be guaranteed, and vertical integration of capital was necessary in order to monopolize the profits divided between the distributor and the theater owner" (D. Y. Lee 2011). As Garnham (2005, 19) points out, the cultural industries were defined as being characterized by "high fixed costs of production and low to zero marginal costs of reproduction and distribution, thus favoring economies of scale, audience maximization and both vertical and horizontal concentration."

Just as the Korean economy has grown primarily with several conglomerates, the Korean film industry is also led by a handful of large chaebol that control all levels of the process, from distribution to exhibition. After first-tier chaebol like Samsung and Hyundai, who had entered the production sector right after the Motion Picture Promotion Law of 1995, retreated in the late 1990s, several second-tier chaebol—such as CJ, Lotte, and Orion—entered the film distribution market through CJ Entertainment (now CJ E&M), Lotte Entertainment, and Showbox, respectively. Two of them operate their own theater chains, too—CJ CGV and Lotte Cinema, the nation's two largest multiplex chains. All three blockbuster movies that opened in August 2014, for example, were distributed and screened by these three distributors and/or exhibitors: *The Admiral: Roaring Currents* (CJ E&M), *The Pirates* (Lotte Entertainment), and *KUNDO: Age of the Rampant* (Showbox; KOFIC 2015a).

The distribution sector is heavily concentrated into a few megadistributors. As table 4.1 shows, four control the Korean market. Among these, CJ E&M has led the market since 2003. Considering domestic films only, in 2015, CJ E&M's share was as much as 40.5 percent, followed by Showbox (31.3 percent) and Next Entertainment World (NEW; 15 percent)—an independent film production and distribution company established in 2008. Including Lotte, these four major distributors have continued to account for more than 90 percent of the market share in most years (KOFIC 2016a).

TABLE 4.1.   Korean film market share by major distributors, 2011–2015

Ranking	2011	2012	2013	2014	2015
1	CJ E&M	CJ E&M	NEW	CJ E&M	CJ E&M
	41.2%	36.8%	29.4%	37.2%	40.5%
2	Lotte	Showbox	CJ E&M	Lotte	Showbox
	26.3%	21.5%	28%	19.6%	31.3%
3	Showbox	NEW	Showbox	Showbox	NEW
	15.6%	16.5%	22.9%	14.5%	15%
4	NEW	Lotte	Lotte	NEW	Lotte
	12.3%	15.8%	13.3%	11.5%	3.9%
Total	95.4%	90.6%	93.6%	82.8%	90.7%

SOURCE: KOFIC (2013, 2014a, 2015a, 2016a).

As only a handful of distributors control multiplex cinemas, the oligopolistic nature of Korean cinema has continued to increase. Vertical integration has also become one of the major causes of screen oligopoly, as will be discussed later in this chapter.

During my interviews, the majority of participants argued this has become one of the most significant barriers to the growth of Korean cinema. KwangWoo Noh explains that "since the late 2000s, CJ, Lotte, Showbox, and NEW have controlled the entire film industry, and Chungmuro[3] has been subordinated to these major players and worked as subcontractors, which resulted in the lack of innovation in the Korean film industries." Chul Huh, a movie director, also claims that "the single most significant problem in Korean cinema is the concentration of power into a few chaebol, including CJ and Lotte, as they control the entire film industry, including production, distribution, and exhibition. Since they invest in venture capital and financial banks, who provide film funds, only a few movies that proven directors create with superstars are able to secure funds." Meanwhile, Darcy Paquet argues,

> the degree to which major releases monopolize screens in Korea is indeed startling, compared to the situation in other countries. There is a "herd mentality" that exists on the part of exhibitors, but audiences too tend to coalesce around the film of the moment with remarkable speed. On one level, you can make the argument that exhibitors are merely responding to the demands of the audience. But this ignores the broader structural imbalances within the film industry which foster this kind of screen monopoly. The dominance of the top three exhibition chains goes virtually unchallenged, and the fact that two of these three chains are tied to major distributors is an obvious problem. There are increasing calls in South Korea to force the major distributors to sell off their exhibition arms, as in the Paramount case of 1948. This would be the ideal first step to take in confronting screen monopolization, but new government policies limiting the scale of film releases would likely also be needed to put a dent in current trends.

As such, what they commonly argue is that Korean cinema cannot prosper without resolving vertical integration and screen oligopoly through progressive cultural policies.

INCREASING ROLES OF MULTIPLEX THEATERS IN THE EXHIBITION INDUSTRY

In both the distribution and exhibition sectors, a recent surge of vertical integration and consequently screen oligopoly has substantially changed the domestic film market. In legal terms, screen oligopoly means that more than 50 percent

of cinemas show the same movie at the same time (S. Y. Cho 2012).⁴ Unlike the
issues discussed previously, the government has not actively intervened to solve
this and other relevant problems via legal power; they have been mushrooming
in the midst of oversight by the government.

Most of all, multiplex theaters have rapidly grown in Korea, as elsewhere. The
history of Korea's multiplex theater chains goes back to 1998, when CJ CGV
opened its first multiplex cinema. CJ CGV, as the largest multiplex theater chain,
held as many as 901 screens as of December 2013 and accounted for 43.3 percent of multiplex theaters. By comparison, Lotte Cinema, the second largest
chain, had 657 screens, followed by Megabox with 438 (see figure 4.1).⁵ As such,
only a handful of multiplex chains have dominated the Korean exhibition market in the early 21st century.

The proportion of multiplex theater chains has rapidly grown since the early
2000s. In 2001, the multiplexes accounted for 20.5 percent (168 screens out of
818), but they increased to 52.6 percent in 2003, and again to 85.7 percent in
2007 (KOFIC 2013). The number of screens at multiplex theaters in 2015 was
13.6 times the number in 2001. The three major chains were 96.3 percent of the
category, accounting for 94.5 percent of all screens, in 2015 (KOFIC 2016b). In
2001, Korea became the country with the highest proportion of multiplex cinemas, 95.2 percent, followed by Japan (83.1 percent), Spain (81.9 percent), the
U.S. (80.1 percent), and the U.K. (60 percent; Bainbridge 2012; KOFIC 2013).

In fact, because of these percentage differences, multiplex theater dominance in the exhibition markets of these countries is not comparable to the
kind seen in Korean cinema. For example, in the U.S., the exhibition sector
has witnessed substantial growth with the rise of megaplex theaters since the

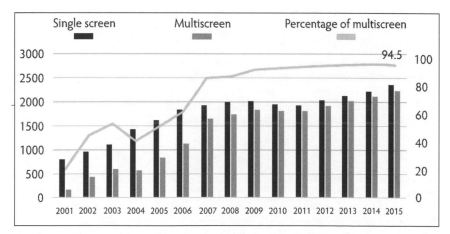

FIGURE 4.1. The rise of the multiscreen in Korean cinema, 2001–2015 (Source: Compiled
from KOFIC annual film industry white papers between 2001 and 2015.)

late 1980s. The number of screens has constantly increased from 10,335 in 1971 to 39,662 in 2012, mainly due to the rapid growth of multiscreen theaters and digital screens (National Association of Theater Owners 2014a). As the number of screens has increased, the film exhibition sector has changed ownership due to financial difficulties in many independent theaters, which has resulted in the concentration of ownership in the hands of a few major players. As of July 2013, the four largest U.S. chains—Regal Entertainment (7,318 screens), AMC Entertainment (4,988), Cinemark USA (4,434), and Carmike Cinemas (2,476)—represented almost half of the U.S. exhibition market (48.4 percent; National Association of Theater Owners 2014b). However, many film theaters have operated in the hands of independent owners for a long time. Of course, independent theaters are increasingly being financed and distributed to by Hollywood studios and large exhibitors, and oligopolistic control never ceased to be a distinguishing feature of Hollywood (Aksoy and Robins 1992; Sigismondi 2012). Regardless this strong foothold in the U.S. market is relatively lower than that in Korean cinema, because the proportion of multiplex screens in the U.S. still accounted for only just over 80 percent in 2011—compared to 95.1 percent in Korea during the same time. Korea shows one of the highest levels of screen oligopoly. Several Korean megahit movies have been made possible because more than 1,000 screens at multiplex theaters simultaneously screen the same movie.

SCREEN OLIGOPOLY IN KOREAN CINEMA

In the exhibition sector, screen oligopoly has become peculiar. The first film to be shown on more than 1,000 screens was in 2009, and as of December 2017, 96 movies had done so (see table 4.2). Among these, 48 are Hollywood movies, while 48 films are domestic; both equally benefit from screen oligopoly. Two movies in 2012, *The Thieves* (1,091 screens) and *Masquerade* (1,001 screens),

TABLE 4.2.   Films shown on more than 1,000 screens, 2009–2017

Year	Foreign movies	Domestic movies	Total
2009	1	0	1
2011	2	0	2
2012	3	2	5
2013	2	3	5
2014	6	4	10
2015	8	8	16
2016	9	11	20
2017	17	20	37
Total	48	48	96

SOURCE: Compiled from KOFIC box-office charts for each year.

became the first local films to be shown on more than 1,000 screens, resulting in an undeniable instance of screen oligopoly, as controlled by a few multiplex theater chains. Korean cinema had learned that Hollywood films, including *Transformers: Revenge of the Fallen* (2009), had become huge hits by utilizing screen oligopoly. Securing more than 1,000 screens for big budget movies became a new business strategy for the Korean film industry. Three movies in 2013 (*Secretly, Greatly; Snowpiercer;* and *The Face Reader*) and four in 2014 (*Miss Granny; The Fatal Encounter; The Admiral: Roaring Currents;* and *KUNDO: Age of the Rampant*) were also screened, one after another, on more than 1,000 screens.

When *The Admiral* was released in July 2014, the movie was screened on as many as 1,586 screens, accounting for 72.6 percent of domestic screens. Screen oligopoly has since become even more common: 8 movies in 2015 and 11 movies in 2016 were also screened on more than 1,000 screens, and many more movies reached several hundred screens. While screen oligopoly in the exhibition sector was already an issue, its degree substantially increased in the 2010s.

This form of screen oligopoly is exactly what Hollywood had in mind when it vehemently pursued the elimination/reduction of screen quotas. Based on their experiences in multiplex cinemas in the U.S., Hollywood studios knew that they could monopolize local theaters with their movies. As explained above, in terms of screen oligopoly, Hollywood movies and domestic movies are seemingly even; however, when we look into detailed information, it is clear that Hollywood has become the major player.

It is certain that the new screen quota has directly related to the expansion of screen oligopoly. On the one hand, the reduction of screen quotas in July 2006 (discussed in chapter 3) became a turning point for Korean cinema in terms of screen oligopoly. As table 4.3 shows, in 2004 and 2005, two Hollywood movies (first *Harry Potter and the Prisoner of Azkaban,* then *Harry Potter and the Goblet of Fire*) made it to the top of the box-office chart in Korea, but until then, the number of screens both Hollywood and domestic films were shown on was not worrisome. Starting in 2007, right after the reduction of screen quotas, the situation significantly changed. In 2007, *Pirates of the Caribbean: At World's End* was screened on 953 screens out of 1,975. Finally, *Transformers: Revenge of the Fallen* (2009) became the first movie ever screened at more than 1,000 screens in Korea, which opened on a large scale the era of screen oligopoly. As Hollywood expected, multiplex screens in tandem with the reduction of the screen quota worked favorably for Hollywood films.

More important, screen oligopoly even more strongly favors foreign movies because both Hollywood majors and domestic distributors release them at as many theaters as possible. In fact, screen oligopoly began with Hollywood films in the 2000s: *Transformers: Revenge of the Fallen* was the first movie to occupy more than 1,000 screens in Korea, and in 2011, *Transformers: Dark of*

TABLE 4.3.   Top movies by number of screens in Korea, 2004–2016

Year	Top movie by number of screens	Nationality of movie	Number of screens occupied	Number of total screens in Korea
2004	Harry Potter and the Prisoner of Azkaban	U.K.	228	1,451
2005	Harry Potter and the Goblet of Fire	U.K.	504	1,648
2006	The Host	Korea	647	1,880
2007	Pirates of the Caribbean: At World's End	U.S.	953	1,975
2008	The Good, the Bad, the Weird	Korea	824	2,044
2009	Transformers: Revenge of the Fallen	U.S.	1,154	2,055
2010	Iron Man 2	U.S.	921	2,003
2011	Transformers: Dark of the Moon	U.S.	1,409	1,974
2012	The Dark Knight Rises	U.S.	1,210	2,081
2013	Iron Man 3	U.S.	1,389	2,184
2014	Transformers: Age of Extinction	U.S.	1,602	2,281
2015	Avengers: Age of Ultron	U.S.	1,843	2,424
2016	Captain America: Civil War	U.S.	1,991	2,575
2017	A Taxi Driver	Korea	1,906	2,766

SOURCE: Compiled from KOFIC box-office charts for each year.

the Moon and Mission Impossible: Ghost Protocol became blockbuster hits in Korea as well via the same means. The story continues. *Transformers: Age of Extinction* was screened at 1,602 screens when it was released in July 2014, and *Iron Man 3* (1,389) in April 2013 also became a megahit movie through screen oligopoly. In 2016, *Captain America: Civil War* was screened at 1,991 screens, which was the highest number of the year for both foreign and domestic films.

This shows that Hollywood has been the most successful at capitalizing on screen oligopoly, as over the 14 years between 2004 and 2017, 11 Hollywood films attained the top position in terms of number of screens occupied. Only three Korean films—*The Host* (2006), *The Good, the Bad, the Weird* (2008), and *A Taxi Driver* (2017)—did the same. Some Korean scholars (e.g., J. H. Kim 2015) believe that the change in the screen quota has had no particular influence on Korean cinema, and that screen oligopoly should not be a negative element because it might develop the competitiveness of Korean films; however, these data (tables 4.1 and 4.2) certainly show its unhealthy effect. As explained in the previous chapter, Korean cinema has been able to manage the new screen quotas in the FTA era partially by developing screen oligopoly, on a smaller scale, following Hollywood's lead.

The Transformers movies were imported by CJ E&M, while *Iron Man 3* was imported by Sony Pictures, but whether they are domestic or foreign films and whether their distributors are domestic or from Hollywood, screen oligopoly is real in Korean cinema. The current screening system at multiplexes reflects "market competition, which drives cinemas to fill as many seats as possible, a market logic that emerged when movie production interests merged with distributors and theaters" (D. Y. Lee 2011). As table 4.4 shows, screen oligopoly has allowed a few select films to break the 10-million-admissions barrier in Korea, which means that it has brought in huge profits—to only a few select movies.

SCREEN OLIGOPOLY ON CULTURAL IDENTITY

In the Korean film industry, a few megadistribution companies wield power over movie production and exhibition. Korean film corporations clearly understand that it is more advantageous to own the whole chain of industry, including production, distribution, and exhibition. Distribution especially is the nexus of power in the film business (Kunz 2007). Hence some producers are connected with certain distributors, leading to an oligopoly in the distribution market and then one on screens. While a few blockbuster movies occupy more than 1,000 screens, many other low-budget movies fail to find screen space, pushed aside by the screening schedules of the major distributors. In this regard, as *Variety* observes, looking at the recent blockbuster trend sweeping the Korean box office, it would be easy to conclude that vertical integration is the driving force (N. Kim 2014).

That vertical integration leads to screen oligopoly is troublesome, primarily because it destroys cultural identity and diversity in the type of films screened and limits distribution channels. The notion of *cultural identity* refers to "the

TABLE 4.4.   All-time box-office rankings of Korean movies by number of viewers until 2016

Rank	Movie title	Opening day	Revenue (₩)	Number of viewers	Number of screens
1	*The Admiral: Roaring Currents*	July 30, 2014	135,753,322,310	17,615,057	1,587
2	*Ode to My Father*	Dec. 17, 2014	110,933,990,730	14,262,199	1,044
3	*Veteran*	Aug. 5, 2015	105,169,264,250	13,414,200	1,115
4	*The Thieves*	July 25, 2012	93,667,250,500	12,983,841	1,091
5	*Miracle in Cell No. 7*	Jan. 23, 2013	91,431,950,670	12,811,213	866
6	*Assassination*	July 22, 2015	98,463,522,781	12,705,783	1,519
7	*Masquerade*	Sep. 13, 2012	88,909.157,769	12,323,408	1,001
8	*Train to Busan*	July 20, 2016	93,167,379,048	11,563,794	1,788
9	*The Attorney*	Dec. 18, 2013	82,872,264,800	11,374,861	925
10	*Haeundae*	July 22, 2009	81,025,734,000	11,324,545	764

SOURCE: KOFIC (2016c).

collective self-awareness that a given group embodies and reflects." It is "akin to the idea of a national or social character which describes a set of traits that members of a given community share with one another beyond their individual differences. Such traits include a constellation of values and attitudes towards life." It therefore incorporates shared premises, values, and beliefs (Adler 2002). Jan Servaes (1989, 383) has already argued that "cultural identity refers to the constitution and cultivation of a reality on the basis of particular values, a reality in which the value system and the social system are completely interwoven and imbued with the activity of each other." He especially emphasizes the relationship "between forms of cultural identity and modes of production and communication that build upon this new perception of culture by emphasizing the macro level of international communication—that is, the cultural imperialism problematic."

However, as Jung Bong Choi (2011, 181) aptly puts it, in our contemporary society, national cinemas are held captive to identity and uniqueness, which does not reflect rapidly changing sociocultural dimensions. For him, "the cinematic contour of a nation can no longer cling to cultural exclusivity but has to acknowledge overlaps and commonality, be they textual, financial, cultural, or material," although "the place these overlapping elements occupy in a society—their respective meanings, significances as well as modes of signification within particular media-cultural landscapes—could vary considerably." Hyangjin Lee (2005, 67) also argues, "The notion of Korean-ness assumes that the collective identity of the nation can be defined by its unique cultural experiences and traditions"; however, "this conceptual artificiality does not accurately reflect the heterogeneity of social reality." What they commonly claim is that contemporary national cinema has been influenced by several elements, and the hybridization of domestic films, of domestic culture with "other" culture, makes it difficult to define national identity. Of course, this does not mean that we do not need to define the notion of cultural identity/uniqueness that we have to protect. Cultural identity with some variations has always been a fundamental cultural value to be protected and preserved.

In the national cinema context, a multiplex may offer diversity and functional integration of space. In other words, "multiplexes are supposed to guarantee an abundant choice of movies at theaters but [companies] are misusing the system, negatively affecting the success of smaller movies" (E. S. Jin 2015). They have become a venue for the most "effective presentation of a small number of hit movies. Having several screens at one site implies a variety of movie offerings, but multiplexes are devoting more of their screens to hit movies only. The screens are not allotted with diversity in mind but according to the movie's popularity: i.e. big hits, somewhat favorable, average, and bomb" (D. Y. Lee 2011). Many domestic filmmakers and producers have long raised concerns that "monopoly would hurt the diversity of films" (*Yonhap News* 2015). It is not difficult to identify the ways in which screen oligopoly hurts diversity and identity in film content.

Most of all, screen oligopoly has resulted in changes in film production. This monopolistic and/or oligopolistic market structure hurts diversity films as well as audiences' rights to select what they want to see, which has drawn much concern. Despite the fact that multiplex cinemas are able to screen them, instead, they focus on a handful of commercially guaranteed films. *Diversity films*, also known as "noncommercial movies"—including independent, art house (auteur), and documentary movies—are not good for companies' bottom lines. It is true that there has been a growth in the number of diversity movies with the development of digital technologies; however, the market share of these in terms of moviegoers seeing them at theaters has continuously decreased. In fact, in 2009, diversity movies accounted for 6.6 percent of films seen in theaters, but it went down to 5.4 percent in 2010, 3.0 percent in 2011, 1.9 percent in 2012, and 1.6 percent in 2013. In 2013, *Jiseul*—the highest-ranked diversity film, had only 144,518 attendees and could be seen on only 81 screens. *Our Sunhi*—the second highest, had only 66,778 attendees and 23 screens (KOFIC 2014b). Paquet (2011, 18) had claimed that "what is special about Korean cinema is its diversity" because Korea's independent film community develops every kind of film people can think of; however, with screen oligopoly's rapid takeover, diversity in Korean cinema could not be sustained, at least at multiplex theaters.

As multiplex theaters increasingly allot their screens to only a few blockbuster movies, films made on shoestring budgets and art house films face certain barriers. Due to the strong dominance of box-office hits in the Korean film market, many art house films and films distributed by small companies end up not being advertised, "being screened during less popular time periods and disappearing from theaters after only a few weeks" (Ahn 2014a). The majority of diversity movies have difficulties in finding investors and theaters; therefore, it has become increasingly hard for them to survive. Although they find some screens, only a few days later, they have to retreat from many because the major theater chains would rather make more room for a few blockbusters.

Another significant issue is the demise of auteur cinema, which engages the humanist vision of a single writer-director. Auteur cinema is often at odds with the box office, but "in Korea, many of the commercial blockbuster films are made by the very auteurs whose ideals are not often incommensurate with that of the entertainment-driven capitalist enterprise" (Kyung Hyun Kim 2012, 182–183). Several film directors like Bong Joon-ho, Park Chan-wook, and Kim Jee-woon attained stardom by fully exploiting their delicate relationships with Hollywood genre films. By fully embracing Hollywood, "their works display hybridity that equally engages national identity and global aesthetics, art and commercialism, conformity and subversion, and narrative coherence and stylistic flair. . . . Although there are differences between their works, what is equally striking in the works of the three filmmakers is the uniform manner signifiers, such as people and nation, from the previous decades are re-authored and even loosened as absolute historical monads" (Kyung Hyun Kim 2012, 186).

Unlike auteur movies, contemporary megahit movies, such as *The Thieves* and *Masquerade*, are primarily entertainment-driven commercial ones. Far from developing from national identity and political traumas, these movies were criticized for their attempted copying of Hollywood movies. Admitting to the contemporary nature of the hybridity of domestic films, these blockbuster genre movies seem to clearly ignore cultural diversity and authenticity to develop the Hollywood formula. As the success of several movies can be made possible primarily due to the nexus of producers' commercial interests and distributors' marketing strategies, it has been difficult to develop diversity films, including auteur movies, in contemporary Korean cinema in the 2010s.

Several parts of society have spoken out about screen oligopoly, and some film directors raise this concern themselves. For example, director Kim Ki-duk unleashed harsh criticism over the practice during a news conference to mark his winning of the Golden Lion award for his savage morality tale *Pieta* at the 2012 Venice Film Festival. He alleged that he and other nonmainstream directors are barred from cinemas by mainstream production companies that own big theater chains such as CGV, Lotte and Megabox (*Yonhap News* 2013). At a Busan seminar held on October 8, 2014, even the producers of some of Korea's biggest-ever blockbusters also voiced concerns about vertical integration and monopolization in the local cinema industry. *The Host* producer Choi Yong-bae warned that the oligopoly has resulted in a lack of creativity: "Investment, distribution and screening are all operated by conglomerates. They are abusing their rights and position, so adventurous or experimental films cannot be made." Choi called on the industry to work together and change the system so fresh material and more creative projects could be produced (Shackleton 2014).

Diversity in developing national traditions and arts is indeed in jeopardy in Korean cinema. Although many young movie fans and critics want to see more art house films at theaters, it is almost impossible. It is certain that the oligopoly of these multiplexes' has limited people's choices as well. Therefore, the film industry and the government together must provide screens where small and midsized film corporations and directors are able to show their films. This is necessary for diverse and unique movies to be able to be produced and thus for the Korean film industry to prosper in the long term. During my interview with Shin Dong Kim, a media scholar, he emphasized that Korean cinema needs to utilize various strategies to secure cultural diversity. Instead of asking film exhibitors to screen low-budget movies, the government and film producers can open public spaces, including schools and government offices, to screen those diversity movies so that many people may easily access them, which eventually will enhance cultural diversity.

CORPORATE SPHERE IN THE SCREEN MONOPOLY

There have been no particular policy measures to resolve this unhealthy industrial structure hurting cultural identity and diversity. There is no screen antitrust law that aims to directly regulate the phenomenon of screen oligopoly and market concentration in the current legal scheme. Consequently, promarket corporations always insist and exploit the free-market system. In 2007, the legislative Promotion of the Motion Pictures and Video Products Act, which would have put a limit on the number of screens a movie could be shown on—no more than 30 percent—was brought to the National Assembly for discussion. However, strong confrontation from stakeholders suspended conversation. As such, the Korea Fair Trade Commission has extended some indirect regulations; however, it has been insufficient and has not changed the industry's direction (S. Y. Cho 2012).

Most recently, in October 2016, People's Party lawmaker Ahn Cheol-soo proposed "a Promotion of the Motion Pictures and Video Products Act amendment that would prevent large companies from being involved simultaneously in distribution and screening. Lotte and CJ are considered the two most prominent examples of combined distribution and screening operations" (J. S. Kwack 2016). However, this movement has lost its momentum in the midst of the political turmoil surrounding President Park Geun-hye and the Ministry of Culture, Sports and Tourism.[6]

The Korean film industry, which is a strong example of a capitalist enterprise, is currently enjoying its free-market ideology with no governmental intervention. Capitalism as an economic system works to "naturalize the concept of an open market economy that the competition of various businesses and industries in the marketplace should be unhindered by governmental intrusion" (Benshoff and Griffin 2009, 9). Korea has no governmental mediation in the case of screen oligopoly, and therefore, the government had actualized the neoliberal capitalist market system. However, the Korean film industry also has no capitalist market competition in which diverse players work together. As McChesney (1999) emphasizes, the Korean film industry, as a capitalist market system with no governmental oversight, has turned into a market oligopoly, where only a handful of corporations benefit from capitalism. The vertical integration of the distribution and exhibition industries has brought about unfair competition because local theaters screen films from their own distribution companies longer than films from other distributors (Y. S. Choi 2007, 86).

Due to increasing criticism in Korea, 26 organizations, including representatives from major film organizations, three major multiplex chains (CJ CGV, Lotte Cinema and Megabox) and four major distributors (CJ E&M, Lotte Entertainment, Showbox, and NEW), gathered on October 1, 2014, to enter into a voluntary industry pact calling for fairer competition. The agreement requires theaters to disclose their screen allotment criteria and to guarantee that all films are screened for at least a week. As expected, however, this kind of voluntary agreement cannot resolve the issues embedded in screen oligopoly. In December 2014, Korea's Fair Trade Commission (FTC) fined Lotte Cinema and CGV ₩5.5 billion after they extended the run periods for their movies. This was a new move by the FTC to boost transparency in the exhibition sector; however, Lotte Cinema and CGV immediately started a legal battle against the FTC and ultimately won the case in February of 2017 (*Yonhap News* 2017). This implies that the government cannot regulate the hegemonic power of a handful of major distributors in Korean cinema, which is a blow to indie and diversity movies. As Andrew Shapiro (2011) argues, even in the U.S., "antitrust laws make it illegal for a large theater chain to manipulate the cutting off of movie supply to independent theaters and smaller chains by threatening to use its larger size to retaliate against movie distributors who choose to supply these pesky competitors." However, the Korean government and the film industry have no particular intention in developing any regulations to counteract these oligopolistic industrial structures or screen oligopoly itself. The corporate sphere, emphasizing investors' logic, cannot be checked and thus Korean cinema deteriorates.

CULTURAL DIVERSITY IN KOREAN CINEMA

Because of business imperatives, neoliberal cultural reforms have not advanced cultural diversity and sovereignty, as can be seen in both the structures of conglomeration and screen oligopoly. Cultural diversity has related to both international trade negotiations and domestic cultural identity. On the one hand, *cultural diversity* is a term that has replaced "the previously employed concept of cultural exception" against the U.S. in international trade negotiations, in efforts to promote the exclusion of audiovisual products from international trade liberalization. Some countries, fearing that U.S. products would dominate their domestic markets and cause the decline of independent, domestic production in the cultural industries, have insisted that "audiovisual products were different from other commodities and hence should be exempted from trade liberalization" (Kawashima 2011, 476–477). Many filmmakers and policy makers certainly argue that preserving and promoting cultural diversity has been important, because cultural diversity is directly related to political freedom and people's equality (G. S. Park 2006).

Several countries have developed cultural policies, including screen quota and subsidies for domestic film production, to secure diverse cultural products and freedom of expression. The proponents of cultural diversity in the realm of film argue that Hollywood produces blockbuster films and aggressively sells them globally, and consequently, more original, creative, and culturally diverse non-Western films have little market appeal, and global cultures become homogenous. In the film context, one could think of this heterogeneity of cultural content in relation to program type (e.g., film genre), language used, cultural tradition, and political orientation (Kawashima 2011, 476–478).

On the other hand, cultural diversity can be analyzed in conjunction with cultural identity. As Malik et al. (2017, 312) point out, what is significant here is that the idea of cultural identity, as the identity or feeling of being part of a group, cannot be considered as a static entity; it is "the idea of cultural identity as a moving phenomenon where new cultural selves are constantly being formed." In other words, cultural identity should be understood as an entity that is constantly being repositioned and reshaped, which means that cultural identities "undergo constant transformation," as Stuart Hall (1990, 225) argues. Thus "we might regard cultural diversity (where diverse cultural identities co-exist) itself as a (mediated) process," which means that "cultural diversity is thus built, and mediated, through these processes of practice" (Malik et al. 2017, 312). As Eugenia Siapera (2010, 6–7) claims, "Cultural diversity is also mediated" and "we understand, and interact with, cultural diversity, and we construct our cultural identities (also) in and through the media." What Siapera emphasizes is that the construction of cultural identity "is not determined, but interactively influenced by the dynamic associated with the media." This is even more important when one considers how cultural diversity has been treated within cultural policy making (Freedman 2008). As N. Burgi-Golub (cited in Yim 2002) also points out, the issue of cultural identity has been considered a major policy objective within many countries, and the notion of it has changed with shifting cultural policies as well.

In the national context, Korea used to deliberate these matters, and the primary cultural policy objectives were to reproduce cultural identity and promote regional culture (Yim 2002). Reflecting the less commercialized eras, the Park Chung Hee regime, for example, launched the first comprehensive five-year master plan for cultural development to be implemented from 1974 to 1979. A priority was to establish a new cultural identity by highlighting a specific cultural tradition. The plan mainly targeted folk arts and traditional culture instead of popular culture like films and television programs (Ministry of Culture and Information 1979, 228). However, in terms of film content, since the Park Chung Hee regime strictly controlled Korean cinema through censorship, many films reflecting Korean culture and history were mainly anticommunist and enlightenment films (films primarily made for educational purposes), which means that cultural diversity was not guaranteed during the military regime.

In the past two decades, cultural diversity has been one of the major subjects, in tandem with the screen quota system and public funding, that has consequently influenced film content. As detailed in chapter 3, the Korean government until 2006 sustained the opinion that the screen quota system was the last resort for cultural sovereignty and diversity (*JoongAng Ilbo* 2006). During the Busan International Film Festival held in 2000, Congressman Shin Ki-Nam clearly stated that "supporting the quota system does not mean we are excluding other films. It is about preserving our uniqueness. Hollywood movies have no difficulty earning money here. What we are emphasizing is that Korean movies should be given an equal chance to survive" (George 2000).

Arguably, the screen quota system protected the local film industry while preserving cultural identity, and Korea's Coalition for Cultural Diversity in Moving Images (CDMI) argued in favor of a cultural exception in international trade (Frater 2000), and the government also did not plan to change screen quotas, on the same grounds. The government and many film scholars feared that the abandonment and/or severe reduction of the screen quota system would lead to the total loss of the Korean film industry and the medium's cultural diversity.

However, several administrations since the early 1990s did not stop to consider cultural diversity because their priority was the film sector's economic imperative. Although they have partially supported small film corporations whose major focuses are cultural diversity and sovereignty, these administrations, from then till now, have emphasized the financial successes of domestic films. When the Korean government pursued the revitalization of the dying film industry in the 1990s, its main interest was an economic matter, not a cultural one. The issue of cultural diversity and identity during the neoliberal era was not seriously considered in devising its policies. In this regard, during my interview with him, Darcy Paquet claimed, "The Korean Film Council previously created a program to financially support the operation of art house theaters and venues devoted to independent films, but the scale and effectiveness of this program was significantly curtailed under the Lee Myung-bak and Park Geun-hye administrations. Another much-discussed idea with potential is to institute a cultural screen quota, requiring all theaters to devote a small number of screenings per year to art house or independent films from around the world."

Meanwhile, the diversification of capital resources in Korean cinema has also not secured cultural diversity and specificity. As is commonly seen in Hollywood, once transnational corporations control the cultural industries, film content can be twisted to reflect their commercial interests instead of enhancing local identities. Venture capitalists and crowdfunding are not much different from chaebol in that they also strongly seek commercial successes. Of course, we cannot claim that transnational corporations and/or venture capitalists ruin cultural specificities with blockbuster movies, as they can still develop films portraying cultural traditions. What we can say is that the blockbusterization of Korean cinema marginalizes indie films, which reflect people's daily activities and struggles. In fact, as Russell (2005) correctly observes, "Korea's weekly top-10 box office chart is regularly chopped down to a top eight—or even fewer—because there have simply been too few films in the theaters to even make up 10 titles. The number of screens has grown, but the variety of films offered has declined." Despite the huge gains made by the local film industry, many film critics, movie scholars, and audiences worry that "success has paradoxically led to a decline in the diversity available to local moviegoers" (Russell 2005). This trend has continued and even intensified due to screen oligopoly, which impedes cultural diversity and identity.

Most of all, the impossibility of developing cultural diversity in Korean cinema, of course, is also directly related to Hollywood's influence. While several concerns have arisen due to Hollywood's hegemony in the Korean film market, two major issues, both in terms of cultural and industrial perspectives, are closely connected. First, Hollywood movies advocate American values and the American way of life, such as commercialization and commodification, thereby threatening national cultures—cultural sovereignty and diversity. As Will Hays, former president of the Motion Picture Producers and Distributors of America (MPPDA), stated in 1923, "Every film that goes from America abroad, wherever it shall be sent, shall correctly portray to the world the purposes, the ideals, the accomplishments, the opportunities, and the life of America" (cited in Glancy 2014, 21). Seeing an important connection between media and national power, Hays encouraged producers to make films with patriotic themes that extolled Americanism. Hays considered his field of operation to consist of more than just the home front: "We are going to sell America to the world with American motion pictures" (Vaughn 2005, 133).

Second, Hollywood advocates the free flow of goods and services because of that policy's core value for the U.S. economy. The MPPDA of old promoted the idea that "Hollywood's international reach had a beneficial effect for the wider American business community" (Glancy 2014, 21). The film industry itself had seemingly infinite commercial promise, generating more income in 1922 than all the public utilities in the U.S. combined (Vaughn 2005, 133–134). In particular, from a critical political economy perspective, it is significant to understand Hollywood's commercial imperatives with "the U.S. government instigating and facilitating capital accumulation generally and screen trade in particular" (Miller et al. 2005, 5). The U.S. has substantially expanded its profits in the realm of films. According to the annual data I compiled from the U.S. Department of Commerce between 1992 and 2016, the U.S. has increased its exports of films and television programs, from only $2.562 billion in 1992 to $17.789 billion in 2015, while its imports increased from $76 million to $4.5 billion in 2015. Therefore, the U.S. has enjoyed one of the highest net profits in the audiovisual industry. As Tamara L. Falicov (2000, 341) points out, the local film industry has increasingly faced a quandary "in reconciling issues around the construction" of national identities on screen, while at the same time trying to "sustain a viable film industry" in the middle of competition from Hollywood.

Since the early 20th century, Hollywood has certainly become a significant apparatus to promote American values through the films they produce while making one of the most profitable industries for the American economy. Due in large part to these ideological and commercial purposes, Hollywood has vehemently encroached on other national film industries, and Korean cinema has been victimized by Hollywood's globalization strategies. While admitting that the idea of cultural diversity and identity can be shifted and modified, one cannot ignore how these several dimensions surrounding Korean cinema have impeded cultural diversity instead of enhancing it.

Therefore, as Won Mog Choi (2007, 283) argues, "Multilateral efforts to harmonize commercial interests with cultural diversity are vital. In this light, the Convention on Cultural Diversity is instrumental to every world citizen, not to mention to cultural activists." By subsidizing film quality, cultural content, and commercial viability, the Korean government could create a competitive domestic film industry that promotes Korean culture. Considering the milieu that currently surrounds the industry, determining how to develop the balance between commercial movies and diversity movies will be a challenge for Korean cinema to overcome in.

CONCLUSION

This chapter has analyzed the structural transformation of the Korean film industry since the mid-1990s in order to determine the overall trend in Korean cinema. It has examined the recent growth of its oligopolistic market structure and investigated the causes of its structural shift toward oligopoly in terms of both its exhibition and distribution systems as well. This chapter has also discussed the impact of screen oligopoly on cultural diversity and identity.

Most of all, Hollywood has continued to influence Korean cinema. After the Korea-U.S. FTA gave direct distribution rights to Hollywood majors and reduced screen quotas, Hollywood movies have benefited from screen oligopoly. Hollywood has implanted its own business model in the Korean film industry to garner maximum capital gains. Their influence on Korean cinema in the realm of exhibition is critical, as Korean filmmakers and multiplex theaters have modeled their screen oligopoly system on Hollywood's.

Some movie critics and producers have said that Korean cinema fought against "the market dominance of Hollywood films in the past and is now combating the screen monopoly of films backed by Korean conglomerates" (Shim 2015). For example, Jeon Chan-il, Busan International Film Festival's programmer, has said, "The problem about the monopoly in the film industry is not limited to Korea. I also think that despite such conditions, Korean cinema is still one of world's most vibrant and diverse [film industries], and the country being the world's 7th largest film market [in 2011] is a telling sign" (S. M. Park 2012). Some in the industry, including multiplex owners, also argue that screen oligopoly is not a problem. However, they likely do not fully understand that the system has been driven by and for Hollywood films, and what they miss is that in the future, Korean cinema cannot continue to prosper without diversity in films and collaboration among film corporations.

More important, it is critical to acknowledge that several blockbuster movies' successes, based on screen oligopoly, have consequently resulted in the lack of diversity seen in both movie genres and the range of choice for audiences, while also restricting competitive pricing and making poor conditions for movie production. With local cinemas screening only commercially viable movies, the phenomenon of wealth disparity is intensifying: the rich getting richer and the poor getting poorer. Content per se matters, but the logics of distribution and competition among distributors matter more in Korean cinema (Song and Im 2013).

Max Horkheimer and Theodor Adorno (1969) have already developed the idea of the cultural industries as part of their critique of the false legacies of the Enlightenment; the term *cultural industry* back then was intended to draw critical attention to the commodification of art. Therefore, it is not easy to emphasize the significant role of culture as art and for diversity; however, it is critical to understand that the film industry will be able to further grow when it develops a well-designed balance between commercial movies and diversity movies. The Korean film industry is relatively strong in regard to the number of movie viewers in the country and the number of films that are domestically produced. However, it is not healthy due to the lack of diversity and Hollywood's continuing dominance. The government and the film industry must understand that long-term prosperity can be made possible only through diversity, not short-term capital gain via screen oligopoly.

5 · PUBLIC FILM FUNDING AND TRANSNATIONAL PRODUCTION

Korean cinema has had a more than century-long history of film production. Since Korea's liberation from Japan, cinema has been closely intertwined with the country's changing cultural policies. The Korean government initiated a few significant measures to support the production sector especially. In an effort to revitalize the almost nonexistent filmmaking industry, Rhee Syngman, the first president of the country (1948–1960), supported the film industry through a few legal and financial strategies, which was the beginning of a unique relationship between the government and the film industry. The Rhee government exempted the film industry from taxation (Y. K. Song 2012), which was recorded as the first government subsidy in the film industry, and in the 1960s, it also supported motion pictures using legal measures. As is also evidenced in histories of film industries in many other countries, including the U.S. and the U.K., Korean cinema's early stage of development and growth could not have been made possible without government assistance (Miller et al. 2001; Wasko 2003).

The Korean government has massively adopted transnational globalization policies since the early 1980s; however, in the midst of this, it has also supported local cinema with financial subsidy programs, resulting in the industry's growth in the early 21st century. Of course, Hollywood has continued to influence Korean cinema in all areas; it has started to produce films in Korea and to directly invest in film production in the 2010s. Therefore, film funding in Korea, which is one of the most significant mechanisms powering Korean cinema, is a complex web of diverse policy objectives, competencies, regulations, and direct and indirect forms of support (Joo 2010).

This chapter attempts to clarify the cause(s) of the changes and goes on to investigate the Korean film industry with a special focus on film funding, including the state public film fund. It historicizes the growth of this fund by exploring the major reasons for its development and its impacts on Korean cinema. It pays particular attention to the ways in which the Korean government has developed the public film fund in the era of neoliberal globalization, analyzing the reasons for its initial establishment. It then discusses the impact of changing film policies on the film business by examining the influx of domestic capital into the film industry. Finally, it documents a recent trend in film production by analyzing the impact of transnational film production—in particular, Hollywood, but not excluding other foreign forces—in Korea while examining the influence of Hollywood majors' direct investments in Korean cinema.

CHANGING ROLES OF THE NATION-STATE IN THE FILM FUND

Cultural industries corporations are mainly private; however, the governments in many countries have supported and/or initiated their growth through several legal and financial mechanisms. As the cultural and economic significance of the film industry has received increasing levels of public attention, the Korean government has similarly developed its own public film fund, starting in the early 1990s, in the midst of neoliberal cultural reform.

Most justification of government support for private film production is given one of two kinds of rationales: cultural or economic. The first is the need to protect and develop the cultural heritage and identity of the nation, thereby enhancing social cohesion and a sense of belonging (Barker 2000; Newman 2009). The second is to provide economic growth and development; the film industry in particular provides skilled, high-paying jobs. In supporting each of these rationales, governments have a number of policy instruments available, including subsidies, regulations, the resources of government departments or agencies, and public-private partnerships (Howlett and Ramesh 1995; Newman 2009). These two factors, of course, significantly overlap, and the form of the support can have profound impacts on the targeted industry (Hesmondhalgh 2013).

Several countries have indeed given financial support to their domestic film sectors since the early stages of film culture. As the largest cultural market, the U.S. government's support for its film industry has been unique. As Toby Miller and Richard Maxwell (2006, 41) argue, "The U.S. government has devoted massive resources to generate and sustain 'private-sector' film in the interests of ideology and money, and the industry has responded in commercial and ideological kind. All in all, this represents a wide array of subsidies, regulations and domestic market protections that neither media studies nor the media-reform movement have yet to subject to a full critical analysis and financial accounting." The U.S. film industry has been aided through decades of tax-credit schemes, representation by the state and commerce departments, Small Business Administration financing through loans in support of independents, currency assistance from the Informational Media Guaranty Program, and a vast array of state, regional and city film commissions coordinated by Film US, as well as hidden subsidies to the film industry via reduced local taxes, free provision of police services, and the blocking of public streets (Miller and Maxwell 2006).

Other major markets are not much different. During the British new wave of films between the late 1950s and the early 1960s, while the attainment of a distributor's guarantee and bank loans were vital sources of funding for film production, the existence of the National Film Finance Corporation (NFFC) eased the pathway to a new pattern of production and distribution (Street 2014). In Canada, federal and provincial governments offer a wide range of financial supports for eligible film and television productions produced in Canada. The Canadian financing available can generally be divided into four categories: (1) federal and provincial government tax credits, (2) incentive programs, (3) private financial assistance, and (4) other sources (including funding restricted to Canadian content; McMillian 2011).

In the late 1980s, the Canadian government switched its emphasis from tax incentives to direct investment and support for international coproduction. Direct financial support for production has been provided through federal government agencies, the Canadian Film Development Corporation (established in 1968) and its successor, Telefilm Canada. The level of direct support increased with the formation of Telefilm Canada in 1983 and again with the establishment of its Feature Film Fund in 1986. For example, in the financial year 1994–1995, Telefilm received a parliamentary appropriation of $122 million (Finn et al. 1996, 152). Likewise, nations ranging from Norway, Denmark, and Spain to Mexico and South Africa keep their small domestic film production industries alive with government subsidies (McChesney 2001). "As the social and economic significance of the creative industries has received increasing levels of attention, publicly funded filmmaking has come under the spotlight" (Blomkamp 2011, 341).

However, with the adoption of neoliberal cultural policies emphasizing the decreasing role of the nation-state, government subsidies to the public broadcasting and film industries have rapidly disappeared in many countries. As Stiglitz (2002, A16) argues, neoliberalism was born from what has been termed the "Washington Consensus," which argued for "a minimalist role for government and rapid privatization and liberalization." It dictated the application of a common set of policies based around fiscal austerity, privatization of publicly owned assets, and market liberalization and became the unanimous recommendation of U.S.-based international agencies like the International Monetary Fund (IMF) and the World Bank for developing countries facing economic difficulties (Flew and Cunningham 2010). In this respect, David Harvey (2005, 2) correctly points out that "neoliberalism is a theory of political-economic practices that proposes that human well-being can best be advanced by liberating individual entrepreneurial freedoms and skills within an institutional framework characterized by strong private property rights, free markets, and free trade."

In the realm of culture, "many governments have no choice but to give up their intervention in the cultural sector, including the film industry. Proponents of neoliberalism in every country argue that cultural trade barriers and regulations harm consumers, and that subsidies inhibit the ability of nations to develop their own competitive media firms" (McChesney 2001). In the global cultural industries—in particular, film industries—there have been two distinctive financing models, either private-driven on the basis of neoliberal cultural policies or government-funded, as Derin (2010, 25) points out:

> The majority of films in the U.S. market can only get made thanks to private investment, provided by big companies and packaged by producers, who all consider the films as consumer goods in the first place. In contrast to this system, where profit always tends to come first, the European film industry is fueled by other motivations. Here, a film often aspires to be a work of art, which conveys a way of life, bears witness to the present or carries a cultural heritage. For this reason, large film subsidies are made available to film-makers by the different governments.

Although this statement does not reflect the pivotal role of the U.S. government as the key player in the growth of Hollywood majors in the global film markets, it at least provides the two basic models for the growth of national film industries. However, unlike the U.S. model and the European model, the Korean film industry is a unique showcase because it has developed its financing system in the middle of the confrontation between neoliberal globalization and state-led developmentalism.

On the one hand, Korean cinema has been restructured under the banner of deregulation and liberalization since the mid-1980s—mainly since the mid-1990s. Therefore, the Korean film sector has experienced increasing influence by Western forces, especially the U.S. government and Hollywood majors. As Paquet (2005, 46) argues, "The government's policies ever since its decision to open up the Korean market to Hollywood, together with the Korean film industry's (eventually) successful response to the market liberalization, have enormously increased the market pressure within the Korean film industry." Consequently, Korean cinema has become a battleground between transnational capitals, in particular, Hollywood majors. With the introduction of neoliberal economic and cultural policies, the concept of the welfare state, with its focus on "big government," has been in a severe crisis. Many governments around the world are short of funds to support encompassing policies, and as in most other policy fields, "government support for the arts and culture is deeply affected by the crisis of the welfare state concept" (Zimmer and Toepler 1999, 35).

What matters is that when the authoritarian regime took a neoliberal turn—that is, toward market deregulation, state decentralization, and reduced state intervention into economic affairs—in the early 1980s, the Korean film industry lost ground while Hollywood majors became main players in the country's film market. In the early stages of Korean cinema, thanks to legal support mechanisms actualized by the Korean government, the Korean film industry experienced a golden age in the 1960s. However, under neoliberal cultural policy, the market share of domestic film reached its lowest point in 1993, and the total number of persons who attended movies significantly declined (KOFIC 2003).

On the other hand, the Korean government has continued to initiate the growth of its national economy through its top-down and export-led policy, known as developmentalism, in most industrial sectors, including the cultural industries. A strong tradition of bureaucratization, centralization, or more specifically, state-led developmentalism is a very explicit feature of public policy in Korea (Oh and Larson 2011). As briefly discussed in previous chapters, since the dawn of Korean cinema in the post–Korean War era, the Korean government has played a pivotal role in the growth of the domestic film industry. The military regimes between 1961 and 1993 used media, including film, as a means to legitimatize political repression and state-led industrialization, while democratic administrations since the early 1990s have been drawn to their economic utility (Joo 2010). This opaque institutional framework essentially is the inevitable consequence of the dual nature of films as both cultural and economic commodities in combination with Korea's state-led developmentalism (Knorr and Schulz 2007).

In the midst of the conflicts between neoliberal cultural policies and state-led developmentalism in Korean cinema, neoliberal cultural policies in the early 1990s were critical to answering the question of whether the government should support the film sector or not at this critical juncture. While it has been controversial mainly due to the nature of neoliberal cultural policy, several theoreticians have discussed the grounds on which government should intervene. In particular, Dick Netzer (1978) makes an argument, based on classic market failure, that the government must intervene. Annette Zimmer and Stefan Toepler (1999, 34) also point out, "Market failure arguments have clearly come to dominate the debate in cultural economics. As a consequence, concerning the arts and culture, public policy research has almost exclusively focused on the role of government. With market failure as a convincing and also convenient rationale for government intervention in the arts and culture, the extent of public support and the ways in which governments are subsidizing the cultural sector became a major focus."

This implies that the national government must play a significant role in the formation of film policy even though the national state is overshadowed by neoliberal transnational phenomena (Maxwell 1995). In particular, film production and consumption are seen as performing an important role in negotiating cultural identity and articulating social consciousness; therefore, "cultural policies that support national film industries in the form of tariffs, quotas, subsidies, and tax credits" may be interpreted "as a forum of cultural resistance to the homogenizing effect of globalization" (Crane 2014, 366; Gao 2009, 423).

In the Korean context, the top-down approach, with the government being the driving force of economic policy, affects every aspect of public life, including the cultural sector. In particular, "the case for support of the arts by the state has been based on market failures, in particular the positive externalities culture provides for society" (Frey 1999, 131). The most significant supporting mechanisms in cultural policies are ostensibly financial, as the industries of culture and arts were first created through subsidies to make up for the deficit made by market uncertainty (S. J. Han 2010). Therefore, it is crucial to understand the rationales underlying public support for the arts and culture—especially, in this case, for Korean cinema.

THE FILM PROMOTION FUND AND THE ESTABLISHMENT OF THE KOREAN FILM COUNCIL

By the early 1990s, an upsurge of interest in a more nationally assertive Korean cultural policy attracted political support accompanied by government funding. In 1973, as the Korean government vehemently intervened in economic growth with its state-led policy, it also created the Korea Motion Picture Promotion Corporation (KMPPC), a special organization entrusted to the Ministry of Culture, aiming to support and promote Korean films through various means. However, during both the Chun Doo-hwan (1980–1988) and Roh Tae Woo (1988–1993) regimes, there were no direct subsidies from the government. Up until the late 1980s, "Korean film companies did not gather funding from banks or any financial capitals because the film business was too risky; instead, they depended on personal seed money, personal loans, and advance money from regional distributors. Regional distributors provided film companies with advance money and received the right of distribution of each region even before some films were completed" (K. W. Noh 2009, 138). As many European countries proved, this first wave of economic intervention by a totalitarian regime was clearly not free from propaganda-related objectives and involved a certain amount of censorship (Lange and Westcott 2004). However, when the Korean government after the military regimes adopted and executed neoliberal economic policies, it liberalized the domestic film market for Hollywood majors, and consequently, the market share of domestic films dropped to 15.9 percent in 1993. The Korean government back then technically gave up its protectionism while widely adopting the neoliberal cultural turn.

On the verge of the demise of Korean cinema, as discussed in chapter 2, the Kim Young Sam government, which was the first democratic government and was inaugurated in 1993, began to change cultural policy. The Kim government introduced several different measures designed to promote the cultural industries. The democratic government continued neoliberal globalization; however, the government's cultural policies—in particular, in the film sector—were very different from those of the authoritarian regimes. The Kim government ironically developed its supporting mechanism as part of its globalization strategy, known as *segyehwa*, in order to advance the film sector as one of the most strategic cultural industries (D. Y. Jin 2006).

More specifically, the Kim government passed the 1995 Motion Picture Promotion Law, which encouraged the investment of domestic capital in film, aiming at the shift "from control to promotion" (J. Y. Shin 2005, 54). One of the major elements of the new law was the Film Promotion Fund. Film importers had previously been required to contribute to a Korean Film Promotion Fund, but this provision was eliminated with the market liberalization in the late 1980s (Joo 2010): "The Kim government pledged to set up the Film Promotion Fund in 1994 as a public fund, with the plan to contribute 100 billion Korean won (comparable to US$10 million) to it by 1996" (D. Kim 2005, 309). Although it was not a direct fund, it exemplified the increasing role of the government in the film industry. In other words, the government began to support Korean cinema through the Film Promotion Fund in 1994, although it was not firmly institutionalized until the late 1990s.

The Korean government started to fully support Korean cinema through direct subsidies in 1999 when it secured $10 million for the Korean film industry. The Kim Dae-jung government (1998–2003) implemented more aggressive and concrete policies based on the principle of "support without intervention." During his campaigns for presidency, Kim promised to give strong financial and regulatory support to the cultural industries. The Kim government enacted the Basic Culture Industry Promotion Law in February 1999, which established the Culture Industry Promotion Fund. Support for the film industry increased noticeably because the Kim government directly invested in the film business between 1999 and 2003.

Again, the local film industry had not been given financial support by the Korean government, but in this age of neoliberal globalization, the government started to help develop Korean cinema. In order to execute its plan, the Kim Dae-jung government set up and implemented the Culture Industry Promotion Five-Year Plan, which aimed at not only strengthening the infrastructure of the cultural industries but also promoting the export of Korean cultural products (J. Y. Shin 2005; Joo 2007). As for the film industry, "the Kim Dae-jung government pledged to contribute $170 million to the Film Promotion Fund by 2003" (D. Kim 2005, 330). Consequently, from 1998 to the end of 2005, "the film industry witnessed the launch of 48 film funds worth $535 million. Such efforts played a key role in the expansion and diversification of Korea's film sector" (Paquet 2009, 77). The government has also contributed vast sums to local filmmaking—not as a direct investor, but as a participant in investment funds. The Small Business Corporation of Korea contributed a total of $121 million to film funds and would often take a heavier share of losses in the event that they failed to turn an overall profit (Paquet 2008).

As table 5.1 shows, independent producers of movies and TV programming started to receive subsidies from the Culture Industry Promotion Fund, which was launched by the government. Entrepreneurs whose firms specialized in computer games, music, and animation were also able to apply for start-up subsidies. The Ministry of Finance and Economy set up the fund using government money in a determined effort to boost culture-related industries. The government also offered tax breaks to firms with creative technology or a high accumulation of knowledge during the same year (Korea Herald 1999).

More important, the Kim Dae-jung government established the Korean Film Council (KOFIC; it was originally called the Korean Film Commission) in 1999, which replaced the KMPPC and expanded governmental encouragement of, and participation in, specialized film investment funds (Paquet 2009). Reflecting "the Kim Dae-jung government's support without control, KOFIC has been allowed greater independence and authority in formulating film policies, even though it is funded by the Ministry of Culture and Tourism" (J. Y. Shin 2005, 55). KOFIC has been involved in a range of activities, from various financial supports

TABLE 5.1.　Culture industry promotion fund

	1994	1995	1996	1997	1998	1999	2000	2001	2002	2003
Government subsidy	0	0	0	0	0	10,000	50,000	40,000	30,000	20,000
Cultural and arts promotion Fund	3,000	3,000	4,000	2,200	2,500	0	0	0	0	0
Others	0	0	0	800	1,500	0	0	0	0	0
Total	3,000	3,000	4,000	3,000	4,000	10,000	50,000	40,000	30,000	20,000

Unit: ₩1 million
SOURCE: KOFIC (2007a 25–26).

for the production of short films, documentaries, animations, and feature films to research on film policies and the industry in order to promote the industry.

An important development with regard to film finance during this time was the creation of the Canadian Co-operative Investment Fund (CCIF), which was stipulated in the Basic Culture Industry Promotion Law as part of the cultural industry investment cooperative (Joo 2007). Though Canada created the first CCIF in 2015, several countries have already introduced this special type of public fund, because "co-operatives have a long tradition of helping one another, and this is an innovative approach that will provide a new source of funding" for film producers (Co-operators 2015). The concept of the fund is that local cooperatives, including investment firms, individuals, and government institutions (e.g., KOFIC and the Small Business Corporation of Korea), invest with the expectation of a modest return but with the additional aim of enabling a new and more flexible source of funding specifically for low-budget movies (Co-operators 2015). In Korea, each cooperative is required to put together at least $1 million and dissolves five years after its creation, thus providing stable funds to film producers (D. Kim 2005, 337–338; Joo 2010): "The Co-operative Investment Fund has been made in the 21st century, and as of 2012, there were 40 CCIFs, which played a key role in funding film production" (Mee Hyun Kim 2013, 71).

Other factors should not be overlooked in generating the current boom of the Korean film industry. Yet it is undeniable that changes in government's policies fostered the growth of film and cultural industries directly or indirectly by providing a favorable legal framework for them, creating public funds, and stressing their importance. In particular, given how the government policies in the military regimes led to the decline of the Korean film industry, the significance of the government's shift in position to its current growth should not be underestimated (Joo 2007). Due to the subsidy stimulus and other contributing incentives, film production experienced an unprecedented surge for a while in the early 2000s.[1]

However, at the same time, it is equally indisputable that these changes in the government's policies have focused on the economic potential of these industries. One of the main concerns of cultural policies during the authoritarian regime was the issue of cultural identity (Yim 2002). Again, for the military regime between 1961 and 1993, the government considered culture as part of national arts. Partially due to an insufficient budget and lack of legal support during the authoritarian regime, "the primary cultural policy objectives were to reproduce cultural identity and promote regional culture" (Yim 2002, 40). When the Park Chung Hee regime launched the first five-year master plan for cultural development, to be implemented during the period of 1974–1979, a major priority was to establish a new cultural identity by highlighting specific cultural traditions. The plan mainly targeted folk arts and national culture (Yim 2002). Yet the horizon of Korean cultural policies during the democratic administrations since the early 1990s has narrowed the goal down to economic values and market considerations for the cultural industries, at the marginalization of other issues and aims.

KOFIC FILM DEVELOPMENT FUND IN LOCAL FILM PRODUCTION

The Roh Moo-hyun government intensified its neoliberal cultural policy by actualizing the reduction of screen quotas as part of his plan to get the Korea–U.S. FTA (Gross 2006). This was for the nation's economic interest, regardless of cultural sovereignty or cultural diversity issues. As discussed in chapter 3, the policy change in the screen quota system supposedly came about as a result of outside pressure in the context of bilateral trade negotiations. This change from state-led protection to neoliberal deregulation implies that the internal conflict between the neoliberal cultural regime and developmental state intervention is not new, and the Korean government has proved its inconsistent position in its treatment of Korean cinema.

This does not mean that the Roh government totally gave up its support for Korean cinema. The Roh government also started to develop a new public film fund to support the film industry in 2007, right after the reduction of the screen quota, although it was a small benefit compared to the screen quota system. Needless to say, the Korean government, including the Roh administration, partially developed the public film fund in order to soothe criticism from the film sector. As table 5.2 demonstrates, KOFIC has continued to increase its film development fund, from ₩46 million in 2012 to ₩55.6 million in 2015. The largest segment is the domestic production support program (KOFIC 2015b).

TABLE 5.2.   Film development funds in the 2010s

Funding categories	2012	2013	2014	2015
Film production and distribution program	19,262	24,491	24,569	29,445
Basic infrastructure support program	12,602	9,007	13,415	11,042
International promotion and marketing program	8,332	9,152	7,542	7,392
Film policy support and the enhancement of film enjoyment right program	6,109	6,203	7,153	7,747
Total	46,305	48,853	52,679	55,626

Unit: ₩1 million
SOURCE: KOFIC (2015a).

To begin with, KOFIC believes that with financial support, more unique and experimental films can be produced, diversifying the pool of movies in the industry. Funds amounting to $1.1 million are available for filmmakers making shorts, features, and documentaries, known collectively as *diversity films*. KOFIC supported 30–40 diversity films with around $700,000 in 2012; this increased to $1.2 million for 50 films in 2013. The number of diversity films had increased from 517 in 2005 to 810 films in 2013 in terms of submissions to the Seoul Independent Film Festival. Consequently, the number of independent films screened in theaters increased from 12 in 2005 to 67 in 2013 (KOFIC 2014b). In order to allow investment funds to continuously flow into the local film industry, KOFIC also put aside $10 million in a venture capital fund, for which their stake does not exceed 50 percent. The investment group decides on which films to support and the amount for each investment (KOFIC 2015a). Of course, despite the increasing role of the KOFIC Public Development Fund, financing is still extremely limited and far from resolving the issue of financing small and mid-sized film producers. Diversity films are "aimed at small niche market audiences," which means that "they rarely get the financial backing" that permits large production budgets (Hick 2010, 32). In most cases, without the public film funds, they are not able to produce films, nor find theaters in which to screen them, which necessitates the increasing role of public financing.

Second, as will be detailed in chapter 6, as part of its international promotion and marketing, KOFIC supports Co-production Promotions and International Offices. KOFIC encourages coproductions between the Korean film industry and foreign industries, especially with the U.S., China, Japan, and France. In terms of support for planning and developing coproductions, there are year-round programs to help connect Korean filmmakers with the U.S. and Japanese industries, create opportunities for one-on-one meetings, and provide consulting, translating, and business matching.

Third, there is a location incentive. KOFIC (2017c) offers a cash grant worth up to 25 percent of production expenses for foreign audiovisual works incurred for goods and services in Korea, with a cap of $1.5 million as of 2017. Feature films and television series produced by foreign production companies in which foreign investment exceeds 80 percent will be eligible for this grant. The shoot must take place for at least three days in Korea and spend a minimum of $100,000 in the country (KOFIC 2015b). As the most prominent example, KOFIC financially supported the *Avengers: Age of Ultron* location shoot in Korea. According to KOFIC, for the 15-day shoot, they got up to 30 percent back on production costs spent in Korea (Jean Noh 2014). Likewise, Korea has increased the number of incentives available for foreign filmmakers in recent years (Russell 2008). KOFIC clearly understood that Hollywood's runaway productions would continue to grow, and it decided to jump into the runaway production market. As several countries—including Canada, the U.K., Australia, New Zealand, and China—compete against each other to attract Hollywood's runaway productions, Korean cinema started to develop several supporting mechanisms to play a new role (see Miller et al. 2001; Burns and Eltham 2010).

There are certainly several ways to support film policies; however, as these new measures clearly indicate, the role of government in creating and developing public film funds has been significant for Korean cinema. As Zimmer and Toepler (1999, 44) point out in their discussion of France, in the European context, "The state's responsibility for, and commitment to, the arts and culture is in many ways a historical legacy. The institutions that the aristocracy built all over the continent were left to the emerging nation states, which seemed to have had little choice but to continue and preserve the tradition. In the French case, the absolutist monarch definitely passed the torch directly to the state bureaucracy. The supremacy of the crown was replaced by the supremacy of the bureaucracy of the government. In the later republics, the centralist pattern of Absolutism remained strongly in place in France."

The Korean government has been developing ways to directly support the film industry, such as the public funding system, since the mid-1990s. In the credits of Korean films, investments are shown to derive from diverse sources, including netizen funds and bank loans, as well as a few conglomerates. Many of these financings have no chance of achieving returns, with a few exceptions (Keane 2006). Under these circumstances, the Korean government has rapidly become the principal supporter, using both its financial and its legal arms. The government has both directly and indirectly supported the film industry, resulting in the recent resurgence of Korean cinema. Although neoliberal globalists continue to emphasize the decreasing role of the nation-state, the Korean government, through significantly developing its unique film policy, has enhanced the performance of Korean cinema.

What is noticeable when examining public film financing is the lack of support provided to theaters that play art house and/or independent films. Since art house films cannot find funding sources and screens, several parts of society—including the government, KOFIC, city governments, and theater chains—need to secure some screens for only these noncommercial films. For example, "in Germany, some theaters rarely screen mainstream blockbusters. On the other hand, art house film can play in small, independent houses that usually screen a given film up to six times on an irregular schedule. Those theatres usually do not belong to a chain and are sometimes run by a city. An example for city support of such theatres is Berlin, a city that arguably has one of the liveliest theatrical (both stage and cinemas) structures of all European metropolis." In fact, in Berlin, people can find theaters that only screen documentaries (Hick 2010, 33).

In this regard, KOFIC has developed the Distribution and Exhibition Support Program, which operates and funds art house theaters.[2] However, they are too limited to accommodate many indie and art films.

Korean cinema has developed in the midst of the conflicts between state-led developmentalism and neoliberalism in the realm of culture. A close look at the cultural politics and political economies in tandem provides a channel to connect neoliberalism and state-led developmentalism, which cannot be separated from each other (Kapur and Wagner 2011). Despite how Korea has pursued neoliberal cultural policies, as indicated by the handover of direct distribution rights to Hollywood majors and the reduction of screen quotas, some of the government other cultural policies, including the financial aid described here, have continued to support Korean cinema. The Korean government has prioritized marketization and liberalization, but it has not given up its concept of state-led tradition, which is a peculiarity of Korea's particular brand of neoliberal cultural policy. Since financial support is one of the most significant standards in terms of the role of the government, the public film fund initiated by the government proves that Korean cinema has been fundamentally influenced by the conflicting interplays between state-led and neoliberal cultural policies: sometimes very positively and at other times very negatively.

INCREASING TRANSNATIONAL INVESTMENT IN LOCAL FILM PRODUCTION

Proactive neoliberal cultural reforms since the late 1980s have substantially influenced Hollywood's investment in the Korean film industry. As the Korean government, sometimes forced by transnational forces and at other times voluntarily, opened the domestic film market, many transnational corporations—in particular, Hollywood studios—played a key role, including in distribution, production, and exhibition. As discussed, several Hollywood studios established their branches for the direct distribution of their own films, and some of them formed strategic alliances with domestic capitals, including Samsung, to produce films in Korea.

The power of Hollywood studios has not been eroded in the early 21st century. The Hollywood majors have developed an elaborate power structure to deal with relations among themselves and also between them and the independent producers, subcontractors, and distributors. In this hierarchically organized power structure, the independents "have represented no real challenge to the strength of the dominant corporations, but instead have either closely aligned with the majors or have had to be content with box office leftovers" (Wasko 1982, 219). They have continued to dominate the local film industry "by holding on to their power as national and international distribution networks" (Aksoy and Robins 1992, 9).

Several transnational corporations in Western countries, mainly Hollywood studios, set up joint ventures with domestic conglomerates—including Samsung, Hyundai, and CJ—on a variety of levels, for coproduction, distribution, and exhibition. As Edward S. Herman and Robert W. McChesney (1997) point out, joint ventures are attractive because they reduce the capital requirements and risk for participants and permit them to spread their resources more widely: "Joint ventures also provide a more flexible weapon than formal mergers or acquisitions, which often require years for negotiation and approval and then getting the new parts assimilated" (Herman and McChesney 1997, 103). One of the largest joint ventures was between Seagram-owned MCA and CJ of Korea. At that time, the CJ Group reached an agreement to take an 11 percent stake in DreamWorks with a $300 million investment. CJ was interested in this deal because the group wanted to use DreamWorks SKG as a foreign movie pipeline for its own movie theaters, while DreamWorks obtained limited Korean distribution rights to the studio's output (Brown 1995, 4).

In the 2010s, Hollywood majors have continued to invest in Korean cinema. For example, *The Age of Shadows*—a very successful historical movie of 2016—was produced and presented in Korean by Warner Bros. Pictures. The Korean supernatural thriller *The Wailing*, produced by 21st Century Fox International Productions, attracted about seven million viewers in Korea; Fox had already produced *Running Man* (2012), *Slow Video* (2014), and *Intimate Enemies* (2015), before *The Wailing*. Boosted by the success of the historical film, including the films produced by Warner Bros. Pictures, 21st Century Fox produced its fifth Korean-language film, titled *Warriors of the Dawn* (*Daeripgun*), which is about young men hired as substitute soldiers for those who want to avoid hard military duty during the Joseon Dynasty. Warner Bros. Pictures is to present *VIP* by director Park Hoon-jung and *Bad Lieutenant* by Lee Jeong-beom in that order following the release of mystery thriller *A Single Rider* starring Lee Byung-hun and Kong Hyo-jin in 2017 (Shim and Cho 2016). Meanwhile, in 2015, Netflix also invested $50 million on the budget of Bong Joon-ho's latest film *Okja*, the follow-up to his global hit *Snowpiercer* (Sims 2015).

The recent success of some movies funded and/or produced by Hollywood majors has substantially changed the nature of Korean cinema, and the massive arrival of Hollywood capital has provided new financial sources. But as Hollywood majors who have their branches in Korea have started to directly produce, fund, and distribute, their market share has increased from 25 percent in 2013 to 39.2 percent in 2016, while four domestic major distributors have lost their market share (KOFIC 2017a). Hollywood investment may also help diversify the subjects of Korean films. However, as movie critic Jeon Chan-il argues, "since the Hollywood investment may be concentrated on relatively high-quality directors and film projects, they will likely be far more aggressive than local investors," which would hurt the Korean film industry (Shim and Cho 2016).

In particular, if Hollywood studios, instead of focusing on direct distribution, continue to produce and directly compete with domestic producers, the Korean film industry may lose some ground in the production sector, as it already has in the distribution sector. Hollywood studios are equipped with capital and global strategies that domestic producers cannot easily overcome.

The impact of Hollywood studios on the Korean film industry in production will only increase, as Hollywood is paying attention to several local directors, like Kim Jee-woon, Park Chan-wook, and Bong Joon-ho. Positive effects could include an increase in production diversity. Since their films will be made through different production structures compared to the existing models established by Korean companies, different kinds of content are likely to be produced. Negative consequences could include an increase of so-called tentpole titles. Korean cinema today is already saturated with tentpoles, and if Hollywood studios add to their number, competition in the market will likely intensify. In addition, some people believe that once these Hollywood studios no longer find Korean production to be profitable, they may quickly exit the market (KOFIC 2006, 30). This means that the debate about Hollywood's influences in terms of both runaway productions, including *Avengers: Age of Ultron*, and direct production, such as *The Age of Shadows* and *The Wailing*, can be framed between two extremes: "internationalists" versus "Korean content" advocates.

Interestingly enough, China has also increased its investments in joint film productions with Hollywood and Korean film companies. Of course, collaboration between Korean and Chinese filmmakers has grown since the early 2000s, when Chinese director Chen Kaige partnered with Korean cinematographer Kim Hyung-goo and Korean producer Lee Joo-ik to make the multi-award-winning feature *Together* (2002). Chen Kaige again employed Korean talent for his historical-fantasy film *The Promise* (2005; Yecies at al. 2011). Chinese funds and corporations had already invested over $2.4 billion in 32 listed and unlisted Korean companies as of September 2015. Of these, 13 were in the entertainment, game, and fashion sectors. As the second-largest box office, only behind the U.S., China needs strong content to appeal to wider audiences and has targeted Korean cultural industries, including webtoons and Korean cinema (H. K. Park 2016). For example, Chinese corporations already promised to produce and distribute *D-War II*, by investing $89 million, while they were in the middle of producing *The Night Man* with $10 million (*Yonhap News* 2016). In fact, Chinese filmmakers want to work with Koreans in the industry to utilize their fresh ideas, stories, and high-quality techniques. Korean cinema has diverse genres and has excellent human resources for producing commercial but quality films.

Admitting that it is significant to secure global financing, we also have to understand that some countries, like Canada and Australia, have totally lost their markets to Hollywood, although they are able to attract Hollywood studios' runaway productions. As David Newman (2008, 296–297) points out, these countries' governments and film agencies brushed aside fears of "Hollywoodization" or "Hollywood South"—a threat now facing the Korean film industry. Transnational capital (mainly from Hollywood, partially from other countries, including China) has become a new funding source for Korean cinema. Bit since Korean filmmakers have difficulties securing funds, transnational capital has started to control the industry, this time in production directly. Since funding is one of the most significant elements in determining the kinds of films that can be made, this new form of Hollywood influence will be a big factor in changing Korean cinema in the near future.

CONCLUSION

This chapter has looked at the roles and policies of the Korean government in tandem with film funds as the underlying dynamic that led to recent shifts in Korean cinema. It analyzed the formation of the public film fund and its impact on Korean cinema, followed by the influences of transnational funding sources. Until the late 1990s, there was little significant financial support in the local film industry (Ministry of Culture and Information 1986). The Korean government later established the Film Promotion Fund, and it began to subsidize the film industry—in particular, production corporations. The fact that many governments around the world spend large sums to maintain a presence in their film industries indicates that films are perceived as "having considerable symbolic and cultural value" (Crane 2014, 365–366).

However, public film funding in Korea has shown no particular relationship with ensuring cultural value. Despite their contributions, the government policies were limited, narrowly focusing on the economic aspect of film. Korea has relied on state-led, top-down policy for the growth of its light industries (and later the heavy ones, like the chemical and auto industries), and the Korean government turned its emphasis toward using the film and cultural industries to boost the nation's economic growth in the 1990s. In other words, the government supported the film industry due to economic imperatives. Accordingly, as Joo (2010, 164–165) points out, "even though the government's view and policies with regard to film and media industries underwent significant changes, they remained strikingly similar to the previous policies in terms of their instrumental approach. In short, the Korean government's cultural policies since the 1990s have been characterized by the uncritical economic approach to culture and film industries. Despite the stated cultural concern, notably the need to protect Korean culture and identity, cultural issues were often conspicuously absent in the government's cultural policies." Indeed, the purpose of supporting the film industry has not been to secure cultural sovereignty but has to do with financial profits.

As Falicov (2000, 341) has already argued, again, "The domestic film industries are increasingly facing a dilemma in reconciling issues around the construction of national and local identities on screen, while at the same time trying to sustain a viable and popular film industry in the face of daunting competition from Hollywood." In particular, as Hollywood has expanded its control over the local film industry, including funding sources, Korean cinema faces a new challenge. It might be beneficial for Korean filmmakers to have Hollywood production and investment in the production sector; however, it may negatively impact Korean cinema.

One cannot deny that it is necessary for Korean cinema to improve the efficiency of its film industry—that is, developing its production system and securing stable investment. However, Korean cultural policy makers and film industry corporations also have to consider how to integrate the specificity and identity of domestic culture into the logic of the global film market—to create both diversity and commercial profits. While it is critical to support large film productions, public film funds are mostly needed for independent movies so that Korean cinema can advance both commercially successful and artistically sovereign domestic films. The Korean government also needs to promote the film industry because films are public goods that carry social benefits. As Liliana Castaneda (2009, 27) argues in the case of the Latin American film industry, "Content presented in films disseminates social meaning and has a symbolic potential to represent the complexity of identities and the context where those identities interact, promoting a sense of belonging or citizenship." As such, the Korean government has to understand that supporting the film industry through its public fund is important not only for the economic benefits it provides but also for such social benefits.

6 · COPRODUCTION AND TRANSNATIONALIZATION OF KOREAN CINEMA

Coproduction in the global film markets has had a long history, and the process has been undertaken often in film since the end of World War I (Selznick 2008). Coproduction in Korean cinema has been lined with the global coproduction trend, as the history of coproduction between Korea and other countries goes back to the early 1930s, when Japan occupied the Korean peninsula and influenced the nascent Korean film industry.[1] Korean-Japanese coproductions of propaganda films, however, do not exactly fulfill the criteria of real cultural exchange (Conran 2015). As Yecies and Shim (2011) argue, while a number of films made in the Japanese colonial period could be called collaborative coproductions, most of them do not have the active the level of cultural diversity and mutual economic benefit that official coproduction efforts embrace these days.

Later, Korea developed coproductions with a few Asian countries. Most prominent of these was *Love with an Alien* (*Igugjeong-won*, 1958)—the first-ever film coproduced by Korea and Hong Kong (Ahn 2014c; S. J. Lee 2019). Codirected by Jeon Chang-geun of Korea and Shanghai-born, Hong Kong–based Tu Gwang-qi and set in Hong Kong in the 1950s, this coproduction film depicts the forbidden love between a Korean composer and a Hong Kong singer. Another, *Last Woman of Shang* (1964), was also created as a reflection of the two growing Asian markets in the 1950s. However, coproductions—particularly with Western countries like the U.S., France, and Canada—started appearing with more frequency two decades ago, and Korean cinema has recently witnessed the substantial growth of coproductions as one of the most significant strategies of transnationalization.

This chapter examines the contemporary trend of coproduction to map out some of the major features in the Korean film industry. It investigates why the Korean government, KOFIC, and film corporations have pursued coproductions not only regionally but with Western countries—in particular, with the U.S. This chapter especially analyzes coproduction as one of the most important transnational strategies in Korean cinema not only as a process that brings products and capital into the country but also as one that sends them abroad. It finally discusses whether Korean cinema has resolved asymmetrical power relations between transnational forces and local players with emerging coproduction movies or if Hollywood continues to dominate the Korean film market through film coproduction strategies.

TRANSNATIONALIZATION IN FILM COPRODUCTION

Coproduction mostly refers to two or more film producers in two or more countries agreeing to collaborate in order to produce cultural products, including films, that one particular country's producers alone could not easily produce (Mirrless 2013). Several advantages are considered as the major reasons for the growth of coproduction in the film industry, including the pooling of financial resources, risk reduction, access to desired foreign locations, and entree to a partner's market (Hoskins et al. 1993). Many governments also provide legal and financial advantages, including tax breaks and the exemption of coproduction films from screen quota, which means the ownership of the film rights would be shared by two or three countries. Meanwhile, private film corporations seek coproduction in order to find talented directors, actors, and crew members as well as film locations.

Film directors and corporations in Korea have utilized coproduction to take advantage of resources such as financial and cultural capital. Coproduction has pursued financial benefits (although the cultural benefits cannot be disregarded), which means that film directors and corporations may attempt to find film funds out of the country as their production costs continue to grow. Coproductions in general also appeal to transnational audiences as they portray local themes, personnel, and locations. Coproduction films, therefore, limit their national peculiarities and reflect global interests (see D. Y. Jin 2019a).

Globally, coproductions are both culturally and financially driven. During the conference titled Chinese Film Market and Asian Cinema held in Singapore in August 2017, however, Melvin Ang (CEO of mm2 Asia) clearly stated that "more than 80% of co-productions occurred due to the financial reason." Coproductions in Asia have been especially driven by financial reasons rather than cultural matters as many parts of the world.

What is at stake regardless of these reasons behind coproduction strategies is that coproduction revolves around the dynamics of globalization and transnationalization. Globalization and transnationalization in the realm of film have interconnected places around the planet. Coproduction has especially become a unique model of globalization because this mode of cultural production "is created as both an economic and a cultural commodity" (Selznick 2008, 2). Coproduction in the film industry has also directly related to transnationalization. As explained in chapter 1, transnationalization is used to describe "a condition by which people, commodities, and ideas cross national boundaries and are not identified with a single place of origin" (Watson 1997, 11). The notion of transnationalism draws attention to the ways in which "the intensifying scale and speed of the transnational flow of people, capital, and media has disregarded, though not entirely, the efficacy of demarcated national boundaries and ideologies" (Iwabuchi 2002, 52). Coproduction has advanced cultural globalization, which could be identified as a process of shifting "from relative heterogeneity and lack of cooperation towards increased cooperation, integration, and convergence" in culture within a given geographical space (Schulz et al. 2001, 304).

Korean cinema has developed coproductions with several Asian countries—including China, Japan, Vietnam, and Thailand—as well as Western countries. The film industry in Korea—once small and peripheral before the early 1990s—has become one of the most significant parts of the global box office in the midst of shifting political (e.g., deregulation in censorship and screen quotas) and economic milieu, as well as due to the Korean Wave. As the Korean film industry has substantially increased its role in the global film market, the Korean government and filmmakers have begun pursuing coproductions with other countries.

Indeed, KOFIC, as a state-supported institution, encourages coproductions between the Korean film industry and foreign industries, especially with China, the U.S., Japan, and France. In terms of support for planning and developing coproductions, there are year-round programs to help connect Korean filmmakers with U.S. and Japanese industries, create opportunities for one-on-one meetings, and provide consulting, translating, and business matching. Under these circumstances, Korean film corporations and directors have formed coalitions with their peers in other countries to enable transnational cultural production. In this regard, coproductions are "a nexus in which creative and cultural capital can be accumulated to exploit the contingencies" of cultural production by taking advantage of cross-border economies of scale (DeBoer 2014, 4). Coproductions in Korean cinema have the potential to create cultural transnationalization as well as globalization. This new trend certainly asks us to ponder whether the issue of Western-driven cultural domination could be resolved, as several Asian countries have become major players in the global film market.

EMERGENCE OF KOREAN-CHINESE COPRODUCTIONS

As globalization is driven by either Western or non-Western countries, transnationalization in terms of the flow of cultural products and capital beyond national territories can be identified in two different forms: going in or going out. The two-way nature of this has been made possible because non-Western countries, including Korea and China, have started to invest in the Western regions. Unlike coproductions before the late 20th century—which were driven by mainly Western countries (in particular, the U.S.) to monopolize capital, talent, and skills—several non-Western countries in the 21st century have equipped themselves with talent and capital. This can be seen in the soaring number of film coproductions driven by these non-Western countries, making them major players in global film markets.

In creating a coproduction, there is, on the one hand, a going-in process, where the local film industry and films are transnationalized by global forces. Since Korea opened its film industry to foreign players, and especially since the late 1980s, several Western film corporations—such as Disney, Warner Bros., and 21st Century Fox—have established their own local branches and directly imported Hollywood films to the Korean market. Many Asian capitals, including several Chinese entertainment corporations, have recently invested in the Korean production sector as well.

But on the other hand, there is a going-out process. Several Korean film corporations and entertainment agencies have recently invested in many other countries to coproduce films, thus avoiding certain regulatory measures while benefitting from the bigger markets. By providing narratives, talented directors, and actors or supplying financial resources, several entertainment agencies, including CJ E&M, have systematically developed going-out transnational strategies. This implies that we need to understand these two processes— going-in and going-out transnationalization strategies—in the Korean context, which has differentiated the nature of transnationalization so that it is consequently not only Western-driven but also locally driven.

Most of all, in the 21st century, several Asian countries have developed coproduction strategies with regional countries, and there are multiple examples of Korean cinema's intertwined relationships with several Asian countries, through either going-in or going-out transnational processes, as part of what has been called "the pan-Asian film market" (N. Lee 2012, 82). Among these, Korea and China have particularly advanced a unique collaboration in the film sector. Their collaborations have evolved from talent loans, such as Zhang Ziyi starring in the 2001 Korean film *Musa the Warrior*, to capital investment (Kil 2015).

While there are several dimensions, three major elements have deeply influenced the growth of the Korean-Chinese coproduction trend. First of all, coproductions between Korea and China, of course, but also other Asian countries as well, are partially booming due to the Korean Wave. As is well documented, Korean cultural content—including dramas, movies, video games, animation, and popular music (K-pop)—have become some of the most popular products in Asia since the late 1990s (Lee and Nornes 2015; D. Y. Jin 2016; Yoon and Jin 2017). As China strongly wants to develop its own soft power by creating China-based cultural products for global markets, the Korean Wave has affected both the government and the cultural industries in the country. In this regard, during my interview with her, Chung-kang Kim argued, "One of the most distinctive aspects in contemporary Korean cinema is the influence of the Korean Wave as co-productions have rapidly increased, meaning several countries, including China have increased their investment in the local film industry." As Joseph Nye (2004) articulates, *soft power* refers to a form of national power that relies on cultural attractiveness and is utilized by the government in international relations to enhance national images and fulfill strategic imperatives. The Chinese government embrace of soft power was "precipitated to a large extent by the rise of cultural content in the region," particularly from Korea (Keane 2015, 5).

In fact, producers from both countries are keen to make the best use of the Korean Wave phenomenon: "As Chinese films become more and more commercial, it is not only actors but also technicians and, more importantly, directors that China is absorbing from Korea. Korean vfx [visual effects] studios have provided service for Chinese films including Feng Xiaogang's *Assembly* and Tsui Hark's *Young Detective Dee: Rise of the Sea Dragon*, while experienced Korean directors have been more extensively involved in directing Chinese films: Hur Jin-ho (*Dangerous Liaisons*), Ahn Byeong-ki (*Bunshinsaba*), and Kwak Jae-yong (*My Girlfriend Is Sick*)" (Kil 2015). For example, Dexter Studios Co., one of the first listed VFX companies in Korea, established a joint venture in China and worked with Tsui Hark as it entered the first phase of VR (virtual reality) content creation (S. J. Song 2017). As Brian Yecies (2016, 784) correctly observes, "In this new cultural and commercial arena, Korea's global experience and success with its own brand of style and technical prowess has been instrumental in developing its collaborative relationship with China."

Second, Korean-Chinese film coproduction can be identified with the emergence of China as a major force, both politically and economically, as China began to work with Hollywood after joining the WTO in 2001 (Su 2011; 2019; Kokas 2017). The removal of several hurdles regulating the importation of foreign films has facilitated transnational film coproduction in China, as elsewhere, regardless of the concern of U.S. invasion.

What is interesting about Korean-Chinese coproduction is that the Chinese public and private sectors have invested in the Korean film industry in the 2010s. Chinese investors have flooded Korea's service sector by increasing their investments by 940 percent over four years, from $100 million in 2010 to $940 million in 2014. One public magazine also reported that China had made deep inroads into Korea's creative economy, investing $2.5 billion in Korean games, movies, and entertainment from 2010 to 2015 (J. A. Song 2016). China Media

Capital—a public fund—decided to invest up to $80 million, and Alibaba—China's largest online platform—was negotiating $100 million in Korean cinema (Lee and Byun 2014). This is largely attributed to China's increasing commitment to Korean media and entertainment. Investors in China use their financial clout in Korea's entertainment industry so that movies and television programs increasingly cater to Chinese tastes.

The cross-border collaboration in Korean media has been increasing due to potential mutual profits (Hailey Lee 2014). For example, Chinese players choose to partner with Korean companies to coproduce content. Showbox's production of the 2012 movie *Mr. Go* involved a 25 percent investment from Chinese film production company Huayi Brothers. Showbox accepted the partnership not only because it needed the money but also so that the movie could be released in both markets and Showbox could learn how to become a global player.

Unlike previous years when Korean-Chinese coproductions mainly relied on the involvement of Korean directors and actors in Chinese movies, China has financially invested in the Korean film industry for the Chinese film market over the past several years. Previously, Chinese cinema needed the directors who had developed creatively in the midst of the Korean Wave because it was having difficulty secure talented local directors as its own film industry exploded. Simultaneously, in Korea, "where the film industry ha[d] plateaued, it [was] natural for film professionals to search for outside opportunities, and the ever-expanding Chinese film industry [was] the perfect market" (Kil 2015). However, even more recently, coproductions between the two countries have further intertwined, as China has secured enough film funds to directly invest in other countries, including Korea. The number of coproduction films and their increasing production costs are certainly the results of these shifting trends.

Finally, in the early 21st century, Korea began signing coproduction agreements with several countries, which has consequently expedited the growth of coproductions. Since Korea signed its coproduction agreement with France in 2006, the Korean government has continued to develop coproduction agreements with other countries, including New Zealand (2008), EU (2011), Australia (2014), China (2014), and India (2015; KoBiz 2017). Among these, the Korean-Chinese coproduction agreement has been the most active and essential. These two countries' filmmakers have actively produced coproduction films since the treaty, as the agreement greatly revolves the quota restrictions.

As for China, KOFIC's Korean Film Business Center in Beijing stands to provide even more intensive support locally. If international funding makes up more than 20 percent of the total production cost for a coproduction project with foreign producers, the film length exceeds 70 minutes, and the budget is more than $1 million, it is then eligible to apply for a 25 percent rebate on production costs (with a maximum cap of $300,000). Against this backdrop, in 2014, Korea and

China signed a pact to expand cooperation in joint film production. Under the terms of the pact, coproductions would be treated as local films rather than more heavily regulated imports and therefore would not come under China's quota of 34 films a year, on a revenue-share basis (Coonan 2014).

One of the major benefits of the agreements between Korea and other countries is the resolution of the designated nationality of some films, thus determining their eligibility for potential benefits. For example, article 2 of the Korea-China agreement signed in 2014 clearly indicates that "a coproduction film made in accordance with this Annex shall be fully entitled to all the benefits which are or may be accorded to national films by each Party under its respective national laws and regulations in force currently or in the future." The Korea-France coproduction agreement (2006) already identified this clause: "Subject to the approval of both competent authorities, a film coproduced in compliance with this Agreement and eligible under the relevant laws and regulations of each Party shall be deemed to be a national film in the territory of each Party and shall thus be fully entitled to all the benefits which are accorded under the laws and regulations in force in the territory of each Party" (article 2). The cultural politics in resolving the nationality of films has become one of the major reasons for coproduction agreements between countries. Coproduction films can be categorized as national films under such agreements, and therefore, they can avoid any kinds of regulations, including screen quotas. Korean films have found themselves shut out of the most lucrative part of the Chinese film market, as China's revenue-sharing quota slots are almost entirely filled by Hollywood studio movies, leaving nearly all other foreign-language movies stuck with flat-fee deals. While the number of Korean films imported into China with flat-fee deals has risen, the appeal of coproductions is that such films are considered local and thus exempt from the quota (Frater 2014).

The coproduction agreement between Korea and China has indeed expedited the process between the two countries. Before the agreement, there were already several movies coproduced by them, such as *The Restless* (2006), *Chongqing* (2008), *Let the Blue River Run* (2008), *A Good Rain Knows* (2009), *Sophie's Revenge* (2009), *After Shock* (2010), *A Wedding Invitation* (2013), and *Mr. Go* (2013). Korea and China had also joined forces with other Asian countries to develop films; for example, Korea, China, Japan, and Hong Kong worked together to coproduce *Battle of Wits* (2006). However, many more Korean-Chinese coproduction films have been created since they signed the agreement in July 2014, including *Meet Miss Anxiety* (2014), *20 Once Again* (2015), *Mermaid* (2016), *The Mysterious Family* (2016), *Passion Heaven* (2016), and *Wedding Bible* (forthcoming).

Such film coproduction deals increase the speed of partnerships—in this case, between Korean companies with film production skills and Chinese companies with abundant investment budgets (Hailey Lee 2014). The Korean-Chinese coproduction agreement has made the nexus of these two film industries stronger than ever, bringing together creative talent involving producers, directors, actors, and visual effects on an unprecedented scale. Furthermore, "these bilateral film encounters have occurred largely without any intervention or guidance from official co-production policy agreement and, as a result, have fallen outside of the aims and objectives of a formal policy instrument" (Yecies 2016, 782).

However, there are growing concerns over Korean-Chinese coproductions. For one, the major concern for many Korean film scholars and filmmakers is how long Korean cinema will be able to sustain its cultural edge as China vehemently tries to tap into the country's territory. Chinese companies have already taken over some Korean producers, including Chorokbaem Media. Competition in the film business "is more about creativity and effective planning than lowering production costs like manufacturing." However, as "China is catching up fast in this industry too," one cannot be sure about how long Korea "can have the upper hand" (J. A. Song 2016). Most of all, political conflicts between the two countries will jeopardize Chinese-Korean coproductions, which is very significant. As Darcy Paquet argued during my interview with him,

In general, one can say that the recent partnerships that have formed between Chinese and Korean film companies have been driven by a desire on the Chinese side to learn from Korea's expertise, and a desire on the Korean side to gain access to a larger market. To a certain degree, both sides have been able to benefit from such partnerships, with many individual Korean filmmakers finding work in China and a number of Chinese-Korean coproductions finding success at the Chinese box office. Nonetheless, the cooling of relations between the two countries over Korea's deployment of THAAD anti-missile defense systems in 2016–2017 brought about a sharp reduction in the number and scale of such exchanges.

What he argues is that "the long-term effect of China's investment in Korean cultural companies is still unclear. The signing of a Free Trade Agreement between China and Korea in 2015 set the stage for more than $86 million being invested in the Korean entertainment sector in 2016, with stakes sold in the distributor NEW and talent company SM Entertainment. This influx of Chinese capital has allowed Korean cultural industries firms to become ever more ambitious in their production of content." However, the significant economic losses that resulted from the THAAD dispute until late 2017, when the two countries started to resolve the situation, served "as a reminder that such partnerships depend on political relationships, which can quickly shift."

The box-office outcomes of coproduction between the two countries have also not been promising. Korean-Chinese coproductions films have not achieved tangible successes, as many coproductions films have technically failed in garnering profits due to lack of interest (S. R. Kim 2016). For example, *Bad Guys Always Die*—a 2015 action comedy coproduced by Korea and China—failed in both markets. Only 14,942 people watched this movie in Korean theaters, although Son Ye-Jin, one of the most famous actresses in Korea, was starring. *Dangerous Liaisons*, a 2012 melodrama, had cast big-name actors like Jang Dong-gun (Korea), Zhang Ziyi (China), and Cecilia Chung (Hong Kong); however, fewer than 300,000 viewers watched the movie in Korea. While several coproduction movies have done well, this clearly indicates that coproduction cannot guarantee financial benefits. In particular, when Chinese film corporations fund coproduction movies, they emphasize Chinese mentalities, ideologies, and emotion, which Korean audiences find unfamiliar. Therefore, it is vital that filmmakers develop cultural collaboration as well as pursuing financial agreements.

COPRODUCTION BETWEEN KOREA AND OTHER ASIAN COUNTRIES

While Korean-Chinese coproductions have been the largest and most significant for Korean cinema in the 2010s, the local film industry has also developed its partnership with other Asian countries, including Japan, Malaysia, Vietnam, and India. In fact, an increasing number of Korean movies, and Asian movies more generally, are being coproduced between Asian companies, and the Busan Promotion Plan—a project market in which new Asian feature films could seek cofinancing and coproduction partners from the Busan International Film Festival—functions as a key platform for the increasing inter-Asian coproduction of Korean (and other Asian) movies (N. Lee 2012).

From Korean cinema's perspective, while Korean-Chinese coproductions have mainly involved capital involvement as a going-in trend, in coproductions with other Asian countries, Korean entertainment corporations have primarily been the ones to invest in these countries. They have also provided necessary resources, including narratives, directors, and talent. One of the most recent of these coproductions, the Korean-Vietnamese *Let Hoi Decide* (a.k.a. *De Mai tính 2*, 2014), broke records for Vietnamese cinema by earning $3.85 million. Korean CJ E&M was a major investor in the film, which opened in 70 theaters across Vietnam in December 2014. CJ E&M has become a major player in Vietnamese cinema; its theater brand, CJ CGV, ranked as the largest cinema exhibitor in Vietnam in the 2010s (H. W. Lee 2015). Korea and Vietnam have also coproduced *Sweet 20* (2015), *The Housemaid* (2016) and *Saigon Bodyguards* (2016) in the 2010s.

Korea and Japan have also developed coproductions in the early 21st century: *Loft* (2005), *26 Years Diary* (2006), *Don't Look Back* (2006), *One Missed Call Final* (2006), *Hana Kage* (2007), *Virgin Show* (2007), *Like a Dragon* (2007), *Oishi Man* (2008), *Dream* (2008), *Higanjima* (2009), *Golden Slumber* (2009), *Tokyo Taxi* (2009), *Café Seoul* (2009), *The Boat* (2009), *Ghost: In Your Arms Again* (2010), and *A Midsummer's Fantasia* (2014). Several filmmakers in these two countries have also developed independent films. For example, in October 2016, filmmakers started shooting a Korean-Japanese coproduction film called *The Goose Goes South*, which is the story of a Korean guy who comes to Osaka and follows his dream of becoming a musician. The director (Baek Jaeho) and the main actor (Kang Du) are Korean, but all other actors and staff members other than the camera crew are Japanese. The first Korean-Indonesian coproduction film, *Cado*, was also released in Indonesia in 2016.

One of the most significant examples of Korean-Asian coproduction is *Miss Granny* (*Susanghan Geunyeo*), which was a 2014 Korean comedy-drama film directed by Hwang Dong-hyuk. Unlike other coproductions, where a single film is made to cater to two or more countries, this film has been reproduced in several Asian countries—China, Japan, Vietnam, Thailand, and Indonesia. A version for the U.S. is also forthcoming.

The original romantic comedy pivots around Oh Mal-soon, a 70-year-old widow who lives with her son, who is a college professor, and his family. Stubborn, controlling, and shameless, one day Mal-soon wanders neighboring streets and comes across a mysterious photo studio named Youth Photoshop that claims it captures the moments of one's youth. When she comes out of the studio, Mal-soon is dumbfounded by her own reflection in the bus window: she is now a fresh, young 20-year-old lady. With no one recognizing her, Mal-soon decides to make the most out of this once-in-a-lifetime opportunity. She renames herself Oh Doo-ri (after her all-time favorite actress Audrey Hepburn), gets a haircut similar to Hepburn's in *Roman Holiday*, and takes advantage of her youth. However, she still acts like a 70-year-old, calling grown men "lad" and patting people on the bum. One day, she attracts the notice of her unknowing grandson, Ji-ha, a college student and a TV music producer. Ji-ha invites her to join his heavy metal band, and she convinces them to switch to more audience-pleasing melodies (for a more detailed plot, see Soompi 2014).

Miss Granny was released in Korea in January 2014, and it garnered 8.65 million admissions, earning ₩62.5 billion (comparable to $62 million) and the number three spot on the box-office chart for the year (KOFIC 2017a). Later, several Asian countries, one after another, including China (*20 Once Again*, 2015), Vietnam (*Sweet in 20*, 2015), Japan (*Ayashii Kanojo*, 2016), Thailand (*Suddenly Twenty*, 2016), and Indonesia (*Sweet 20*, 2017) produced this film as a form of coproduction. CJ E&M is also working with Tyler Perry Studios'

34th Street Films and 3Pas Studios to coproduce U.S. and Spanish versions. With six Asian renditions, the two additional remakes will make *Miss Granny* as the world's most-adapted film with a total of eight versions.

As Jinhee Choi (2017, 153) points out, "As film practice, regional remakes of commercially viable films of another country are not new: one saw the regional (and Hollywood) remakes of horror films, such as the Japanese *Ring* series, shortly after its success in the original country." *Miss Granny* is an important film as it is one of the first Korean films to implement this tactic.

What is interesting is that *Miss Granny* has made its global success not because of financial collaboration but because of cultural consideration. One of the major differences in the success of *Miss Granny* could be found in that "the production company of *Miss Granny*, CJ E& M, does not merely sell the remake rights to other countries, but coproduced the remakes," through a strategy that CJ calls "one source, multiple territory" (Channel CJ 2016), CJ E&M has thus promoted a new global project, which emphasizes the flexibility of the source material to be adapted to appeal to local tastes (J. H. Choi 2017).

For example, *20 Once Again*, *Miss Granny*'s Chinese version, is the result of CJ E&M's global going-out project as the company, from the starting point, planned to develop a Chinese version. *20 Once Again* is the first official remake under the 2014 coproduction agreement that does not feature the original Korean director. Both films were produced by CJ E&M, while *20 Once Again* was also produced in collaboration with China's Beijing Century Media Culture (Soh and Yecies 2017). The Chinese version maintains *Miss Granny*'s original storytelling, but the production team selects some details that Chinese audiences symphonize with, like family values and sensuous audiovisual effects. In Vietnam, CJ E&M and HK Film in Vietnam coplanned *Miss Granny*'s local version, *Sweet in 20*, emphasizing its comedic components as comedy has been one of the most popular genres there. The production team recruited several local comedians for several supporting actor positions while adding slapstick elements as well. In this regard, the popularity of these coproductions "coincides with the emergence of other commercial production modes such as genre hybridization," which has resulted from changes in the regulatory, economic, and technical environment of the cultural industries (Baltruschat 2002, 14–15).

Meanwhile, CJ E&M and Japan's Nihon TV and Shochiku (a movie production company) together produced another version of the film, *Ayashii kanojo*, targeting middle-aged female audiences, a primary group of moviegoers. The movie modified the plot to focus on maternal relationships (grandmother and her single daughter, who is raising children alone). Of course, it also reflects Japanese humor codes, as expected (Channel CJ 2016). As such, cross-border activities have transnationalized popular culture as a form of coproduction.

As *Miss Granny* certainly proves, transnational, localized films may follow the same overarching narrative; however, they each embody diverse cultural nuances, and each country's version includes its own national cultural elements. When Asian countries make films together, they are driven not only by the desire to resolve funding difficulties but also because they share similar cultural grounds; the really successful coproductions have emphasized cultural elements more than financial factors. However, cultural producers also must keep in mind is that they also need to respect national uniqueness, which can be preserved and developed.

KOREAN CINEMA'S PRESENCE IN HOLLYWOOD VERSUS HOLLYWOOD'S CONTINUING DOMINANCE

There are some controversies regarding which was the first film coproduced by Korea and the U.S. However, the history of coproduction between these two countries dates back to 1970, when they coproduced *Northeast of Seoul* (*Seoul Affair*). The *Dong-A Ilbo* (1970) reported that actress Anita Ekberg was in Seoul for a joint American-Korean production titled *Seoul Affair*, set to start filming with director David Rich and Korean actors Shin Young-kyun and Choe Ji-hee on October 15. While the record indicated that it was first released in 1972 as a thriller and action adventure, this movie was actually renamed *Catherine's Escape* and released in April 1974 (KMDB 2017).

Setting aside this early attempt, Korea-U.S. coproduction films have been made mainly since the early 2000s. For example, the 2005 movie *Love House* was directed by Kim Pan-soo as a crime film. However, *Never Forever* (2007), directed by Gina Kim and starring Vera Farmiga and Ha Jung-Woo, is largely considered the first official coproduction between the U.S. and Korea. *Never Forever* engages the generic conventions of melodrama to examine facets of gender, sexuality, race, and class for both women and Koreans in America, as indicated in her online bibliography. It was released theatrically in Korea, the U.S., and France.

Later, several films were made through Korean-American coproduction and sometimes with a third country, like China. They are *Fetish* (2007), *August Rush* (2007), *West 32nd* (2007), *D-War* (2007), *Thirst* (2008), *The Forbidden Kingdom* (2008), *American Zombie* (2009), *Haeundae* (2009), *Late Autumn* (2010), *The Yellow Sea* (2010), *The Warrior's Way* (2010), *Final Recipe* (2014), *Seoul Searching* (2015), *The Age of Shadows* (2015), *Last Knights* (2015), and *Okja* (2017).

As this list exemplifies, coproduction between Korea and the U.S. mainly started with the reduction of the screen quota in the Korean film market in 2006. While until 2006, only a handful of films were made, film corporations in these two countries have since frequently worked together, as the Korean film market has become more lucrative. As the reduction of screen quotas symbolizes deregulation in the local film industry, many American film corporations have shown more interest in the Korean film market.

There are two different types of coproductions between Korea and the U.S. On the one hand, several Korean companies and filmmakers, as well as actors, are heating up their American dreams by partnering with Hollywood majors. American distributors like Warner Bros., MGM, and DreamWorks have started to purchase the rights to remake successful Korean films, such as *My Sassy Girl* (2001), *Addiction* (2002), *A Tale of Two Sisters* (2003), *Sympathy for Lady Vengeance* (2005), and *The Host* (2006).

In the early 2000s, "some Korean actors also started to make their entry into Hollywood. Singer-turned-actor Rain was cast in 2008 in the Wachowskis' *Speed Racer*, and in 2009 in *Ninja Assassin*. Actress Jun Ji-hyun starred in *Blood: The Last Vampire* (2009), and actor Jang Dong-gun was in *The Warrior's Way* (2010), although neither of these films made commercial success." Among these, "actor Lee Byung-hun is one of the few actors who seems to have found his place in Hollywood," although his roles seem limited to stereotypical Asian characters. He made his Hollywood debut in the 2009 blockbuster *G.I. Joe: The Rise of Cobra* and reprised his role in the 2013 sequel *G.I. Joe: Retaliation*. Actress Bae Doona was chosen in 2012 by the Wachowskis' for *Cloud Atlas* (Rousse-Marquet 2013).

In terms of capital investment, CJ E&M partnered with Warner Bros. on the movie *August Rush*. CJ E&M already distributed Paramount and Dream-Works product in Korea, and through these connections, CJ hoped to facilitate the crossover of Korean directors and actors in Hollywood (Paquet 2007). CJ E&M put up $1.5 million of the film's $30 million budget and secured coproduction credit plus Korean distribution rights. The movie opened on 318 screens in November 2007 and grossed $5.8 million for the first few weeks (S. H. Han 2007).

CJ E&M's transnational model in the U.S. market is not new, of course. Starting in the late 1980s, several Japanese cultural corporations have invested in the American cultural industries, including the film and music sectors, in order to pursue both profits and insight into the Byzantine ways of Hollywood (Stevensen 1989). As such, several Korean entertainment agencies, including CJ E&M have slowly invested in the U.S. market—a form of going-out transnationalization.

On the other hand, however, the going-in model has been dominant. Hollywood already started to fund a few Korean movies, and in 2015, for example, two of the best films were produced by Hollywood studios. Na Hong-jin's *The Wailing* and Kim Jee-woon's *The Age of Shadows* were produced by Fox International Productions (FIP) and Warner Bros., respectively. FIP had already invested in local productions in 2010 with a 20 percent stake in Na's *The Yellow Sea*. Warner Bros. financed and distributed its first-ever Korean-language movie with *The Age of Shadows* (*Mil-jeong*), which is a 1930s period drama starring Song Kang-ho.

This made Warner Bros. the second Hollywood studio to greenlight a Korean-language movie, following Fox Korea, which had backed *Intimate Enemies* (2015) and *Slow Video* (2014) and been involved in *The Yellow Sea*. *The Age of Shadows* had an $8.62 million (₩10 billion) budget, which Warner Bros. almost fully financed. Warner is a direct distributor in the country and therefore handled the Korean theatrical release (Kil and Frater 2015). In 2013, 20th Century Fox fully financed *Running Man*, starring Shin Ha-kyun and directed by Jo Dong-ho. Warner Bros. Korea also financed the low-budget film *Single Rider* starring Gong Hyo-jin and Lee Byung-hun, released in 2017.

Among those coproduction films, *Okja* (2017)—an ungainly mix of benign monster movie, action comedy, and coming-of-age fable—was a new form of coproduction between the two countries in that it was the joint work of the local film sector and the U.S. streaming platform Netflix. *Okja* features a star-studded cast of both American and Korean talent, including Jake Gyllenhaal, Seo-Hyah Raj, Tilda Swinton, Woo-sik Choi, and Paul Dano. This Bong Joon-ho film is a near-future science fiction love story, the tale of a young farm girl named Mija (Ahn Seo-hyun) and a massive genetically engineered monster named Okja (Tiffany 2017).

Netflix backed *Okja* to the tune of $50 million, as the streaming giant was looking to expand its footprint in Asia. This meant the film, one of the first Asian features to be financed by Netflix, had just under the company's biggest movie production budget to date (Trumbore 2015). Likewise, *Okja* certainly exemplifies a recent trend of coproduction: the emergence of media platforms as new financial sources.

For the Hollywood studios and media platforms, it makes sense to enter the Korean market. Koreans on average see four films per year; two of which are local films, with total annual theater admissions surpassing 200 million in the past four years (Bechervaise 2017). Admissions per capita in 2013 reached 4.25, up from 1.1 in 1998 and 2.98 in 2005; this surpassed the U.S./Canada combined figure (4.0), making it the highest in the world (KOFIC 2008; 2014a; Motion Picture Association of America 2014). A further incentive is found when one considers the abundance of talent found in Korea—and not just in terms of directors. Actors, actresses, cinematographers, writers, producers, composers, and so forth make an immense contribution to the overall tapestry of Korean cinema. For Hollywood majors, it makes sense to invest in local content (Bechervaise 2017). As Sonia Kil and Patrick Frater (2015) correctly observe, "Korea has one of the most vibrant film industries in the world. Thanks to high rates of cinema-going, it is the world's sixth largest box office territory, with a cumulative gross last year of $1.52 billion, that puts it far ahead of much larger countries including Russia and Germany. In most years recently local films have accounted for most of the box office, prompting Hollywood studios to examine co-production or investment strategies in Korean-made titles." The characterizations of these coproductions are the result of a combination of financial and cultural, as well as political, factors. Korean cinema has begun to collaborate with other cinemas, both regionally and globally.

However, it is crucial to understand that cultural coproduction does not guarantee cultural globalization in content (Jin and Lee 2007), as the asymmetrical power relations between the parties have continued and sometimes intensified. The coproduction process between Korea and the U.S. is "exclusively linked to Hollywood's hegemonic, imperialist politics, whose ultimate aim is worldwide cultural homogenization" (Bergfelder 2005, 323–324). We cannot deny that within the contemporary frameworks of transnationalization between Western and non-Western countries, popular culture is considered a significant tool for spreading ideology and global capitalism (Selznick 2008). As the case of *Okja* proves, Netflix as a media platform supported the coproduction partially because it planned to increase the number of the subscribers of Netflix in Korea, which will be eventually beneficial for the platform.

Some film directors, like Chul Huh, certainly believe that coproduction is the most viable path for Korean cinema, as it provides necessary funds and resources like scripts, talents, and audiences. For example, Chul Huh argued that a new method of distribution and exhibition, as shown in the case of *Okja*, has been necessary because "new media platforms, like Netflix, are identified as an alternative to a few giants, like CJ and Lotte." As Netflix is expected to coproduce both blockbuster movies with top-tier directors and low-budget movies focusing on national themes in order to penetrate the Asian markets, there will be no other choice but to rely on these new platforms, Chul Huh and KwangWoo Noh claimed during their interviews. What they believe is that the new situation may help the enhancement of cultural diversity, although Netflix is a transnational, mainly because domestic-based film giants focus too much on financial benefits instead of developing cultural identity. However, this new development needs to be carefully analyzed.

As Pieter Aquilia (2006, 442) has already pointed out in the case of Southeast Asian coproductions, in an era of transnational cinema, "cultural specificity is often underestimated in the race for popular movies that will resonate with international audiences" *The Maid* (2005), one the first coproductions to be instigated by Singapore, suggests the increasing hybridization of the nation-state's films: it exchanges cultural uniqueness for Hollywood and East Asian horror verisimilitude, in return for significant economic gains in the global film market. As Western forces are always pursuing profits, they do not care about local specificities and. However, instead of hastily pursuing the U.S. market through locally financed coproductions, Korean entertainment sectors should carefully consider both the financial and cultural benefits, as the latter will be a vital component for the success of this form of coproduction in the long run.

CONCLUSION

This chapter has analyzed the soaring trend toward coproduction in Korean cinema in the early 21st century. The Korean film industry has continued to develop coproducing films with not only Asian countries but also Western countries, including the U.S. and France, and this chapter has documented such recent coproductions by emphasizing their major trends and cultural politics. Coproductions in Korean cinema have shown a unique trend, as local film and entertainment corporations have developed a two-tiered strategy: first coproduction within the Asian region, followed by coproduction in the Western region. Coproductions have also shown two different forms of transnationalization: either going-in or going-out models, which have fundamentally differentiated the nature of Korean cinema.

Transnationalization implies that, because talents, commodities, and ideas are crossing national boundaries, audiences cannot identify the origin of cultural products; in this way, Korean cinema has substantially achieved its transnational goals through going-out coproduction. Many directors and actors have started to work in international film industries, and some local entertainment corporations have invested in global film markets to develop coproductions. Korea has also developed these films by putting capital into several Asian film markets.

Most of all, coproductions with other Asian countries focus on cultural elements, as these films have developed based on sharable cultural content among Asian audiences, as shown in the case of *Miss Granny*. As Nikki Lee (2012, 90) clearly states, Asian transnational ventures through coproductions have produced "movies designed to respond to the cultural tastes of particular groups of local Asian audiences. In order to do so, they both engage with and facilitate the cultural fantasies and desires of those audiences." Moreover, the cinematic embodiment of Asian countries presented in coproduction films marks out "a set of spatial and temporal mappings of Asian locations." In other words, cultural transnationalization and globalization in Asian invoke and reproduce "a multitude of different and often conflicting cultural imaginations of Asia within Asian film and media markets" (N. Lee 2012, 90). Looking at Chinese cinema specifically, Chris Berry (2010, 124) also argues,

> The specificity of transnational cinema can be grasped by distinguishing the earlier international order of nation states from the current transnational order of globalization, and that the primary characteristics of "transnational cinema" can

be best understood by examining it as the cinema of this emergent order. However, it has ended by insisting that any proper consideration of this transnational order must not only take into account the economic forces of global capital in the cinema, but also the fact that by understanding that the spaces opened up in the course of accommodating those forces have also allowed a host of other cinematic activities to develop and thrive, often with no primary consideration of profitability at all.

However, coproductions with the U.S. and China mainly emphasize financial goals. Consequently, coproductions with these two major countries have not fulfilled cultural integration because the major players are still the U.S. and China: several Hollywood majors and other platforms, like Netflix, have increased their influence by providing necessary resources to Korean filmmakers, and China has also significantly extended its influence in the domestic market. Although Korean filmmakers and entertainment corporations have pursued cultural integration in several Asian countries, Korean cinema is subordinate to U.S. and now Chinese dominance. Cultural transnationalization and globalization have not been equally achieved, as these two large countries, thanks to investments made by Hollywood majors and media platforms as well as Chinese forces, have wielded their power through capital.

Overall, the transnationalization of film culture is tied to cultural bondage and economic structure at the same time, as transnational filmmakers aim for both benefits. Coproductions in the realm of film can be conducted in pursuit of financial profits at some times and, at others, in search of cultural integration. Coproductions may be financially driven; however, since film production assists in "negotiating cultural identity and articulating social consciousness," filmmakers should engage with these issues as well (Gao 2009, 423; Soh and Yecies 2017). How to advance a balance between financial and cultural goals will be a new agenda for Korean cinema in the midst of these increasingly transnational dealings.

7 · TRANSNATIONALIZATION OF FILM GENRES

Korean cinema has become one of the most significant parts of the local cultural industries. Due to the swift development of domestically produced films, the Korean film industry has been considered a very distinctive non-Hollywood cinema. As the soaring number of movie attendees—the highest in the world—shows, Koreans enjoy local films partially due to their high quality and blockbuster style. While the structure surrounding the industry, including the increasing number of multiplex theaters and screen oligopoly, has contributed to the recent boom in the local market, the quality of local films' content—which can be compared with Hollywood movies in terms of genres, themes, digital technologies, and scripts—certainly drives the popularity of domestic films in Korea.

The industry has substantially advanced the quality of its films through various strategies, such as the transnationalization of local film content, changes in film genres and themes, and coproduction. Among these, I am especially inclined to examine genre because it is one of the most significant aspects in understanding major characteristics of film. Ever since the first stage of the development of film in the late 19th century, movie directors in Hollywood have advanced movie genres and developed certain types of films according to them. Producers and directors in other countries have also developed their films by utilizing genres, which have been adopted mainly from Hollywood. Since the inception of motion pictures, many in Asia and Latin America, as part of Third World Cinema—non-Western "cinemas opposed to imperialism and colonialism" (Tyrrell 1999, 261)—have developed their own unique movie genres, such as Korea's particular take on melodrama, which mainly reflects people's daily struggles and hardships. What is interesting in Korean cinema is that local filmmakers have recently revised the major movie genres and themes of domestic films in the midst of its interactions with Hollywood.

This chapter explores the primary characteristics of content in contemporary Korean cinema, analyzing films between 1971 and 2016 in terms of their genres so as to understand how they have systematically changed.[1] By analyzing 460 movies, which were the top-10 highest-grossing movies of each year in this period, it first categorizes major film genres to determine how they have shifted. It then maps out the nature of these changing patterns and the major reasons for these variations in Korean cinema—in particular, in relation to cultural policies and Hollywood's influence. Finally, it analyzes the nature of hybridity in terms of genre-bending by investigating whether it has created new cultures, distinct from Hollywood, or it has represented transnational cultural traits. In other words, it discusses whether genre-bending movies have developed unique local styles or are extensions of Hollywood formulas.

FILM GENRES IN TRANSNATIONAL CINEMA

There are several dimensions to consider in understanding the nature of film. While structural aspects, such as financing and government policies, are significant to the growth of any cinema tradition, movie viewers go to the theaters to watch movies mainly because of content, which can be identified by genre. As Ralph Amelio (1976, 48) argues, "The genre approach is one of the best ways to understand the popular film," and films are influenced by films. Therefore, it is critical to examine the nature of Hollywood films in terms of genre and whether non-Hollywood cinemas have developed their own unique films or simply copied famous Hollywood genres. Despite the fact that the transnational production and consumption of disseminated genre formats and styles have been essential parts of the development of those same genres in film, previous works in genre studies have not paid attention to this. However, in this book, we will be interrogating "the transnational flows of genre aesthetics, styles, and industrial practices and examining film genres as sites for transnational struggles over meanings and identities" so that we can determine Hollywood's influence on film content (D. H. Kim 2009, 6–7).

Movie genres are continually evolving; therefore, it is not easy to classify some movies, especially contemporary movies. Nevertheless, film scholars, filmmakers, and audiences classify films into groupings for critical appraisal, easy identification of subject matter, or quick clues as to the films' nature (Lopez 1993). Categorizing films is important because it may elucidate what producers and audiences of films do (Staiger 2003). As *genre* refers to a specific type of fictional film, it is usually exemplified by the western, the gangster film, musicals, horror films, melodramas, and comedies (Benshoff and Griffin 2009). On occasion, the term *subgenre* has been used to refer to specific traditions or groupings within these genres: romantic comedy, slapstick comedy, gothic horror, and so on. As Hollywood has been the most significant industry in global markets, including in terms of developing new genre movies, film producers in many countries learn not only new techniques and skills but also these genres from Hollywood. Therefore, genres have tended to focus on mainstream commercial films in general and Hollywood films in particular. While we do not need to exclude noncommercial or non-feature-length films such as the documentary, the animated short, the avant-garde film, or the art film, genres in have usually focused on commercial feature films, especially Hollywood's (Neale 2005, 7). Genres also perform several economic functions: "They enable the industry to meet the obligations of variety and difference inherent in its product. But they also enable it to manufacture its product in a cost-effective manner, and to regulate demand and the nature of its output in such a way as to minimize the risks inherent in difference and to maximize the possibility of profit on its overall investment" (Neale 2005, 218–219).

Of course, "genre films deal just as surely and deeply with social issues, considerations of life and death and the unknown, as do art films," although they are not the major interests of film producers and companies (Kaminsky 1985, 3). Movie genres can also be defined as various types, categories, or groups of films that are recurring and have familiar and easily recognizable patterns in terms of subject matter, theme (e.g., contemporary social issues), mood, and motif. For example, theme is "a basic conceptual or intellectual premise underlying a specific work or body of works" and "motif is a dominant, generally recurring idea of dramatization designed to enhance the theme or themes of the director" (Kaminsky 1985, 9). These terms are sometimes separated from genre but often work as parts of genre. Therefore, it is critical to acknowledge these patterns as well.

Understanding genres, themes, and motifs is significant because they represent some of the major features of a country's cinema, as "theorization around cinema and globalization has largely been structured in terms of a basic opposition between Western commercial and culturally imperialist cinema, and the Third World's non-commercial, indigenous, and politicized cinema" (Tyrrell 1999, 260). In fact, national cinema tends to concern itself with the lives and struggles of people in the nation (through, for example, melodrama), while entertainment predominates in Hollywood's commercial genres, including comedy, action, adventure, and horror. What we have to consider is whether commercialized films also touch on significant national themes, such as ideological conflicts, political issues (e.g., political corruption), and traditional culture (e.g., national history and arts; Abelmann 2003; D. Y. Jin 2016).

In order to understand the major characteristics of Korean cinema, it is beneficial to know the primary features genre in Hollywood films, which provides a useful point of comparison. According to the data provided by Statista (2016), the most popular genres in North America between 1995 and 2016 were comedy ($41.49 billion total grossed), adventure ($40.97 billion), action ($33.46 billion), drama ($31.46 billion), and thriller/suspense ($16.36 billion). Others include romantic comedy, horror, musical, documentary, and black comedy (see figure 7.1).

There are several reasons comedy, adventure, and action are popular in Hollywood movies: "For better or worse, Hollywood strives to present the universal to global audiences. As Hollywood markets its films to more non-English speakers, these films become more general. Action films are favored over movies with subtle dialogue. Comedy revolves around slapstick rather than verbal puns" (Cowen 2002, 93). Luckily, from the cinematic perspective, "the American values of heroism, individualism, and romantic self-fulfillment are well suited for the large screen and for global audiences" (Cowen 2002, 94). This paradoxically explains that non-Hollywood cinema industries would not focus on some genres that Hollywood emphasizes because they are primarily targeting domestic audiences; however, as they learn film production from Hollywood, they cannot avoid these successful Hollywood genres even when targeting smaller markets.

UNDERSTANDING FILM GENRES IN KOREAN CINEMA, 1971–2016

Film genres in Korean cinema in the 21st century are complicated because they are continuously changing. Korea's film industry "reveals itself to be open to

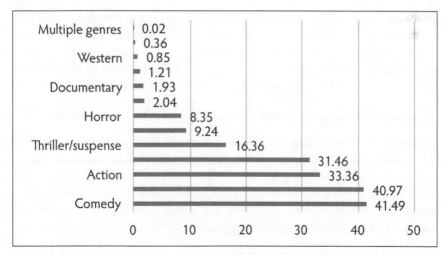

FIGURE 7.1. Most popular movie genres in North America by box-office revenues, 1995–2016 (Source: Statista 2016.)

(Unit: $1 billion)

struggle over its meaning and status at home and abroad," so "questions of genre have a crucial role to play" (Stringer 2005, 95). As Yecies and Shim (2016, 209) point out, "Given the dominance the Hollywood film industry has maintained in Korea for around a century, genre appropriation and transformation are necessary and constructive processes of development for a national cinema." This is significant because "in a globalized and increasingly complex film market—in which Korean cinema now enjoys major status—the transnational flow of film genres is a significant step toward recognizing and celebrating the diversity of contemporary Korean cinema."

While the sample films selected for this analysis were produced domestically between 1971 and 2016, I will start with an overview of earlier films. The films produced between 1945 and 1970—from the first stage of U.S. influence right after the liberation of the country from Japan to Park Chung Hee's Yusin System—provide a good point of comparison. During this early period, Korean cinema produced 2,124 films. Due to the Japanese colonial period and the Korean War, followed by the socioeconomic milieu of the war-torn country, the number of films domestically produced were few, usually fewer than 30 per year until 1957. Then, during the golden age of Korean cinema from the late 1950s to the late 1960s, more than 150 were made annually—sometimes reaching up to 200.

Among these, drama/melodrama was the largest genre (1,116 films), consisting of 52.5 percent of movies, followed by action (297, 13.9 percent), comedy (194, 9.1 percent), history (92, 4.3 percent), anticommunism (92, 4.3 percent), war (57, 2.68 percent), classic (56, 2.63 percent), bibliography (41, 1.9 percent), thriller (40, 1.88 percent), and enlightenment (38, 1.78 percent; KMPPC 1977, 46–48; table 7.1). The top three genres—drama (in particular, melodrama), action, and comedy—accounted for as much as 75.5 percent of films produced. However, as a reflection of the societal mood right after several historic ordeals, war, enlightenment, history, and anticommunism movies also accounted for 13.1 percent, which was relatively significant (KMPPC 1977).

This trend has continued until recent years with some variation, according to the analysis of the films selected. For this book, I chose only the top-10 highest-grossing films per year, based on annual reports by the Korean Film Council because only a few films on a large scale dominated the market. In other words, I identified the top-10 highest grossing movies of each year between 1971 and 2016, and among these 460 films, slightly more than half were dramas (233, 50.6 percent). Drama was followed by action (64, 13.9 percent), comedy (57, 12.4 percent), horror/thriller (28, 6 percent), and melodrama/romance (22, 4.7 percent). Others were history (20, 4.3 percent), crime (9, 1.95 percent), science fiction (8, 1.7 percent), family (4), and war (4).

TABLE 7.1. Korean films by genre, 1945–1971

	Drama/ melodrama	Action	Thriller	Comedy	History	Horror	Classic	War	Anticommunism	Enlightenment	Bibliography	Music	Marshal Art	Religion	Others	Total
1945										5						5
1946	1									1	1				1	4
1947	3	1								3	2				2	13
1948	8	2			1					3	1	1		1	5	22
1949	9				1				5	2	1				2	20
1950	1							1	1							5
1951	1				2				1						3	5
1952	1	1					1			3				1		6
1953	2							2	1							6
1954	2							3	3	4					6	18
1955	7						2	2	3	1						15
1956	16	1		4	5			2			1			1		30
1957	26	4	1	3	1						2					37
1958	59	2	2	7	1		2		1							74
1959	85	2	1	12	4		1		1		5					111
1960	64	6	1	8	2	1	3		1		1					87
1961	47			8	4	1		1	5	1	3				10	79
1962	57	11	3	13	8	1	1	5	2		6			2		112
1963	82	14	7	19	7	1	2	4	2	3	7					148
1964	82	20	2	11	12	1	1	2	3		2			1		137

(continued)

TABLE 7.1. Korean films by genre, 1945–1971 (continued)

	Drama/ melodrama	Action	Thriller	Comedy	History	Horror	Classic	War	Anticommunism	Enlightenment	Bibliography	Music	Marshal Art	Religion	Others	Total
1965	91	24	1	12	6	1	7	9	6		1			1	2	161
1966	86	26	5	16	4	2	2	11	10	3	4				3	172
1967	89	29	3	11	10	7	14	7	5	4	1	1			4	185
1968	96	26	4	18	16	3	2	3	22	4		3	9		6	212
1969	106	55	4	24	4	6	9	3	11		2	2		1	2	229
1970	95	73	6	28	4	6	4	2	11	1	1					231
Total	1116	297	40	194	92	31	56	57	92	38	41	7	9	8	46	2124

SOURCE: KMPPC (1977, 46–48).

There were also some adult (3), fantasy/adventure (3), animation (2), documentary (2), and western (1) films, which means that 15 genres have been popular in Korean cinema since the early 1970s, with three genres—drama, action, and comedy—accounting for as much as 76.9 percent of the highest-grossing movies (see table 7.2). As such, in Korean cinema, between 1945 and 2016, drama—melodrama in particular—has continued to be the dominant genre, followed by action and comedy, and their proportions have remained relatively constant. However, horror, thriller, crime, and science fiction have replaced the anticommunism, war, and enlightenment genres.

This shows that Korean moviegoers like drama, action, and comedy, and film producers have heavily focused on these few successful genres. While adventure has been one of the most popular genres in Hollywood, it is not significant in Korean cinema, perhaps mainly because of the lack of film funds to make blockbuster-scale adventure movies. Other than that, though, the Hollywood and Korean film industries show similar trends in that drama, action, comedy, and horror/thriller have become the top genres. Of course, unlike Hollywood films, in Korean cinema, drama has been the largest and the most significant genre, although the situation has changed over the past several decades. This seems to confirm that drama's popularity is due in part to its ability to portray specific qualities of Korean society and people.

In fact, the dark age of the Korean film industry in the 1970s, which was due to several social-economic changes such as the introduction of the television, provides a clear historical background against which to compare the change and continuity of Korean cinema thereafter. The changing cultural policies amid neoliberal globalization in the 1980s and 1990s were crucial in the reconstruction of the Korean film industry, and there were several major historical events—political, economic, and cultural—that directly influenced Korean cinema. Therefore, this part of my analysis divides the entire period into five major eras based around several significant historical turning points.

First, during the military regime between 1971 and 1979, Korean cinema experienced the worst recession in the midst of several regulations, including severe censorship. In the ruling period of Park Chung Hee, state power endeavored to exclude possible dissent in order to impose a uniform schema of political opinion from above. To this end, "the Park government managed the culture industry as the system to fashion a collective feeling that bound the nation together and legitimized political centralization. Cinema was required to function as a means to block heterogeneous narratives and representations impairing cultural and political unities, with support from the state, the public, and the industry itself" (S. H. Park 2012, 54). Under the Yusin System, the military regime controlled the local film industry through censorship and other legal measures, which resulted in a deep recession.

TABLE 7.2. Top 10 Korean films by genre, 1971–2016

	Drama	Action	Comedy	Horror/mystery	Melodrama/romance	History	Crime	Sci-fi	Family	War	Adult	Fantasy/adventure	Animation	Documentary	Western
1971	4	2			2	2									
1972	4	4	1		1										
1973	3	5			2										
1974	3	3			4										
1975	3	4	1	1	1										
1976	6				2	1						1			
1977	6				1	1		1	1						
1978	8	1			1	1									
1979	8				1								1		
1980	8	1						1							
1981	8					1		1	1						
1982	8					1			1			1	1		
1983	7			1				1							
1984	9								1						
1985	9					1									
1986	7			1		2									
1987	8					1		1							
1988	6	3			1										
1989	7				2						1				
1990	6	3			1										
1991	8	1	1												
1992	7	2								1					

Year													
1993	8			1									
1994	5	1	1	2							1		
1995	6	1	2								1		
1996	4	4	2										
1997	4	2	3	1									
1998	5	1	2	2									
1999	3	3	1	2				1					
2000	4	4	1	1									
2001	3	1	6										
2002	2	1	5	1				1					
2003	1	1	5	2						1			
2004	4	2	2	1						1			
2005	7		2	1									
2006	5		5										
2007	4	3	3	2				1					
2008	5	3	1										1
2009	3	1	2	1	1							1	
2010	3	2	2	2		1	1						
2011	4	3	3	2		1							
2012	1		3	1	1	2	2	1					
2013	1	2	1	1		1	3	1					
2014	4					3	1		1			1	
2015	3	2	1	1		2	1						
2016	1	3	2	2		1	1		1			2	1
Total	233	64	57	28	22	20	9	8	4	4	3	3	2	1

SOURCE: Compiled from KOFIC annual film industry white papers between 1971 and 2016

Second, the Chun Doo-hwan regime (1980–1987) continued to control the cultural industries, including the film sector, in order to avoid any kind of political or social contest against the military regime. Despite some supportive measures, Korean cinema during this period did not make any tangible recovery.

The third period (1988–1994) was characterized by the inception of neo-liberal globalization—in particular, policy changes that gave direct distribution rights to Hollywood. The Korean government opened the film market to Hollywood major studios in 1988, and they began to penetrate the Korean market. Local cinema, which was in recession in the 1980s, further descended into a dark period.

The resurrection of Korean cinema and the second golden era of the Korean film industry epitomized the fourth period (1995–2006). During these years, the film industry fluctuated based on the influx and withdrawal of conglomerates, including Samsung. With the Motion Picture Promotion Law of 1995 and consecutive supporting film policies, Korean cinema built a new environment. The fourth and fifth periods have some overlap, because in both, filmmakers adopted Hollywood styles, skills, and capital, resulting in the blockbusterization of local films.

However, independent producers, instead of chaebol, were the major players during the final period (2006–2016), which started with the change in screen quotas in 2006 as a part of the Korea-U.S. FTA The fifth period is important because, through it, we can evaluate the results of reduced screen quotas. We are also able to determine the nature of local films in terms of their content and whether they have developed a national identity—a sociopolitical agenda characterizing Korean society—or only advance Hollywood-style blockbuster themes aiming at commercial imperatives.

FILM GENRES DURING THE MILITARY REGIMES, 1971–1987

Under the Park Chung Hee regime, Korean cinema experienced a dark age due in large part to repulsive film policies during the rise of the television era. After the 1960s, Korean cinema entered a deep recession in both production and exhibition. Movies produced domestically were limited to only a few genres, such as drama (45 movies, 50 percent), action (19 movies, 21 percent), and melodrama/romance (15 movies, 16.7 percent). These three major genres were responsible for 87.7 percent of films among the 90 films produced in the 1960s. Comedy (2), horror/thriller (1), science fiction (1), family (1), fantasy/adventure (1), and animation (1) were the remaining genes, which were not significant. Since melodrama and romance are usually considered subgenres of drama films—dealing in particular with human emotion as part of strained familial situations, tragedy,

TABLE 7.3.   Korean film by genre during major periods

	Drama	Action	Comedy	Horror/thriller	Melo/romance	History	Crime	Sci-fi	Family	War	Adult	Others	Total
Park Chung Hee regime, 1971–1979	45	19	2	1	15	4	0	1	1	0	0	2	90
Chun Doo-hwan regime, 1980–1987	64	1	0	2	0	5	0	3	3	0	0	2	80
Direct distribution, 1988–1994	47	11	2	2	5	0	0	0	0	1	2	0	70
Motion Picture Promotion Law, 1995–2005	43	20	31	11	0	0	0	2	0	2	1	0	110
New screen quota, 2006–2016	34	13	22	12	2	11	9	2	0	1	0	4	110
Total	233	64	57	28	22	20	9	8	4	4	3	8	460

SOURCE: Compiled from KOFIC annual film industry white papers between 1971 and 2016

and emotional hardship—drama might be considered the only standout during this period.

Dramas—and in particular, melodramas—displayed national specificity in their focus on ordinary lower-middle- and working-class citizens, as opposed to Hollywood's gravitation toward upper-middle-class bourgeois housewives and widows (Abelmann 2003; D. Y. Jin 2016). The 1960s were the starting point of the development of Korean melodramas, and the limelight was the broad range of experimental genres that appeared (N. Park 2009). Director Yu Hyun-Mok's *An Aimless Bullet* (*Obaltan*, 1961) attests to the existence of genuine native realism in Korean cinema by depicting the poverty and hopelessness of the nation after the Korean War. Director Kim Ki-Young's *The Housemaid* (*Hanyo*, 1960) presents virulent sexual fantasies sustained by hybrid stylistics that "act out the psychological angst and anxiety behind the nation's rapid pace of industrialization" (Kyung Hyun Kim 2005, 208): "Both film-makers kept expanding their styles—realism and modernism respectively—in the ensuing decades, but the origin of their creativities is rooted in the vibrant atmosphere of the 1960s" (N. Park 2009, 45). The Korean society of the 1960s was "torn apart by postwar poverty and chaos, so melodrama sided with underprivileged masses suffering social and familial alienation in the shadowy margins of modernization and economic development" (H. S. Chung 2005, 119). As Darcy Paquet (2000) points out, throughout Korea's film history, "the melodrama has dominated popular film. In any given year [until the late 1990s], 50–70% of the films produced in Korea were classified (rather broadly) as melodramas. Popular movie stars were often best remembered for their roles in heartwrenching tragedies. In an ironic way, melodrama seems to have influenced many Korean art films as well." He continues,

> The word "realism" is often used in conjunction with arthouse films intended for intellectuals and the festival circuit. Leaving a movie camera on a street corner for two hours would produce a highly realistic work, but not necessarily an interesting film. When critics use the word, they often imply the political orientation of the work—its portrayal of the neglected corners of society—or, in regard to form, the extent to which it rejects the conventions of the popular melodrama. In the melodrama, exaggerated feelings and circumstances work to arouse empathy in the viewer, whereas in most Korean art films, directors have filled their works with the mundane. In place of the throbbing, seductive music of the melodrama, we hear little to no music at all. The melodramatic hero's floods of emotion form a polar opposite to the bitter, silent hero of the art film. In this way, the genre of melodrama has had an indirect influence on many of the works that make up Korean film history.

As a reflection of the significance of dramas, during the period of 1971–1979, the highest-grossing movies of each year were dramas. These included

Heavenly Homecoming of the Stars (1974), *Winter Woman* (1977), and *Heavenly Homecoming of the Stars 2* (1979), which were considered melodramas and adapted from famous novels. Many of them touched on social issues and general struggles through the tragic lives of female protagonists, such as hostesses, housemaids, and workwomen. Several of the less erotic movies during this period also targeted older teenagers and people in their early twenties. *Graduating School Girls* (1975), *Mischief's Marching Song* (1977), and *Yalkae, a Joker in High School* (1977) were some of the most successful movies targeting this audience. Consequently, the 1970s were marked as a period of "low-quality" films, earning it the blanket categorization of "dark age" (Jang, cited in N. Park 2009). These deprecating terms label "the many tear-jerking melodramas, misogynistic barmaid (or 'hostess') films and action films produced at this time containing prosaic anti-communist overtones" (N. Park 2009, 46).

The situation continued through the Chun Doo-hwan military regime of 1980–1987. During this second period, out of the 80 films analyzed, drama (64) as the single largest film genre accounted for 80 percent of Korean cinema. History (5 movies, 6.25 percent), family (3 movies, 3.75 percent), science fiction (3 movies, 3.75 percent) and others followed. Interestingly, there were no comedies produced and only one action film made at this time. Other than *The New Travelog to India* (1983, fantasy), which was a Korea–Hong Kong coproduction, the highest-grossing movies were dramas. These dramas, including *Madame Aema* (1982) and *Deep Blue Night* (1985), were considered melodramas—although some of these, like *Madame Aema*, could be considered adult movies.

In 1980, when General Chun Doo-hwan became the new military-leader-turned-politician, the new Chun regime made it clear that it would encourage the growth of TV—perhaps on the assumption that this would distract people from politics. In this desperate situation, filmmakers found a solution as old as humanity itself—sex. Under the Park Chung Hee regime, censorship was very strict, and all indecent scenes were cut away. In the 1980s, the situation changed, mainly due to the political instability of those days. As Andrei Lankov (2007) explains, "The Chun government harbored serious doubts about its own legitimacy. The Gwangju Revolt of May 1980 and its bloody suppression were still fresh in everybody's memory." But it found a solution to this in films like 1982's *Madame Aema*:

> The government approved the so-called 3S policy. The 3S stood for sex, screen, and sport. . . . Mass entertainment should distract the people from politics, and *Aema* fitted the new policy line perfectly well. The success of *Aema* paved the way for a tidal wave of erotic movies. When the studios were losing money, an erotic show looked like a sure winner. Sex sells, and does not require a large investment. The erotic video boom did not outlive the military regime which was largely

responsible for it. The Korean studios continued to produce cheap erotic films, but from the early 1990s serious Korean cinema was reborn, and soon garnered great success (Lankov 2007).

However, other top-grossing dramas continued to touch on social issues and general people's daily struggles, such as *Whale Hunting* (1984), Lee Chang-ho's *Baseball Team* (1986), and *Youth Sketch* (1987). This period also produced movies like *A Fine, Windy Day* (1980), which depicted the lives of three young working-class male friends, and *People in a Slum* (*Kkobangdongne salamdeul*, 1982), which portrayed the lives of people in a poor neighborhood of Seoul. They also sometimes realized social justice: *Human Market, Small Devil—an Autobiography of a Twenty-Two-Year-Old* (1983) clearly portrayed several societal issues rampant in those years.

FILM GENRES AFTER DIRECT DISTRIBUTION RIGHTS OF HOLLYWOOD STUDIOS, 1988–1994

Korean cinema came under Hollywood's direct influence in the late 1980s, primarily when Hollywood obtained direct distribution rights. This period was still undergoing the worst recession in Korean cinema; however, the nature of it was much different than it had been the previous periods. Hollywood's was making inroads, and domestic filmmakers could not challenge Hollywood studios because they could not find funds to produce films on the same scale. Korean cinema was totally unprepared for such unmitigated competition (J. Y. Shin 2005).

Genre had not changed much, although it started to in the early 1990s. During the period from 1988 to 1994, drama was still the most significant and largest genre at 67.1 percent (47 films), and when including melodrama/romance (5), it consisted of as much as 74.2 percent of Korean cinema. However, action had leapt into second place (11 movies, 15.7 percent), although comedy and horror/thriller were still marginal. As a continuation of the previous years, dramas comprised the largest portion of domestic movies each year. In 1988 and 1989, there were only two genres in the top-10 highest-grossing films: seven dramas and three action films, then nine dramas and one adult movie. The situation was exactly the same in 1993—dramas were still receiving most of the attention from audiences in Korea; a few from the top 10 were *My Mellow Rose* (1988), *Rainbow over Seoul* (1989), *All That Falls Have Wings* (1990) and *Seopyonje* (1993). In particular, melodramas and historical films with soft-core pornographic elements were the major trend until the very early 1990s.

Although not as popular yet, several action movies—including *General's Son* (1990), *North Korea's Southern Army* (1990), *General's Son II* (1991), *General's*

Son III (1992), and *Two Cops* (1994)—made it to the top 10 in the box-office charts in their years they were exhibited. Some of them were even number one, which drove the Korean film industry to seriously consider them, unlike during the 1980s, when only a couple of action movies had even made it onto the top-10 list. Meanwhile, the adult movies that characterized the previous decade began to disappear from the rankings.

The *General's Son* films are especially some of the most famous works of director Im Kwon Taek in the early 1990s: "The *General's Son* trilogy, which was based upon a novel by Hong Sung Yoo, certainly sees Im at the top of his game, being a great mixture of not only history, politics and themes of Korean national identity, but also of action and spectacle, and are packed with bloody, exciting fight scenes. Originally released back in the early 1990s when the Korean film industry was at a particularly low ebb, all three films in the trilogy were huge hits at the domestic box office, and provided a template for the country's new cinematic wave" (Mudge 2006). Interestingly, the trilogy is set during the Japanese occupation of Korea and based on the life of Korean independence activist and fighter Kim Doohan (played by Park Sang Min, who later appeared in the action blockbuster *Tube*). A young man who is actually the son of a famous general, he rises to rule the Jongno area in Seoul and wage his own war against the brutal Japanese invaders: "As the years go by and the Japanese, led by the cruel Yakuza Hayashi (Shin Hyun Joon) gradually tighten their grip, Doohan's struggle grows ever more difficult as he finds himself up against all kinds of evil schemes and betrayals, often only with his own two fists to rely upon" (Mudge 2006).

One of the first gangster movies in Korean cinema was *Gallant Man* (1969), and following this, a flurry of such films were released, highly influenced by contemporaneous Japanese Yakuza pictures. During the Chun Doo-hwan regime, gangster films faded from Korea's movie landscape, but they made a comeback in a big way in the early 1990s (Modern Korean Cinema 2011).

In this era, many dramas touched on social issues and national values as major themes. For example, because Korea had finally achieved a democratic government after the military regime in 1993, many domestic films started to deal with sociopolitical agendas, including the Vietnam War, student movements, and class issues (*Chisu and Mansu*, 1988; *Human Market* and *Oh. God!*, 1989; *White Badge*, 1992). Since commercial Hollywood genres were not yet popular, Korean cinema still primarily developed dramas, but it started to create comedy and action movies too. Since there were no capital investments from local or foreign-based transnational corporations yet, domestic films were primarily funds-sensitive and touched on the struggles of people.

KOREAN FILMS DURING THE MOTION PICTURE PROMOTION LAW ERA, 1995–2005

Korean cinema in terms of its genres fundamentally changed after the Motion Picture Promotion Law of 1995. As the Kim Young Sam government vehemently pursued neoliberal globalization, the number of Hollywood-style comedy and action movies soared, while dramas significantly decreased. Among the 110 films analyzed, dramas still accounted for the largest share; however, their number had decreased to 43 (39 percent, compared to 67.1 percent in the previous period), while comedy and action movies took off. Comedy (31, 28.1 percent) became the second-most significant genre in the box office, and action, the third largest, consisted of 22.2 percent (20 films). Comedy and action together accounted for 46.4 percent of the top-10 highest-grossing films, which was a new phenomenon in Korean cinema history. Horror/thriller also became significant at 10 percent during this period. Hollywood's major genres between 1995 and 2015 were comedy, adventure, action, drama, and horror/thriller; therefore, it is not dicey to argue that Korean cinema became similar to Hollywood (outside of its lack of adventure films).

During this period, several filmmakers focused on crime and cop stories. They started to produce similar genre movies, including *The Terrorists* (1995) and *Two Cops 2*, which ranked first among the top-grossing films of 1995 and 1996, respectively. Of course, film producers did not entirely give up on melodrama; they incorporated melodramatic elements into big-budget blockbuster films like *Shiri* (1999; Paquet 2009, 19). Melodrama is also part of commercial movies; genre films are generally commercial rather than art films. Local filmmakers began utilizing more entertainment-driven devices to guarantee the profitability of their films.

As comedy became the second-largest genre, many filmmakers attempted to create them one after another, with some variations. On the one hand, in the latter part of the 1990s, filmmakers emphasized romantic comedies *Dr. Bong* (1995), *Mister Condom* (1997), and *Jjim* (1998) signaled the arrival of this new, very popular genre, which often involved sexual discourse, in the late 1990s. On the other hand, in the early 2000s, the focus shifted from romantic comedies to action comedies like *Kick the Moon* (2001), *Oh! Brothers* (2003), and *Marrying the Mafia 2* (2005), which rapidly became one of the major genres of the early 2000s.

Action movies themselves plummeted because the conglomerates who made blockbuster-style action films (e.g., *Shiri* by Samsung) had left the film industry after their failure to profit from it. Comedy movies dealing with gangs became a popular trend, partially as production corporations with smaller budgets turned their focus from expensive action movies to more affordable action comedies (D. Y. Jin 2016). Horror/thriller movies also became popular in Korean cinema at this time. There were only five top-ten horror/thriller movies between 1971 and 1994; however, the number increased to 11 during this period.

Consequently, themes touching on social issues faded as dramas gave way to crime, action, and comedy movies. However, a few movies, like *Shiri* (1999) and *Joint Security Area* (2000), dealt with North Korea–South Korea issues, while *A Petal* (1996) portrayed the brutality of the military regime in Gwangju in 1980. *A Beautiful Youth Chun Tae Il* (1995) also touched on the labor movement. Filmmakers could emphasize these issues, mainly because they were free from severe censorship (D. Y. Jin 2016, 81), and "the concept of a Korean cinema was a counter-practice to the dominant films—commercially oriented U.S. films—in the domestic market, and a revolt against the oppression of the government's strong censorship. Korean filmmakers have begun to actualize the concept and the task of national cinema, dealing with subject matters that had been prohibited by censorship" (Min et al. 2003, 11). However, filmmakers began to emphasize entertainment and commercial values much more than cultural identities. "With a renewed emphasis on the box office," Korean cinema may be said to "have experienced an artistic downturn in the new millennium" (Rist 2004, 44). The Korean film industry after the late 1990s had "scrupulously followed the path of Hollywood and has shown more interest in making deals and formulaic genres than in innovating and devoting itself to the creation of art" (Kyung Hyun Kim 2004, x).

In the latter part of the 1990s and the early 2000s, Korean cinema aimed to reinvent itself. As previously discussed, the local film industry underwent a profound change after the 1997 financial crisis, with the exit of the largest chaebol, including Samsung, that used to dominate the industry. Venture capital replaced the conglomerates, and young filmmakers began to transform the film industry (Paquet 2000). In early 1999, the blockbuster *Shiri* smashed the domestic box-office record previously held by *Titanic* to become the most successful film in Korea.

There are several ways in which the films of the early 2000s tried to distance themselves from their predecessors. In this respect, Paquet (2000) argues, "newer films tend to have a glossier feel to them, and as the technical capabilities of the industry have expanded, directors have started to employ sophisticated digital imagery and special effects. Many newer directors have been schooled in Korea's booming short film industry, and have thus brought some of the techniques and feel of short film to their feature debuts" As such, Korean cinema in the early millennium witnessed a fundamental shift in film genres.

KOREAN CINEMA IN THE POST–SCREEN QUOTA SYSTEM, 2006–2016

The success of Korean cinema did not last for long. During the final period I will discuss, 2006–2016, the situation changed greatly due to the reduction of screen quotas, which influenced film content. Dramas were still the major genre with 34 movies (30.9 percent) out of 110 films analyzed. Comedy (22 movies, 20 percent) and action (13, 11.8 percent) followed, and these two genres together consisted of 31.8 percent. As a continuation of previous periods, horror/thriller movies slightly increased to 12 (10.9 percent). However, the proportion of the top three genres—drama, action, and comedy—decreased from 85.4 percent during the fourth period to 62.7 percent in this period. Instead, history (11, 10 percent) became the fifth largest, followed by crime (9, 8.1 percent).

In the 21st century, science fiction and horror/thriller became major genres worldwide, and both sci-fi/fantasy (*D-War*, 2007; *Snowpiercer*, 2013) and horror/thriller (*Moss*, 2010; *Deranged*, 2012; *The Wailing*, 2016; *The Handmaiden*, 2016) were also getting popularity in Korean cinema. Interestingly, the nature of drama also changed. Unlike during the 1970s and 1980s, dramas between 2006 and 2016 were not just melodramas. Instead, they were more often connected to crime, like street gangs and rotten cops (*The Terror Live*, 2013; *The Divine Move*, 2014; *Inside Men*, 2015), like many Hollywood movies. Another interesting trend is the production of thriller movies. For example, in 2016 alone, Korean cinema produced three of the highest-grossing thrillers in its history, *Train to Busan* (2016), *The Handmaiden* (2016), and *The Wailing* (2016).

Four significant trends have emerged, closely related to the sociopolitical environment surrounding the Korean film industry. Most of all, local films have been hybridized through genre-bending, resulting from their mixture with dominant Hollywood entertainment genres. In drama, for example, many movies contain elements of both comedies and romantic dramas, or history films and dramas. Likewise, many contemporary Korean films have at least two genre characteristics: for example, history and action, horror and drama, or comedy and action.

Genre-bending "challenges generic conventions, expanding the definition of a specific genre by mixing it with another, thus creating a new kind of experience." Genre-bending is a global phenomenon—easily detectable in Hollywood genre cinema and other film industries as well (Berliner 2001; Utin 2016, 49): "This practice only challenges the spectator's experience to a certain limit, since such films tend to preserve their systematic tone by using a narrative and stylistic strategy that dissimulates genre mixing. Genre-bending has provided some interesting and creative results and may prove to be a suitable description of the strategies of Korean films like *Shiri* (mixing action and melodrama) and *The Quiet Family* (mixing horror and comedy)" (Utin 2016, 49).

In Korean cinema, one of the key ways in which film producers have attempted to create a new image for the industry is in the blending and bending of old genres. This started in the late 1990s and became very common in the 2010s:

Many of the major Korean hits in recent years have provided an interesting twist to their genre. *Shiri* (1999), for example, shrewdly combines the Hollywood action blockbuster with the Korean melodrama to result in a film which appeals to a wide spectrum of viewers. *The Quiet Family* (1998) provides a funny and sick dissection of human nature in a fusion of the horror film and the comedy. This tale of a family-run lodge in the mountains is at turns playful and horrifying, and its enigmatic ending only further distances itself from the typical genre film. *Christmas in August* (1998) is a melodrama in name but it rewrites the conventions of the genre by replacing emotional excess with understatement and encouraging its viewers to recognize death not as a tragedy but as a phenomenon which must be accepted with grace. (Paquet 2000)

Nevertheless, during this period, only a few films could be categorized as touching on themes such as sociocultural matters.

Second, during this period, the history genre has become one of the most significant in Korean cinema. Seeking to draw in younger viewers with spectacle and older viewers by harkening back to older times, filmmakers put forward a litany of pricey period films (history genre).[2] Following the success of *Masquerade* (2012), Joseon-era (1392–1897) films remained a top choice for producers; no fewer than six such films came out in 2015. Set slightly earlier, but aiming for the same crowd was the Goryeo-era (918–1392) epic *Memories of the Sword* (2015). Several films set during Korea's colonial era (1910–1945) started to gain traction on the charts in 2016 as well. *Assassination* (2016) was easily the most successful (Conran 2016, 23). Due to big budgets and major stars, which often guarantee success in the box office, period genre films became a new favorite of Korean cinema in the 2010s. Several films, like *War of the Arrows* (2011), *The Face Reader* (2013), *The Admiral: Roaring Currents* (2014), and *The Last Princess* (2016) were all very successful. Such films reflect some of the most significant historical events but also people's hardships (as in melodrama).

Spirit's Homecoming (2016), which portrays comfort women—women and girls forced into sexual service during the Japanese occupation of the Korean peninsula—became a top-20 box-office hit with 3.58 million viewers. Many people, including in the film world, had been concerned the movie would not be a success because they were not sure that Korean audiences would be interested in this kind of agonizing movie. However, although it is not one of the greatest local hits, it was still attractive to many movie viewers, which proved the potential of movies touching on sociocultural and political issues with a low budget.

Third, some patriotic films like *Ode to My Father* (2014), *Northern Limit Line* (2015), and *Operation Chromite* (2016), which could be classified in the drama and/or war genres, have been very successful. However some have criticized them as a continuation of the military regimes' propaganda films, which were made to boost anticommunism, nationalism, and social morale, as these recent movies, which appeared under the Park Geun-hye government, portrayed similar themes. During our interview, Chung-kang Kim argued, "Recent Korean movies portraying nationalistic content, including Japanese colonial legacy or historical contents, including the abolishment of political controversies under the conservative administrations, have rapidly increased. This trend certainly implies that film content and contemporary Korean politics have closely connected; however, there are too many films representing nationalistic tendency. In fact, in Korean film history, the 2010s marks the second major period that witnesses the rapid growth of films portraying Japanese colonialism—since the 1960s, when Manchurian western movies were popular—which is not healthy for Korean cinema."[3]

Finally and interestingly, in the past 5 to 10 years, "the stylistic range of films made outside of the commercial system has expanded (The term 'diversity film' or *dayangseong yeonghwa*, used by the Korean Film Council in connection with their funding policies, has been resisted by many filmmakers)." Many in the industry still reserve the term *dayangseong yeonghwa* to refer exclusively to activist-tinged work. "In the meantime, *dokrip yeonghwa* has come to simultaneously shoulder both the broader and the narrower connotations" (J. W. Kang 2017). As the number of low-budget movies has increased in the 21st century, Korean cinema has expanded its potential to achieve diversity. The number of so-called diversity films increased from 82 (56.2 percent) in 2011 to 163 (70.3 percent) in 2015. For example, *Old Partner* (*Wonang sori*, literally "Sound of a cow bell," 2009) became the first documentary to be on the top-10 highest-grossing movies of the year chart. *My Love, Don't Cross That River* (2013) also had a meaningful box-office presence, which proves the possibility for these low-budget movies to achieve success.

Overall, domestic movies have increasingly adapted Hollywood genres and themes, to focus on entertainment. Hollywood films, as the global standard, reign supreme; local cinemas copy or follow. The primary trajectory of globalization—in terms of capital, system, and content—is still from West to East (D. Y. Jin 2016). Of course, blockbuster movies also reflect some significant social issues, as shown in *Inside Men* and *Veteran*; these films successfully "fed off the public's discontent with corruption in the media, politics, and big business" (Conran 2016, 24).

In Korean cinema, many directors have one after another tried to produce and even copy Hollywood's action movies. As one film critic points out, "The Korean cinema is heading for Hollywood-style blockbusters as if the globalization of domestic films lies in the copy of Hollywood" (K. H. Choi 2005). As this study of the genres most often used in Korean cinema demonstrates, many local film producers have in recent years developed previously neglected movie genres, such as comedy and horror. Several directors have also utilized a style that "mixes indigenous cultural elements with regional and Western influences" (J. Y. Shin 2005, 56–57). The majority of hybrid movies, including those that exercise genre-bending, have become commercially oriented entertainment movies instead of developing aesthetic and social themes. As Homi Bhabha (1994) posits, hybridity presumably allows for the emergence of new identities, and it should oppose those that hegemonic power desires to create locally. However, this implies that hybridity must be the site of resistance against imperial power (Kraidy 2002), and Korean cinema has not been able to resist Hollywood's dominance over its content.

CONCLUSION

This chapter has analyzed film content in terms of genres. By analyzing the 460 highest-grossing films between 1971 and 2016, it not only determined the nature of film genres and movie themes but also traced Hollywood's influences. The Korean film industry has developed several major genres, including drama, action, comedy, and horror/thriller. Other than adventure, which is the second-largest genre in Hollywood, genres in Korean cinema are similar to Hollywood's. Historically, Korean cinema has focused on dramas, including melodrama; Korea has modernized and democratized in a surprisingly short time, and melodrama is good at portraying how rapid swings in fortune, or difficult societal conditions, affect individuals (Paquet 2011). however, in the 21st century, it has rapidly developed comedy and action, and in the 2010s, horror/thriller. Based on movie genres, both Hollywood and Korean cinema have emphasized these proven genres because they guarantee commercial successes.

The content of domestic films in the realm of theme has also consequently shifted, formerly emphasizing serious social issues, now utilizing commercial entertainment formulas. As is rampant in Hollywood, Korean filmmakers have also tried to blend genres to attract many audiences. The cultural factors displayed in these genre-hybrid Korean films are often Western-centric and neglect local sociocultural values to fit Western tastes. As the structure of Korea's film industry has become similar to Hollywood, the contents of its films have adopted the latter's norms and formulas. Therefore, some critics and film scholars have criticized "the lack of unified and collective efforts to enable the cinema to function as an authentic culture" in Korea because "Western ideas of cinema along with Western views of men, women and the world had been transplanted to Korea without any critical or active filtering, and imitated without any subjective conceptualization or reflection" (Jeong 2016, 1).

As film genres and themes have changed, some argue (e.g., E. M. Kim 2010) that Hollywood's influence has provided inspiration, strengthening the local film industry. Sun Jung (2011, 12) claims that "the cultural imperialist perspective is inadequate to explain the current phenomenon of hybridity in Korean cinema because it ignores the hybridized presence of Korean cinema through the articulation of difference through postcolonial mimicry." As postcolonial scholars (Bhabha 1994; Appadurai 1996) argue, the U.S. influence has been constructive in helping Korean filmmakers be able to create quality films comparable to Hollywood's.

However, this optimism ignores the struggles Korean cinema continues to face in both structure and content; "the representation of the local culture" has given way to "connotations and value standards" based on transnational ideas (Wang 2008, 60). The flow of globalization is still uneven and markedly one-sided in its power (Shome and Hedge 2002). As seen in Korean cinema, in many cases, local producers cannot guarantee diversity because they are accustomed to creating a limited number of genres, particularly commercially driven Hollywood genres. In the 2010s, many diversity movies have been created and earned some popularity and profit; however, these are still marginal. The uneven power relations between the U.S. and Korea is still felt, since Korean content needs to be "modified to the taste and style of Hollywood"—although Hollywood's dominance has decreased as it has also embraced Asian content (Iwabuchi 2010, 203).

In Korean cinema, while several movies continue to develop cultural specificities, the majority of commercial films do not focus on social and national values as they reproduce dominant Western cultural genres. Therefore, in the future, it is critical for Korean cinema to develop local films not only mixing Korean stories and Hollywood styles but also creating new local formulas.

8 · TRANSMEDIA STORYTELLING OF WEBTOONS IN FILMS IN THE DIGITAL ERA

The Matrix—a science fiction / action film—was released in 1999. The first film turned out to be very successful, and two more films were produced, *The Matrix Revolutions* and *The Matrix Reloaded*, in 2003. As the films were extremely popular, later, comic books, video games, and animations were produced one after another. When *Avatar*, another science fiction film, was released in 2009, it was also adapted into books, games, and merchandise almost simultaneously.

Transmedia storytelling has had a long history. This phenomenon—in which one particular cultural form, an original, births other cultural forms, as described above—has become one of the most significant trends in the global cultural industries in recent years. Already at the dawn of the 1940s, the U.S. film industry was already "exploit[ing] other media in order to maintain a firm understanding of the sorts of products that were appealing to audiences at any particular time" (Freeman 2015, 226). The evolution from a single media text to "transmedia texts and the incorporation of affective economics as an audience strategy has additional implications with respect to the production context" (Simons et al. 2012, 27).

Though it has a longer history, multiplatform storytelling has rapidly grown and changed. In previous decades, "the rise of each new medium—print, motion pictures, radio, and television—introduced new forms of communication and entertainment. Often, the new medium initially replicated what came before. Many early movies were filmed stage plays, and early television programs were based on their radio antecedents" (Knowledge@Wharton 2012). However, the current multichannel and multiscreen era has given rise to a new form of storytelling, dubbed *transmedia*, which unfolds a narrative across multiple media channels. A single story may present some elements through a television series or a motion picture, with additional narrative threads explored in comics, digital games, or even Twitter feeds (Knowledge@Wharton 2012). As Ian Gordon and Sun Lim (2016, 301) argue, "Transmedia storytelling thus leverages a constellation of diverse and dispersed media platforms to tell a series of interconnected stories, each of which can also be stand-alone." Matthew Freeman (2017, 1) also points out, "The proliferation of content across multiple media is now so commonplace that the contemporary creative industries—be it the entertainment industries, the advertising industry or consumer and heritage sectors—are now calling upon transmedia consultancies to more effectively engage their audiences across multiple media." Of course, transmedia storytelling has not been owned and developed by only Hollywood and the U.S. In Japan, many cultural forms like film and digital games have relied on manga and/or animation. As such, transmedia storytelling has been advanced in various ways in several parts of the planet.

Korea has especially developed a new type of transmedia storytelling in the early 21st century, as webtoons (comic strips largely read on smartphones) have gained popularity. The Korean cultural industries, including film and broadcasting, have attempted to adapt webtoons into films and television programs. In Korea, the rapid growth of webtoons has created one of the most unique youth cultures, and the local entertainment industries have in fact depended on these comics as new sources for their own media. Several movies based on webtoons—such as *Secretly, Greatly* (2013); *Incomplete Life: Prequel* (2013); *26 Years* (2012); *Inside Men* (2015); *Along with the Gods: The Two Worlds* (2017); and *Along with the Gods: The Last 49 Days* (2018)—were huge successes, and many film directors and television producers intend to continuously develop webtoon-based films and television dramas. Many webtoonists also create their works for multiple purposes, which means that they develop one particular cultural work to make several products (comics, films, dramas) at the same time. Previously, many cultural producers transformed popular books and manhwa (more traditional comic books) into audiovisual products; however, in the 2010s, Korean film corporations began to create webtoons and directly produced films simultaneously.

By employing media convergence as a major theoretical framework, this chapter analyzes a crucial element characterizing the emergence of the contemporary Korean film industry—transmedia storytelling. It especially investigates the recent emergence of webtoons as the source of this development and historicizes the evolution of Korean films according to the surrounding digital media ecology. It explores changes and continuity in the manhwa industry—now focused on webtoons—over the past 15 years. It then considers whether local films utilizing transmedia storytelling have played a major role in the global cultural market in the 2010s.

NEW TRANSMEDIA STORYTELLING IN THE DIGITAL ERA

Storytelling, as one of the most ancient forms of communication, has been a significant component in the media and/or cultural sector. Transmedia storytelling, also called either cross-media or cross-platform storytelling,[1] is now a popular technique in cultural production. It identifies narratives that develop across multimedia platforms, which means that narrative forms can be changed depend on the platform (Giovagnoli 2011). As Lothar Mikos (2016, 52) clearly explains, "Transmedia storytelling is the process of telling a story on different media outlets which is planned by a producer or author. From the beginning the diverse narrative and aesthetic possibilities of different media outlets are part of the development of the story." For Giovagnoli (2011, 8), "Doing transmedia means to make the project's contents available on different technological platforms, without causing any overlaps or interferences, while managing the story experienced by different audiences."

One of the most significant aspects of transmedia storytelling is media convergence. As Freeman (2015, 215) points out, "Transmedia storytelling is perhaps the most aesthetically theorized component of media convergence, and one that has gained significant academic presence over the last decade. . . . Transmedia storytelling here has been contextualized most prominently as a product of the contemporary landscape, typically in relation to digital convergences and the horizontal integration of the media conglomerate."

Most explicitly theorized by Henry Jenkins (2006, 334), this form of storytelling is itself the convergence of textual forms and involves the telling of "stories that unfold across multiple platforms, with each medium making distinctive contributions to our understanding of the story world," a more integrated approach to franchise development. He points out that media convergence is "the flow of content across multiple media platforms" and, in recent years, has been actualized through transmedia storytelling (2006, 2–3). What Jenkins (2011) also points out is that "transmedia storytelling represents a process where integral elements of a fiction get dispersed systematically across multiple delivery channels for the purpose of creating a unified and coordinated entertainment experience. Ideally, each medium makes its own unique contribution to the unfolding of the story." In other words, media convergence is about the mix of digital technologies and content for achieving endless transformation to maximize the benefits to both producers and customers. The term *transmedia* itself and relevant practices are connected to processes of convergence (D. Y. Jin 2015). In this regard, Jenkins (2011) argues, "Transmedia storytelling reflects the economics of media consolidation or what industry observers call synergy. Modern media companies are horizontally integrated—that is, they hold interests across a range of what were once distinct media industries. A media conglomerate has an incentive to spread its brand or expand its franchise across as many different media platforms as possible. . . . The current configuration of the entertainment industry makes transmedia expansion an economic imperative, yet the most gifted transmedia artists also surf these marketplace pressures to create a more expansive and immersive story than would have been possible otherwise."

While there are several cultural forms that utilize media convergence and transmedia storytelling, webtoons are one of the most recent and exemplary cases, mainly in light of how "the emergence of digital modes of content creation and distribution has led to the digital integration of the production and circulation of narrative content across media" (Smith and Pearson 2015, 1). As Kalogeras Stavroula (2014, 28–29) argues, "Technology advancements have created new forms for stories," and "a digital story is a short form of a digital production narrative. Digital stories combine moving images with voice, music, sound, text, and graphics." Webtoons, one of the latest and the most significant forms of Korean media, are thus a good example of transmedia storytelling.

With an eye toward filmmaking, the Producers Guild of America (2010) indeed identifies transmedia storytelling as follows: "A transmedia narrative project or franchise of three (or more) narrative storylines existing within the same fictional universe on any of the following platforms: Film, Television, Short Film, Broadband, Publishing, Comics, Animation, Mobile, Special Venues, DVD/Blu-ray/CD-ROM, Narrative Commercial and Marketing rollouts, and other technologies that may or may not currently exist. These narrative extensions are not the same as repurposing material from one platform to be cut or repurposed to different platforms." Stavroula (2014, 34) also points out that "the theory of transmedia is especially contextualized from a film perspective because films are key components of transmedia productions."

Several scholars (Jenkins 2011; Chang and Oh 2015; J. M. Ha 2016) use the term *one source multiuse* (OSMU) to explain transmedia storytelling; however, the trend relevant to webtoon-based films and dramas is not limited to the perspective of OSMU. One source multiuse, as a creative idea based on efficiency and productivity, is where a single piece of media content is utilized in various applications to create maximum value with minimum investment (Chang and Oh 2015). The OSMU is not the same concept as transmedia storytelling, as discussed above, because the idea of multimodality encompassed in OSMU is a different affordance that diverse media have (Kim and Kang 2013; S. E. Seo 2015; D. Y. Jin 2015). As Jenkins (2011) in fact argues, the general definition of transmedia storytelling as equivalent to "one source multiuse" is inadequate.

Going beyond simple OSMU—for example, webtoons transformed into films and dramas after becoming hugely popular, as briefly mentioned previously— some webtoonists have begun to utilize a truly transmedia storytelling strategy, in which their webtoons immediately adjust to other media formats (Song et al. 2014). Many local webtoonists realize that transmedia storytelling, describing one logic for thinking about the flow of content across media platforms almost simultaneously, can be actualized (D. Y. Jin 2015). The following discussion, focusing on the realm of webtoons, will shed light on the current debates on transmedia storytelling in the film industry.

WEBTOONS AS TRANSMEDIA STORYTELLING CONTENT

While manhwa has a long history in Korea (as comic books in general have else-where), webtoons have had a relatively short one. It is commonly agreed that *Kwang Su's Thoughts*, which ran in the *Chosun Ilbo* between 1997 and 2002, was the first webtoon, as it was popularized through the internet, although it ran in a physical newspaper and was not called a "webtoon" at that time. Webtoons primarily "started in 2005 as a collage of drawings that netizens could enjoy as light-heartedly as enjoying a snack and was thus referred to as snack culture pop media" (D. H. Ko 2015). In the early 2000s, several webtoons gained popularity, including *Sunjeong manhwa* by Kang Full, which was transformed into the movie *Hello Schoolgirl* (2008). Later, in the smartphone era, starting in 2009, webtoons rapidly became one of the most enjoyable forms of culture for Korea's youth (see D. Y. Jin 2019b). The webtoon market in 2014 increased 14.5 percent from the prior year (KOCCA 2015).

With a new awareness of the increasing role of webtoons as transmedia sto-rytelling, the Korean government started to support the manhwa industry—in particular, the webtoon sector—in the early 2010s. However, its support has not been substantial. When the Ministry of Culture, Sports and Tourism announced its five-year plan for the industry in May 2014, it did not involve any significant financial support, though there were a few minor financing projects (MCST 2014b). Furthermore, the five-year plan did not include any tangible policy mea-sures for the development of media convergence to utilize transmedia storytell-ing strategies. In 2016, the government announced that it would provide only ₩15 million to support webtoon-based content production between February 2016 and July 2017, which is not promising. Government support has been rela-tively less substantial to the webtoon sector than in other areas.

Nevertheless, webtoons have remained popular due in large part to several factors: diversity in subject and genre, speedy publication and easy access, and optimization for smartphones. These elements, alongside the rapid growth of mobile technologies, have greatly contributed to the swift growth of webtoons.

To begin with, the major reason for the popularity of webtoons is easy acces-sibility. Webtoons are not simply another version of print comics. It is a whole new, different cultural form tailored for the smartphone age. The introduction of smartphones in 2009[2] was a watershed moment for webtoons (H. W. Jung 2015), as, along with tablets, they provided platforms that "support[ed] a wide range of visual, narrative and interactive media" (Goodbrey 2015, 54). As all comics, including webtoons, rapidly leave behind the trappings of print and embrace those of the screen, "it becomes necessary to re-examine the fundamental storytelling practices of the medium in the context of these changes" (Goodbrey 2015, 54). In fact, anybody with a smartphone, internet access, and a few spare moments is able to enjoy webtoons anywhere. Webtoons specifically are especially optimized for mobile devices, which means that webtoonists create the pages vertically and show one panel at a time; the audiences simply scroll down to read them. As Hyung-Gu Lynn (2016, 13) aptly puts it, "The digital infrastructure of broadband Internet, mobile access, and smartphone create the preconditions required for the diffusion of webtoons." In other words, the transmedia phenomenon started with the evolution of high-speed internet and prospered with smartphones in tandem with the digitization of cultural content. At this present moment, it is digital convergence that "hold transmedia story worlds together while pointing audiences across media" (Freeman 2017, 3).

Second, webtoons have diverse topics. Initially, webtoons were usually romance stories, but webtoonists have since developed fantasy, thriller, drama, history, and sci-fi narratives as well. Webtoons have especially gained popularity due to the portrayal of social minorities colloquially known as "losers"—such as bullied students or those still unemployed despite endless efforts—in contemporary Korea. Youth in the country have been struggling with several hardships in recent years—severe competition in school, difficulty finding jobs, and soaring housing prices—and so many feel like they are losers. This is the reason many young Koreans—in particular, those in their teens and twenties—show sympathy with webtoons that deal with the "loser" characters (S. K. Park 2013). For example, *Misaeng: Incomplete Life*, a webtoon-based drama and/or movie, portrays intern workers, precariously holding onto their positions. What makes people enjoy it is the plot, which is compelling for many office workers who struggle to survive. For them, the drama is rather realistic, so that they feel like they are not alone in suffering office hardships like long working hours, a mountain of work, and endless internal conflicts in their workplaces (Ahn 2014c). Several webtoons, like *Inside Men* and *Secretly, Greatly*, touch on key social issues, such as political corruption and the division between North and South Korea, but in these cases, the main characters still play the part of "losers" as an act. Webtoons, in their multitude, can attract many readers with diverse tastes.

Third, webtoons allow for extensive communication between webtoonists and readers (D. Y. Jin 2015). Webtoon readers are able to rate each episode, and the ratings and the number of clicks on any episode, provide immediate feedback to both the webtoonist and the webtoon platform. These measures serve as barometers for cultural producers to potentially adapt them into movies or television series (J. Y. Sohn 2014). Of course, there are some variations of communication among the various webtoon providers. Lezhin Entertainment, which provides fee-based webtoons, does not feature a comment function, while Naver and DaumKakao do.

Webtoons have gained popularity as one of the major forms of culture in Korea and started to become one of the primary resources for others. Movies to television dramas can use webtoons' story lines as tracks to follow, as they provide ready-made ideas, characters, and even scripts for numerous forms of popular culture, as well as attract diverse fans. Webtoons have thus significantly enhanced their fame by becoming new sources of movie scripts and drama stories.

WEBTOONS AS A NEW TRANSMEDIA STORYTELLING FORMAT

As webtoons have grown in popularity, many cultural producers in film, broadcasting, and gaming have developed products based on webtoons.[3] The Korean film industry, suffering from its ongoing lack of new ideas, often looked to other forms of culture. Japanese manga adaptations continuously failed in the Korean market, and so content producers turned their eyes to locally made webtoons in the 2010s. They found that webtoon stories are well-designed, structured, and easy to transform into movies and dramas. In addition, since many Koreans already enjoyed webtoons, content producers were able to attract audiences. As the drama *Misaeng*'s producer Lee Jae Moon states, "Webtoons are great resources for content producers because the original messages and episodes are already strong, and it is easy for us to add dramatics" (J. Y. Lee 2015).

The first popular film to be based on an original webtoon was *APT* (2006), which was made from Kang Full's webtoon of the same title. However, it was not a box-office success, and neither was another webtoon-based film released in the same year, *Dasepo Naughty Girls* (J. M. Ha 2016): "When *APT* was screened in 2006, the number of attendees was only 540,539, and it ranked 42nd in the box office that year. In this regard, it was not until *Moss* that movie adaptations of webtoons started to achieve success" (C. I. Park 2016, 246). *Moss* (2010) was based on Yoon Tae-ho's webtoon of the same name. *Moss* is a thriller that depicts the cruelty of human nature, set in a small village in the countryside. The film was directed by Kang Woo-suk (see D. Y. Jin 2019b).

Adapting the webtoon's powerful characters and narrative onto the screen, *Moss* attracted 3.35 million movie attendees nationwide to become the fourth-highest grossing movie of the year (J. M. Ha 2016). The movie organized the scenes in a visual format that maximized the aesthetics of the original cartoon's vertical-scroll-based presentation unlike the previous movie adaptions (Han and Hong, cited in C. I. Park 2016). Since the success of *Moss*, film adaptions of webtoons have also emphasized the characteristics of their original format, expanding on the attraction of webtoons.

Several movies, from murder thrillers to films about political corruption, show off the diverse genres and styles of films based on webtoons. For example, webtoonist Jang Cheol-soo's *Secretly, Greatly*—about a North Korean spy in a neighborhood, disguised as a mentally deficient young man—had good box-office results when it successfully transferred its story to the big screen, recording the highest number of movie attendees in 2013: with three young movie stars, including Korean Wave icon Kim Soo-hyun, the film accumulated 6.95 million viewers nationwide (J. M. Ha 2016; see table 8.1). Similarly, the political thriller flick *Inside Men*, starring Korean actor Lee Byung-hun, was also received well in 2015. In fact, it was with *Inside Men* that the craze for webtoon-based movies reached its zenith.

TABLE 8.1.   Korean movie adaptations of webtoons

Movie release year	Movie title	Webtoon title	Webtoonist
2006	*APT*	*APT*	Kang Full
2006	*Dasepo Naughty Girls*	*Dasepo Naughty Girls*	B Class Dal-gung
2008	*Ba:Bo*	*Ba:Bo*	Kang Full
2008	*Late Blossom*	*Late Blossom*	Kang Full
2008	*Crush on You*	*Crush on You*	Kang Full
2008	*Hello Schoolgirl*	*Love Story*	Kang Full
2010	*Moss*	*Moss*	Yoon Tae-ho
2011	*I Love You*	*Late Blossom*	Kang Full
2011	*Pain*	*Pain*	Kang Full
2012	*Fist of Legend*	*Fist of Legend*	Lee Jong-gyu
2012	*The Neighbors*	*The Neighbors*	Kang Full
2013	*The Fives*	*The Fives*	Jeong Yeon-sik
2013	*Horror Stories II*	*The Cliff*	Oh Seong Dae
2013	*Incomplete Life: Prequel*	*Misaeng: Incomplete Life*	Yoon Tae-ho
2013	*Montage*	*Montage*	Dan Woo
2013	*Secretly, Greatly*	*Secretly, Greatly*	Jang Cheol-soo
2014	*Fashion King*	*Fashion King*	Gian 84
2015	*The Cat Funeral*	*The Cat Funeral*	Hongjakga
2015	*Inside Men*	*Inside Men*	Yoon Tae-ho
2015	*Steel Rain*	*Steel Rain*	Yang Woo-seok
2017	*Along with the Gods: The Two Worlds*	*Along with the Gods*	Joo ho-min
2018	*Along with the Gods: The Last 49 Days*	*Along with the Gods*	Joo ho-min

SOURCE: Compiled from diverse written materials, including KOCCA (2014).

Due to these successes at the box office, movie rights for moderately popular webtoons began to be bought up in their early stages (J. M. Ha 2016), which means that many more webtoon films are currently in development. According to data from the Korea Creative Content Agency (KOCCA), as of December 2014, the publication rights of 73 cartoon works, up from 30 in 2013, were sold for dramas, films, and performances (Baek 2016; MCST 2014a). The numbers continued to grow: 52 webtoons from Naver and 279 webtoons from DaumKakao were transformed into books, films, and games by the end of 2015. Among these, 115 webtoons were transformed into audiovisual cultural materials, including films and television dramas. Furthermore, CJ E&M, one of the largest film distributors, established its own webtoon division to create webtoons for movies (J. A. Shin 2015). Webtoons thus have become transmedia platforms, creating a cycle in which cartoon characters and stories can move through television, film, and digital games simultaneously and have come to play a key role in sustaining the Korean cultural industries (H. K. Park 2014).

The Korean movie industry had been suffering from dwindling popularity in the early 2010s, as local films were overshadowed by Hollywood blockbusters, but webtoons have provided crucial sources for ideas in cinematic productions (A. Y. Chung 2013). Bringing webtoons to the big screen offers more opportunities to filmmakers, who can take advantage of the original ideas along with their solid fanbases and familiar story lines: "This trend [of creating movies based on webtoons] will likely continue because webtoons are now a treasure trove of original stories. They come with an established fanbase and the format itself is a narrative and visual map that the producers can use as a foundation" (You and Kang 2016). Several audiovisual cultural industries corporations have realized that webtoons are able to attract broader audiences, both in and of themselves as a format and as an already established database of stories that are ready to be turned into other content (You and Kang 2016).

In fact, many film producers and corporations are keen because well-made webtoons are often colorful and have detailed pictures, providing detailed information for how they will look as movies. The demographics of webtoon fans is another positive aspect. Unlike manhwa, whose major audiences are between their midteens and early 20s, webtoons' audiences vary, from young teens to those in their late 30s—which overlaps with the primary audiences sought by filmmakers. Furthermore, since webtoons are distributed through online portals, the movie producers and corporations can obtain the rights to these original stories for much cheaper than from other resources, including novels (Y. S. Song 2012). In May 2012, for example, movie producers paid only $20,000–30,000 to adapt a webtoon into a movie (Y. S. Song 2012); however, as webtoons' popularity as transmedia storytelling has soared, the royalties have been increasing.

CULTURAL POLITICS OF TRANSMEDIA STORYTELLING: THE POLITICAL ECONOMY OF *INSIDE MEN*

While there are several successful examples of transmedia storytelling based on webtoons, *Inside Men* (2015), which was developed from Yoon Tae-ho's incomplete webtoon, is one of the most successful. Yoon, best known for his webtoons like *Moss* and *Misaeng: Incomplete Life*, serialized *Inside Men* in a newspaper (*Hankyoreh Shinmun*) for three years from 2010 to 2012, but abruptly stopped releasing the political thriller because he could not handle the sensitive story any longer. During our interview, conducted in June 2018, he stated, "I stopped writing the series because of my own political conflicts. The webtoon was politically sensitive, and I thought that I could not delicately express real political situations. On top of that, I felt that my position was relatively conservative compared to webtoon characters, so I was not sure I could end it well."

Directed by Woo Min-ho, the film version of *Inside Men* is somewhat different from the original webtoon, which observes how society becomes ultimately corrupted by power through characters in the world of media by chaebol, national politics, and political hoodlums (Baek 2015b).[4] Instead of featuring a freelance photojournalist with a strong sense of social justice, as in the webtoon, Woo created a policeman-turned-prosecutor who sends shockwaves through an establishment that controls everything in the country, making the screen version the tale of a man's desire to overcome challenges to realize social justice. Director Woo said, "The original cartoon was very strong, and I tried to keep that strength in my plot." While the cartoon focused on the corrupt systems existing in Korea, the film focused on the intense competition between the characters themselves (H. J. Won 2015). Regarding these changes to his story, Yoon Tae-ho expressed, "The movies adapted from webtoons should have their own directions and plots, which are different from the original text. Webtoonists cannot and do not intervene in the production process because, once the rights are sold for big screen production, film directors and drama producers have their own rights to modify the themes, subjects, and characters. Produc[ing] big-screen cultural products and creating webtoons are not the same, and transmedia storytelling itself allows this kind of modification for the dramatization of adapted culture."

The movie *Inside Men* (which is called *Naeboojadul* in Korean, meaning "whistleblowers") is a political thriller revolving around three protagonists— Lee Kang-hee (played by Baek Yoon-sik), a chief editorial writer at an influential conservative newspaper who manipulates public opinion by pulling strings with political figures; Ahn Sang-goo (played by Lee Byung-hun), a gang-leader-turned-political-henchman who takes revenge against political, business, and media moguls; and Woo Jang-hoon (played by Cho Seung-woo), a prosecutor with no promising background in terms of money, family, and education who later joins hands with Ahn to investigate political and business tycoons. The social issues of deep-rooted corruption and injustice take center stage as *Inside Men* deals with the close relationships between politicians, businessmen, and the media (Bechervaise 2016).

Inside Men deftly portrays the unlikely partnership of a prosecutor and a gangster as both fight to unmask a corruption chain centered around Jang Pil-woo (Lee Kyoung-young), a congressman pursuing the presidency. The first half of the movie concentrates on displaying how society has been corrupted, as the movie starts with retired gangster Ahn Sang-goo holding a press conference to spill the beans about a slush fund set up by Hanyul Bank and Mirae Motors to bankroll the presidential campaign of Jang Pil-woo. With a grotesque flourish, Ahn takes off his glove to reveal a prosthetic hand (M. Lee 2016).

The film flashes back to two years ago, when ambitious district attorney Woo Jang-hoon has cornered Mirae accountant Moon Il-seok to get evidence of the slush fund, only to be beaten to it by Ahn, then a small-time gang leader in the pocket of Mirae president Oh Hyun-soo. However, Ahn makes the mistake of passing a copy of the documents to Lee Gang-hee, chief editorial writer of the most powerful newspaper company. This leads to the film's most sensational scene, when Ahn gets his hand sawed off by Oh's henchmen (M. Lee 2016).

The triangle of bribery among these three powerful men is well portrayed in the movie. For example, during their meeting, the CEO of Mirae Motors tells the chief editorial writer, "It is good to have a marketing partnership between a media company and a private corporation." Since the media are expected to perform a watchdog function, they ought to keep their distance from businesses; however, this particular conversation clearly implies the unhealthy nexus of these two powerful institutions. Worse, they are shown to have also created a close relationship with a congressman, Jang Pil-woo, by providing illegal political funds and editorial support in return for the future protection of their companies and themselves. The role of Ahn Sang-goo is to protect both the congressman and the CEO of Mirae Motors. However, once he learns that he has been being used by editorial chief Lee Kang-hee, whom he saw as an elder brother figure, he decides to take revenge on the powerful elite.

The actors who play Woo Jang-hoon and Ahn Sang-goo—Cho Seung-woo and Lee Byung-hun—coordinate the inimitable ensemble of the two characters in hostile and corresponding partnership as they act as inside men who are whistleblowers. Ahn reveals the massive bribery connections—the dirty tricks that manipulate public opinion—through a press conference. However, because he is a gang leader, he is not trusted; the three established and powerful men disclose his gang activities, including his sexual behavior and acts of murder, to the media. Despite the significant evidence he presents, he cannot effect change. Therefore, Ahn teams up with the prosecutor Woo to secure irrefutable evidence by having Woo temporarily becomes a puppet of the corrupt cabal by giving up the evidence he already possesses. In this way, Woo himself becomes another inside man and eventually reveals the web of bribery in another press conference, which finally brings the powerful men to justice.

This might seem like nothing new: by 2015, Korean cinema had witnessed its fair share of movies discussing rampant corruption and collusion. As Horkheimer and Adorno (1972, 126) have argued, "Real life is becoming indistinguishable from the movies," which means that contemporary films show "the growing concordance between its products and everyday life under capitalism" (Gunster 2000, 43). Films, with some special effects and techniques, ultimately duplicate the society they are a part of; *Inside Men* was like a reality show for many Koreans.

There are several elements that contribute to the success of the movie version of *Inside Men*. To begin with, all three of the main actors were already familiar with the webtoon; therefore, it was relatively easy for the production team to utilize a transmedia storytelling strategy. Two of the main actors, Lee Byung-hun (gangster Ahn) and Baek Yoon-sik (editorial chief Lee), decided to act in the film because after they read the script: "Based on the script and the original cartoon work, I attempted to create my own version of the editorial chief before shooting" (Baek, quoted in Baek 2015a). Actor Cho Seung-woo, who took the role of prosecutor Woo, said that he refused to join the cast three times—because his character was not originally in the webtoon version. He said, "Frankly, I am an avid fan of Yoon's work. I have read all of his cartoon work. So, when I was cast for the film at first, I had to turn the offer down as there is no reference to my position because there was a photojournalist in the cartoon instead of prosecutor." However, he confessed that he decided to appear in the end due to director Woo's persuasion (Baek 2015a). In Korea, as this anecdote illustrates, webtoons have become major sources for scripts in part because some directors and actors are already familiar with—and even passionate about—the stories.

Inside Men's success was made possible not only because of a well-made webtoon script but also because of the political milieu surrounding Korean society in the mid-2010s. In 2015 and 2016, there was "a steep rise in political thrillers that lambast unholy alliances between state departments, politicians, chaebols, and the media" (M. Lee 2016). *Inside Men* features, for example, a newspaperman with ambitions of being a political kingmaker, and for many Koreans, that no longer felt like fiction. Koreans had become increasingly frustrated by cronyism among chaebol (like Samsung, Hyundai, and Lotte), top-tier politicians (including the president), and even the media (e.g., conservative newspapers like *Chosun Ilbo*). As Anthony Kao (2015) indicates, "This might explain the film's relative success at the Korean box office. Though dramatized, the movie's story has elements that have timely precedent in real-life Korean politics." In particular, right after the movie's release, in 2016, Koreans witnessed the second presidential impeachment in their history—and it was because of a chain of corruption that connected the government (in particular, President Park Geunhye), chaebol (mainly Samsung), and the media.

In contemporary Korea, citizens keenly relate to social injustice that has occurred due to social corruption, and so they sympathized with the movie. They have been disappointed by reality but get vicarious satisfaction from the movie's just ending. Although the main protagonist is a gangster, movie viewers have applauded his role in breaking the chain of corruption—they want to see this kind of action in real life. People believe that social justice has been thwarted by politicians, prosecutors, and the media, three major powerful but unchecked agencies. Media and prosecutors, who are sworn to protect society, have not played their proper role, People are satisfied with seeing this in movies, but that is a sign that they also want to achieve this kind of justice in real politics.

Overall, webtoon-based movies and dramas are popular because webtoons reflect diverse lives that people can easily sympathize with. Unlike film writers, who are trained in film schools, webtoonists' backgrounds are more varied, and they portray their own unique worldviews, which attracts both content providers and audiences. Yoon Tae ho himself is, as of 2018, only a high school graduate, but he has taught at the university level due to his successful webtoons.

There are now an incredible amount of webtoons that people can easily access and enjoy. For example, Naver and DaumKakao have 50–60 new webtoons daily, with page views of 8–9 million on average. As such, there are many webtoons that content producers consider adapting, with subjects that range from romance to labor issues (H. J. Park 2014). As discussed, some movie production companies have already developed their in-house webtoon production arms in order to use them immediately for film production as well. As movie audiences have flocked to webtoon-based films reflecting cultural politics, film producers will likely continue to create new films like *Inside Men*, establishing another type of genre movie in Korean cinema.

TRANSNATIONALIZATION OF KOREAN WEBTOONS IN MEDIA STORYTELLING

With the soaring popularity of webtoon-based movies in Korea, global entertainment industries are also interested in Korean webtoons. As a reflection of these global interests, domestic webtoon service portals like Naver, DaumKakao, and Lezhin Entertainment are providing English, Chinese, and Japanese translations for the world market. With these entering the global markets, the copyright market is expected to be active as well. For example, Kang Full's *Witch* will be turned into a film in Korea and China at the same time, as the film rights have been sold to both countries. A Chinese production company has signed for the films rights to *Gi-gi-goi-goi*, and Michael E. Uslan, the producer of the recent *Batman* films, also plans to turn *Pick, Tribe X* and *A Watch Repairman* into films and TV drama series (J. M. Ha 2016).

More specifically, the two major internet portals for reading webtoons, Naver's Line Webtoon and DaumKakao's Daum Webtoon, have recently developed globalization strategies. Line Webtoon is seeking to produce television and movie adaptations of its most popular webtoons. The division of Korean internet and search giant Naver signed with the Creative Artists Agency (CAA), which now exclusively represents Line Webtoon's U.S. portfolio of comic titles. Some of these include the young adult series *Dents* from 2 *Broke Girls* star Beth Behrs and Broadway actor Matt Doyle; fashionista-superheroes comic *Heroine Chic* from David Tischman and Audrey Mok; fantasy-romance *Siren's Lament* from Kaitlyn Narvaza, and the New Brooklyn superhero universe created by a group of writers and artists that includes Dean Haspiel. Line Webtoon's Korean comic series such as *Noblesse, Tower of God,* and *Orange Marmalade* are also represented by the CAA for English-language adaptations (Spangler 2016). JunKoo Kim, founder and head of Line Webtoon, said in a statement, "Our portfolio of comic series across every imaginable genre has garnered huge success in both the U.S. and internationally and we know that fans are going to be incredibly excited to see their favorite titles brought to life on screen with the help of the CAA" (Spangler 2016).

In February 2016, Line Webtoon also released one of its biggest global digital comic series, *Noblesse: Awakening,* as a 30-minute animated film, which marked Line Webtoon's first entry into video content in the U.S. Additionally, the franchise will expand further in digital comic format as Line Webtoon launches a 10-episode limited-edition spin-off series entitled *Noblesse: Rai's Adventure.* Created by Son Jeho and Lee Kwangsu, *Noblesse* first debuted on Line Webtoon in Korea in 2007 and globally in 2014, quickly gaining momentum as one of the platform's most popular titles. The series is about Cadis Etrama Di Raizel, who wakes up from an 820-year-long sleep and starts a new life as a high school student. The series has amassed almost 400 episodes and accumulated more than 2 billion page views since its debut.

As Line Webtoon's first video to launch in the U.S., *Noblesse: Awakening* offers fans a new way to relive the series' original story arc. The film was produced by acclaimed Japanese anime studio Production I.G, known for their work on the animated films *Psycho-Pass: The Movie* and *Ghost in the Shell,* and directed by Shunsuke Tada and Kazuto Nakazawa (Line Webtoon 2016).

Meanwhile, in March 2016, DaumKakao announced that it had partnered with Huace Group, China's comprehensive film and TV media conglomerate, to bring five of its popular Daum Webtoon titles to the screen in China.

Through this deal, select Daum Webtoon titles are reproduced as movies, TV dramas, or web dramas and distributed across China. Titles include *Girl in the Mirror, Help! Breakup Ghost, Just One Shot, Cashero,* and *My Boss Dies Once a Day*. All are proven hits in Korea and are expected to appeal to Chinese fans thanks to their engaging, unique story lines and high adaptability to Chinese culture (beSUCCESS 2016). Of course, several small venture capitals have sought webtoons with such global appeal. For example, *Peak*, which is a Korean comic series, might be made into a film as its provider Rolling Story—a Seoul-based webtoon start-up—signed a film production deal with a U.S. entertainment agency in October 2015. Shortly before the production deal, the web comic had launched on Spottoon, Rolling Story's English platform for Korean webtoons (W. Y. Lee 2016).

After successfully navigating the transition of the comic book industry to mobile services in the smartphone era, Korean webtoon providers have started to eye global viewers through multilingual services and to look for more opportunities in global markets, such as remaking webtoons into films and television dramas (W. Y. Lee 2016). Webtoons, and consequently other webtoon-based forms of culture, have come to characterize the contemporary Korean cultural industries, and Korean cinema has greatly benefited from the recent growth of webtoons. Consequently, webtoons have rapidly become one of the most significant parts of the new Korean Wave, developed by emerging transnational cultural industries through the convergence of digital media and content. Previously, the Korean cultural industries exported separate cultural products and/or digital technologies; however, they have now started to export webtoons as transnational storytelling, a strategy that is not only new but also innovative. Korean webtoons have opened new possibilities; the convergence of old media with this new form is creating new cultural products to flow into global markets.

CONCLUSION

This chapter has analyzed transmedia storytelling based on webtoons. By developing the concepts of media convergence through digital technologies—particularly in relation to smartphones and the content made for them—it discussed the possibility of webtoons as sources of transmedia storytelling in Korean cinema. Although transmedia or cross-media storytelling has been common in Hollywood, Korean cinema—and in general, the local cultural industries—have recently developed a unique form of transmedia storytelling due to the rapid growth of webtoons in the era of smartphones without government support. Many cultural producers—such as film directors, television producers, and game developers—are keen to adapt and transform webtoons into films, dramas, and games.

This kind of transmedia storytelling has been building speed since the mid-2000s. As the stories in webtoons are amusing and fresh, with visual images that immediately show how they could appear on the big screen, the adaptation of webtoons has become increasingly popular. As Emily You and Chloe Kang (2016) point out, the webtoon's format is

> visually engaging and when done right, contains a story world filled with interesting characters that people can get emotionally attached to but at the same time it does not demand a huge commitment from readers. All webtoons are broken down into succinct episodes that people can read at their own leisure. The Koran film industry has developed these webtoon-based films, and this trend will likely continue because webtoons are a treasure trove of original stories. They come with an established fanbase and the format itself is a narrative and visual map that the producers can use as a foundation. Companies are beginning to realize that webtoons can appeal to broader audience outside of Korea, both as a format and as an already established database of stories that are ready to be turned into other content.

Korean webtoons are also receiving attention overseas, including from Hollywood, as some of Korea's webtoon films have had strong results in the global markets. As discussed in previous chapters, Koran cinema has been deeply influenced by Hollywood studios and films; however, now that Korea has developed its own unique transmedia storytelling model based on webtoons, it has gradually expanded its infiltration into global markets. This new trend is significant because it implies that Korean cinema will be able to develop films in tandem with webtoons and therefore penetrate other countries' cultural markets. What Korean cinema should do is develop its local, unrivaled popular culture and transmedia storytelling, using the growth of webtoons as a new model for its other cultural industries.

In sum, as Freeman (2017, 199) points out, "The future of transmedia storytelling seems contingent on acknowledging the very multiplicity of transmediality and its many possible potentials." The transmedia phenomenon cannot be analyzed by isolating it into one category or one industry—or one media: we should be "broadening our understandings of the transmedia phenomenon," as the webtoon example implies, "beyond the singular and quite limited framing of convergence culture" (Freeman 2017, 199). As Christy Dena (2009, 327) claims, "Just as a transmedia project cannot be created with one medium, the phenomenon cannot be understood through the lens of one research field." In other words, "the transmedia phenomenon has been made possible by digitization of content"—the development of smartphone technologies in particular, in the Korean context (Stavroula 2014, 44).

The Korean cultural industries have been greatly influenced by webtoons, and many webtoonists are trying to develop their creative works for several mediums, including films, while both domestic and foreign cultural producers pay close attention. In the era of digital media, Korean cinema has substantially shifted its attention to webtoons as primary resources, and the convergence of new media with old (e.g., webtoons with films) through transmedia storytelling has created a new stage in Korean cinema, especially in terms of its potential power as a local-based transnational force, in the early 21st century.

9 · CONCLUSION

Korean Cinema's Future
in Digital Technologies

This book has analyzed contemporary Korean cinema as the film industry—including the production, distribution, and exhibition sectors—has rapidly grown to become one of the major local-based cinemas in global film markets. By mainly employing the theory of political economy, emphasizing a historical approach, and partially utilizing textual analysis and expert interviews, this book has attempted to identify the major characteristics transforming Korean cinema. It has discussed several of the dimensions that greatly contributed to the changes, such as transnationalization in Korean cinema (focusing on its relationship with transnational forces, both Western and non-Western) and digital technologies embedded in transmedia storytelling.

In particular, it has examined the structural changes in Korean cinema due to shifting cultural policies, particularly in tandem with U.S. influence, including those that provided direct distribution rights of Hollywood studios, reduced screen quotas, and allowed for Hollywood to directly produce and invest in local films. It has also addressed fluctuations in film genres and themes, identified as part of genres, in order to determine whether local film content has advanced national identity and specificity or mainly adopted Hollywood norms and formulas.

Based on this, I believe that Korean cinema has fundamentally changed according to a few major dimensions: inconsistent and unstable cultural policies; Hollywood's consistent hegemonic dominance in the local film market; and rapid changes in Korean political economy, an ecology that Korean cinema is part of, and in digital technologies. All are closely connected, and these major dimensions together have created and recreated contemporary Korean cinema.

SHIFTING CULTURAL POLICIES

Korean cinema has shown unpredictability and irregularity partially due to the country's cultural policies. The local film industry has exhibited noticeable growth over the past several decades. A small country in East Asia with no particular cultural industries until the 1980s has greatly advanced its cultural sector since. The local film industry especially has become one of the most significant for both local cultural industries and Hollywood, as Korea is now the sixth largest box office in the global film market. However, the contemporary accomplishments of the local film industry raise several significant questions, as Korean cinema has had several ups and downs that have created a high degree of uncertainty and volatility.

Korean cinema has indeed achieved remarkable growth in a few areas. Several films have reached 10 million admissions, which means Korea has the highest admissions per capita in the world. Some Korean movies and actors/directors have received film awards in international film festivals, and there are several such festivals held in the country, including those in Busan and Puchon, which have boosted the reputation of Korean cinema. Seeing this growth in the industry, Hollywood majors have remade local films, and some famous actors and actresses are regularly cast in Hollywood movies.

However, the local film industry has certainly experienced some unpleasant shifts as well. Foreign exports have been diminishing, and profits are not guaranteed, while foreign films—in particular, those made by Hollywood majors—continue to dominate. The Korean film industry cannot penetrate the global film markets, especially the North American market. A collapse in exports, both before and after the 2006 change in the screen quota, was a setback that Korean cinema has only perhaps partially recovered from. Making inroads into the Western markets, in both North America and Europe, seems to have been the major challenge. Film financing has also been troublesome.

While there are several causes for this, one of the most significant is the Korean government's neoliberal policies. Beginning in the 1980s, these have profoundly affected the film industry, resulting in Hollywood's overwhelming influence on the local film market. Amid neoliberal cultural reform, Hollywood, as a primary force for the transnationalization of Korean cinema, has rapidly encroached on the local market and continued to be a major player.

With the adaptation of neoliberal reforms to resolve the trade disputes with the U.S., the Roh Tae Woo regime allowed the direct distribution of foreign films—of course, mainly Hollywood studios' films—in 1988. Partially due to this, Korean cinema experienced the worst recession in its history in the early 1990s; however, when the government introduced the Motion Picture Promotion Law of 1995, which emphasized governmental support to the film sector, the local industry was able to find the momentum to reverse this downturn. The rapid pursuit of globalization by civilian governments since 1994 has indeed positively influenced the film sector because new cultural policies equipped with legal and financial aid contributed to the swift structural change of the film business. When the Kim Young Sam government began to adopt such measures, applying the logic of globalization to the cultural industries, it consequently initiated the further resuscitation of the film business. The Kim government followed a neoliberal strategy, which usually implies a small government; however, the government still supported the film sector. These contradictory approaches have been unique in the Korean context because they have largely driven the different changes that Korean cinema has experienced (D. Y. Jin 2016).

Korean cinema has continued to experience some seesaw-like shifts. The government changed its position on the screen quota system, which substantially influenced the local film market. As can be seen in the exhibition sector, the government has also not taken any measures to control the negative effects of the rise of screen oligopoly. This implies that the Korean government has developed its unique cultural policies while grappling with the conflicts between state-led developmentalism and neoliberal cultural reforms, which both sometimes work positively and at other times negatively for the country's cinema. Of course, these unstable cultural policies have developed because of its complicated relationships with both foreign forces, including the U.S. government and Hollywood studios, and local-based transnational corporations, such as Samsung, Lotte, and CJ. The Korean government has developed several supporting mechanisms of domestic film; however, due to its inconsistent and unpredictable policies, the Korean film industry has experienced a roller-coaster-like ride over the past several decades.

HOLLYWOOD'S DESTINY IN KOREAN CINEMA

Korean cinema has been deeply influenced by Hollywood's consistent and hegemonic dominance. The success of the local film industry has always fluctuated whenever transnational forces, including Hollywood, expand their control over it. The U.S. government and Hollywood, equipped with neoliberal globalization politics, have penetrated the local film market, resulting in a swift change in both the structure and content of Korean cinema. In fact, Korean cinema's interplay with Hollywood has been intriguing and complicated, because Korean cinema has developed its film industry in the midst of conflicting relationships with the U.S. government and Hollywood majors. As the film industry has been one of the most significant components for the U.S. economy and ideological hegemony, the U.S. government has vehemently asked other governments, including Korea's, to open the film market to foreign companies and films—and of course, in particular, to Hollywood studios. Since the U.S. government first exercised control over the Korean film market at a very early stage in the 1940s, with the United States Information Service (USIS), it has continued to be a major player in the Korean film market.

Hollywood's major studios, backed by and lobbying the U.S. government, have also developed unique forms of hegemony in the Korean film market. Hollywood majors have gained substantial control over the Korean film industry—including distribution, exhibition, and production—through direct distribution rights, capital investment, and/or film (co)production. Korean cinema almost completely collapsed under the heavy influence of U.S. forces after the local government removed barriers for imported films in 1988 (J. Y. Shin 2005).

Since the mid-1990s, some filmmakers and scholars as well as government officials have argued that Korean cinema developed its unique system due to an influx in capital from major companies, including chaebol and investors. They argue that the result was the rise of domestic films, up to 50–60 percent of the market share. As the Korean Film Council (2016b, 29) itself points out, the Korean film market, at least for a while, put Hollywood distribution companies on the backburner. However, the council also clearly indicates that the contemporary Korean film industry is very different from several decades ago, when Hollywood studios started to directly distribute their films: "Back then Korean film companies were more like film offices rather than full-scale companies, and the market share for domestic films was much lower than that of foreign imports. Direct film distribution by Hollywood studios began in this environment, and the negative forecast seemed to come true at first: the Korean film market was invaded by Hollywood films through direct distribution. However, Korean films gained sophistication, slowly but surely."

What is significant is that the ostensible growth of Korean cinema does not imply the decreasing role of Hollywood in Korean cinema. The local film market in the 2010s has witnessed a new level of U.S. influence: in addition to Hollywood's existing distribution rights and benefits under screen oligopoly, Hollywood studios can now produce films in Korea. In fact, Warner Bros. and 20th Century Fox have already started doing so. Korea's domestic film market has significantly widened and is now a $1.8 billion industry, and at this stage, it is difficult to be an active player in the market just through direct distribution, so local production has become a key element for success. Since this development, Hollywood major studios have become important players in the Korean production field (KOFIC 2016b, 29).

The Korean film industry in the 2010s has become fearful of the possibility of Hollywood's dominance over the entire film sector. Unlike several decades prior, when Hollywood studios focused on distribution, they are now expected to expedite film production in Korea, which will change the map of local cinema. As Korea's film producers have often had difficulties finding major investors, some see Hollywood's involvement in Korean film production as a new financial resource; however, it is still another serious invasion by Hollywood, which may result in its hegemonic control over the entire industry in Korea. According to the Korean Film Council's box-office chart, in 2016, when two Hollywood-produced films (*The Age of Shadows* and *The Wailing*) became top-10 hits, Hollywood films also accounted for 28 out of the top 50 movies (Korean films were at 21, followed by one U.K. movie). Based on the huge successes of these two movies, several Hollywood studios and Netflix started production on several films, which might also end up being game changers in Korean cinema.

For Hollywood, the Korean film industry has become a cornucopia; it controls, dominates, and garners capital through the entire market, from distribution to exhibition to production, which is unprecedented. Unlike other countries like France, which firmly resist Hollywood in order to protect their cultural identity and sovereignty, Korea has sometimes voluntarily and actively initiated Hollywood through policy changes regarding the screen quota system and direct film production. In other words, Korea has sometimes been coerced by and at other times worked with global forces, mainly the U.S. government and Hollywood studios, in the course of its film industry's development. Due in large part to this unique but asymmetrical interplay between global and local forces, the Korean film industry has lost its strong position as a concrete and independent Third World Cinema.

Of course, it is necessary to understand that Hollywood is so influential in part because the Korean government and domestic film corporations also want to work with U.S. film corporations. As the Korean Film Council (2016d) states, some Korean film companies prefer to work with Hollywood in creating coproduction. For example, Showbox has partnered with Blumhouse and Ivanhoe Pictures, with which it has established long-term plans. One is a five-year agreement (between 2017 and 2021) to coproduce thriller and horror movies with Blumhouse. Previously, Ivanhoe Pictures, which has recently worked with 20th Century Fox, invested in *The Wailing*. Encouraged by the warm reception of *Operation Chromite* in the North American market, Taewon Entertainment is also planning on producing *The Blob* along with Goldcrest Films and A-List Corporation.

KOREAN CINEMA IN CONTEMPORARY POLITICAL ECONOMY

Culture, in terms of both structure and content, has always been a reflection of society. Although culture itself is able to influence and change society, in most cases, popular culture is also substantially influenced by continuity and change in society. Korean cinema has especially proven the close relationship between society and culture. As Tom O'Regan (2008, 244) argues, "By virtue of its public visibility and industrial character, politics and government tend to exercise a defining influence upon filmmaking." Korean cinema is an example of how it is "at one and the same time a textual and aesthetic system, an economic institution, an object of government and a social institution."

As already discussed, two key dimensions—shifting cultural policies and Hollywood's influence—have been major factors in the Korean film industry. However, Korea's changing political economy has also been the backbone of these two major dimensions. In the Korean cinema, from its earliest stages, the government has had no choice but to work with U.S. forces. In particular, the Chun Doo-hwan regime and the Roh Tae Woo regimes opened local markets, including the cultural market, to foreign players—of course, mainly the U.S. forces. The military regimes until the early 1990s had no political legitimacy, and for them, it was crucial to secure U.S. support in order to stabilize domestic politics and economy. Some civilian administrations in recent years have also needed this support to actualize their own political agendas, and therefore, they have changed several key policy measures, including the screen quota system.

Against this backdrop, the Korean government has not had the momentum to fully resist U.S. dominance in the film sector. The state has applied Hollywood's capitalist model to the Korean film industry, and with some exceptions, the Korean government has not been a leading actor of change in Korean cinema, serving instead as a resource for Hollywood majors. But this does not mean that the Korean government has totally given up its role as a facilitator for the growth of the local film industry. Through financial and legal support, it has certainly advanced it; however, due to its unique political philosophy, the Korean state has not shown a promising and consistent commitment to domestic cinema.

Korea's rapidly changing political economy has also substantially influenced film content. Although the Korean film industry has achieved ostensible success in several fields, its contemporary accomplishments have relied on only a few blockbuster movies that make money through oligopolistic market structures. The Korean government has not taken any measures to break up the screen oligopoly, unlike many other countries. Because of the changing nature of domestic films in terms of genres and themes, with some exceptions, filmmakers also cannot develop unique local films representing cultural identities and specificities due in large part to the adaptation and development of Hollywood-style commercial and entertainment formulas. At the height of Korean films' global popularity in the early part of the 2000s, again, the Korean government and filmmakers were optimistic that they would create a solid and independent film sphere separate from Hollywood cinema; however, this reality has not come about yet. Contemporary Korean cinema in the 2010s recuperated from the recession right after the change in the screen quota system, as proven in its boom in the local box office; however, this does not guarantee the certainty of Korean cinema, both financially and textually.

Overall, Korean cinema has grown in the midst of interplays between local forces and global forces and between the government and domestic transnational corporations, as well as Korea's changing political economy. These dimensions have contributed to the industry's ups and downs, and in particular, the complicated and convoluted relationship between Korean cinema and Hollywood has largely worked to commercialize and marketize local films—at the sacrifice of national identity. While it is still a marginal player, China has also gradually increased its influence as an investor as well as an outside market for Korean films, which may greatly change the roadmap of the local film industry going forward.

CLOSING REMARKS

The effect of the flow of cultural products, including movies, on cultural sovereignty has been at the core of debates over globalization, transnationalization, and the exercise of economic and cultural powers. In Korea, confrontational negotiations have become real between local producers calling for continued governmental protection and their governmental counterparts, who are pressured by U.S. trade negotiators demanding the abolishment of such barriers (E. M. Kim 2010). In the past decade, there have been enormous changes in the organization and content of the media in many countries, particularly in Asia, as can be seen in the case of the Korean Wave. These developments raise the question of whether and how U.S. popular culture continues to play a dominant role in global culture. "The global film market is a strategic site for examining these issues. Thus, the global domination of the American film industry exemplifies one of the major criticisms of globalization, the potentially homogenizing effect of global culture, which constitutes a threat to the distinctiveness of national cultures" (Crane 2014, 365).

Due to the recent growth of Korean cinema in the early 21st century, some argue that Korea has overcome Hollywood's hegemony. In other words, due to the tangible growth of Korean cinema, some scholars and news media (Russell and Wehrfritz 2004; E. M. Kim 2010; Parc 2016) claim that Hollywood no longer rules Korean cinema. In fact, regardless of reduced screen quotas, one of the major neoliberal cultural policies, in July 2006, Korea has continued to sustain its percentage of the market share (which is in the high 40s and 50s) in the 2010s. What these scholars and new media argue is that the one-way flow of popular culture, in this case movies, from the West to the East—in particular, from the U.S. to the rest of the world (D. Schiller 1969)—has disappeared because Korean cinema has developed its own strong film industries amid neoliberal globalization.

What they have not considered, however, are recent features of the trans-nationalization of cultural industries, as well as intensifying U.S. dominance in global cultural markets. The U.S. has continued to develop its unique strategies to maintain this position, including over Korean cinema. Hollywood studios have diversified their influences in Third World Cinema with not only their films but also their capital. U.S. dominance in films has never decreased in the global film markets; its revenue from global box offices is resting at about 70 percent in the late 2010s. Its dominance through capital and industry has greatly increased as neoliberal globalization has evolved. The rise of Western corporate power is represented through the flow of not only cultural products but also capital and the organization of the industry, which thus transmits cultural and economic values, including commercialism, to large numbers of developing nations around the world (Chadha and Kavoori 2000). Third World Cinemas do not have the muscle to compete against Hollywood. Dan Schiller (1996) and Annabelle Sreberny-Mohammadi (1997) both argue that, in addition to cultural dominance in terms of the exports of American popular culture, including Hollywood films, another profound carrier of American values and a major outcome of colonial contact is the development and spread of U.S. capital, which reinforces commercialism.

While Hollywood's global domination seems to be almost cliché and Hollywood's global hegemony is nothing new (Joo 2007), American cultural industries, with the U.S. government, have continuously and massively developed ways to enter into non-Western markets. As Wendy Su (2016, 166) points out with the Chinese film industry, the capital alliance between local and U.S. governments has led to "hypercommercialism and an overemphasis on market value and box office returns. As a result, the [local] film industry has tilted in favor of purely commercial movies, while social realist movies and artistic movies have been marginalized."

We cannot deny the positive aspects of global influences because they provide high standards that local filmmakers must meet to make globally competitive films. However, Hollywood studios can sweep the local market, impose a homogeneous film format, and pose a threat to domestic film production in many cases. The consequence of the interplay between the U.S. and Korea is still one-sided, with both American films and capitals dominating the Korean film market. Although Korean cinema has continued to penetrate the North American market, its influence is not considerable yet. With the exception of several remakes of Korean films by Hollywood studios[1] and the increasing role of webtoon-based transmedia storytelling, Korean cinema has not yet established a significant global presence.

In the era of globalization, Western cultural industries have changed their strategies to adjust to the changing global environment: "Instead of solely focusing on exporting their cultural goods, they have invested in cultural industries in devel-oping countries. In this way, they are able to continue to dominate the world cul-tural market, while also introducing and reinforcing the commercial ideologies of Western countries" (D. Y. Jin 2007, 765–766). A discussion of the content of recent Hollywood films shows that, while the U.S. still dominates global film markets through a form of economic imperialism, the cultural and symbolic sig-nificance of American films has changed. Hollywood's strategy of augmenting its profits by attracting global audiences has led to important modifications in the content of Hollywood films (Crane 2014).

As mentioned above, Hollywood exemplifies a form of global culture that emphasizes violence, action, sex, and fantasy that other countries try to imitate on a smaller scale. The "blockbusterization" of some commercial films has been a model that local filmmakers emulate through violence and sex, which have been embraced by many Korean filmmakers, "leading to increasingly monotonous films and the loss of an indigenous cultural tradition that makes more sense" to domestic audiences (Su 2016, 166). Furthermore, Hollywood's dominance is still evident in films about controversial topics:

> In some cases, American values and the American way of life are imposed on remakes of films from other countries in a process of delocalization. The American film industry and American film policy have important effects on other national film industries whose cultural policies represent a form of resistance to American dominance. Changes in the content of American films in the direc-tion of transnationalization and deculturalization have occurred in response to Hollywood's increasing need for box office receipts from other countries. Similar changes are occurring in other countries, because films, which are less culturally specific, represent the most viable means of communicating with audiences that are widely distributed across the globe. (Crane 2014, 379)

Korean cinema has never been free from Hollywood, and it cannot be free from Hollywood's influence in the near future, which makes the local film industry vulnerable. This complex nature of Korean cinema's transnationalization asks us to contemplate the future of the Korean film industry from diverse perspectives.

Regardless of some hesitations, I believe that transnational—in particular, Hollywood's—dominance has continued and even intensified in the film indus-try. Hollywood has developed several new strategies to control local film markets. Hollywood started to transnationalize the Korean film market from its birth, as part of U.S. political-economic influence since the liberation of the country from Japan, and Korea has had no choice but to accommodate American demands regarding direct distribution rights screen quotas, and direct production in Korea, resulting in changes to genres and themes in the local industry. In addition, several administrations were particularly vulnerable—mainly because of their unstable political legitimacy (e.g., military regimes), economic uncertainty (e.g., the 1997 economic crisis), or a new economic and cultural direction toward neoliberal reforms (e.g., the Korea-U.S. FTA)—which have provided incredible opportunities for the U.S.

The increasing influence of Hollywood hegemony in Korean cinema, is more complicated and nuanced, however. Hollywood has cultivated a close relationship with the U.S. government, and these two major transnational forces have worked together to open global markets, including Korea's. The cultural industries have become some of the most significant in the U.S. economy; therefore, the U.S. government has represented Hollywood abroad. Hollywood has relentlessly continued and intensified its influence over the Korean film industry. Regardless of the recent growth of Korean cinema in terms of domestic production and blockbuster movies, "Hollywood production capacity, system and format are becoming ubiquitous in the producing of original national cultures in East Asia," including Korea, and therefore, "it is highly dubious that the rise of Korean cinema fundamentally challenges the existing global cultural power configuration" (Iwabuchi 2010, 203).

Korea should develop relevant cultural policies and identify necessary elements for the growth of its film content in order to challenge Hollywood studios and compete with their films. Both the local government and film corporations must work together to create domestic films that still portray local traditions and realities while being commercially reliable in global markets as well. Korean cinema needs to create some crucial mechanisms to sustain the balance between the efficiency of the Hollywood model and its own cultural sovereignty. In the globalized cultural market, it is crucial to recognize and understand working relationships between the foreign and local forces in order to create new forms of popular culture.

Another significant element for Korean cinema in the near future to develop is digital technology. As foreign media platforms, including Netflix, have attempted to increase their role in the Korean market, and webtoons based on the growth of the smartphones have become a major resource for transmedia storytelling, advancing new digital technologies for both production and exhibition is a timely and important task. In fact, several film experts, during their interviews with me, commonly argued that Korean cinema must develop virtual reality (VR)[2] and artificial intelligence (AI) for the enhancement of the contemporary film industry. KwangWoo Noh, for example, emphasized that "interests in digital technologies, in particular VR and AR (augmented reality) are increasing in the film industries. It is not easy to predict how these digital technologies change traditional paradigms in the film sector; however, as Marvel Comics and DC Comics, working with Hollywood, have become some of the major film production companies in the U.S., several domestic digital giants and content creators, like DaumKakao alongside filmmakers should be able to develop digitally-driven films."[3] Junhyoung Cho also claimed that "in the long run, how to develop and utilize new technologies will be one of the most urgent tasks for Korean cinema as several contemporary technologies, including VR, will change the nature of films, as the digitalization of movie content over the past decade has shifted production, editing, distribution, and exhibition process[es]."

In fact, as new technologies like these have become increasingly prominent elements in the movie industry, Korean cinema has already prepared for the new era. For example, the Busan International Film Festival held in October 2017 organized a special section for movies produced with VR technology. This separate screening venue showed 36 movies, including 19 animated films (e.g., *Arden's Wake: The Prologue, Invasion, Asteroid!*, and *Rainbow Crow*) using VR technology. As they see it, the convergence of VR technology and cinema is only natural and mutually beneficial (BIFF 2017).

Similarly, in the inaugural year of the Venice International Film Festival's virtual reality competition in September 2017, for example, Gina Kim's 12-minute film *Bloodless* was selected as the winner in the Best VR Story category. Twenty-two films, in genres spanning from documentary to science fiction, were in competition in the Venice Virtual Reality program, and three prizes were handed out. *Bloodless* traces the last living moments of a real-life sex worker who was brutally murdered by a U.S. soldier at the Dongducheon camp town in Korea in 1992. In doing so, *Bloodless* transposes a historical and political issue into a personal and concrete experience. The film was shot on location where the crime took place, bringing to light ongoing experiences at the 96 camp towns near or around the U.S. military bases. During the an interview with the Associated Press in October 2017, Gina Kim stated, What she really wanted for the audiences "was to not necessarily experience the horror of being murdered," but "genuine sympathy and empathy." She believed that it could be possible with VR. "Virtual reality can tell the story of the marginalized and the underprivileged in a more powerful way than any other medium in film history" (Y. K. Lee 2017).

Just as Netflix has played a key role as a new platform for both importing and funding Korean films, we cannot overemphasize the importance of future digital technologies as new resources for the growth of Korean cinema. While cutting-edge digital technologies have always been a major part of film production, contemporary Korean cinema is increasingly dependent on digital platforms and storytelling—from production to distribution to exhibition. How digital technologies and storytelling, as well as financing, is used will make a significant difference to the local film industry.

Meanwhile, it is critical to guarantee the leading role of domestic filmmakers as transnationalizing agents to make locally specific but globally oriented films, which is only possible when they can advance their own unique cultural identity. Korean cinema has already shown its potential as a transnational cultural force; several well-made Korean films have become popular in global markets, and a few local filmmakers and transnational corporations, including CJ, have been working with other countries' film corporations on coproductions.

In the near future, Korean cinema has to develop its national identity—reflecting local mentalities and emphasizing sociocultural values—which would also, in fact, be the most effective business strategy. As the recent emergence of webtoons as transmedia storytelling sources has demonstrated, once Korean cinema advances films based on the country's local uniqueness—in combination with the swift growth of digital technologies, and therefore, the convergence of digital technologies and popular culture—the film industry will be able to achieve huge successes, both commercially and culturally, in the global markets. Korean cinema should keep in mind that it will be able to achieve this not by mimicking Hollywood-style commercial successes but though creating its own unique films, embedded in local tradition and culture.

NOTES

CHAPTER 2   STATE FILM POLICY AND THE POLITICIZATION OF CENSORSHIP

1. Many film scholars have different interpretations of Korea's first film due to the nature of its content, and the debate about the first Korean movie is still ongoing. According to the Korean Film Archive (2017), the foremost problem is that *Fight for Justice* "is not completely a dramatic film but a screen-and-stage play, where a performance on an outside stage was recorded on camera and displayed on screen. . . . It was a film to be played in a small section out of the whole theatrical performance so the question about whether this should be regarded as a true film in itself still remains." Nevertheless, the Korean film industry views October 27, 1919, as the date of its birth, and October 27 is commemorated as Film Day.

2. During Japanese colonization, Korean cinema "could not but be heavily dependent upon the Japanese film industry and its infrastructure, due to the lack of Korean capital and workforce. Ironically, even though Korean filmmakers regarded cinema as an art form expressing a nation's spirit, they were still heavily dependent upon Japan's technology. Japanese film policy and its changing attitudes toward the Korean filmmaking industry also had a great impact on the Korean filmmaking process during the colonial period" (C. K. Kim 2010, 26).

3. For example, USIS-Korea hired local filmmakers and was churning out localized propaganda films, as well as the weekly newsreel film *Liberty News*, since the major goal of USIS was to align public opinion abroad with U.S. security objectives (Heo, cited in S. J. Lee 2017).

4. Against this backdrop, venture capital invested by several financial banks and corporations also flowed to the Korean film industry, and they rapidly become major players. For example, Hana Bank, one of the largest financial banks in Korea, launched a public film investment fund titled "The Hana Cinema Trust Fund No. 1" in December 2001, marking the first involvement of the banking sector in Korean film financing. In the early 2000s, when economic prospects were gloomy, investors of all kinds were keen to invest in the film industry, which was booming (Paquet 2001a).

5. Between the late 1990s and the early 2000s, another form of financing film, the netizen fund, played a key role in Korean cinema by raising cash from individual investors over the internet between the late 1990s and the early 2000s. It was a program in which Koreans invested in film projects through the internet for a return based on the movie's success after release. The netizen fund began in 1999 when the production house Bom invited movie netizens to participate in an $85,000 fund (Mi Hui Kim 2002, 19). Other projects that employed netizen funds include *Friend* (2001) *Libera Me* (2000), *The Humanist* (2001), and *My Sassy Girl* (2001). Netizen funds have decreased since late 2001, because several films (such as *The Humanist, Jakarta,* and *Tear*), which were partially produced through netizen funds, failed to make profits and could not return the capital. Nevertheless, netizen funds played a role as marketing strategies for film producers—that is, as PR via the internet (C. K. Oh 2002).

6. Many artists, including filmmakers and actors, complained about this new form of censorship. In July 2017, a Korean court sentenced former presidential chief of staff Kim Ki-choon and former culture minister Kim Jong-deuk to prison for blacklisting artists and denying them state support. The court agreed that many of the blacklisted artists were unjustly

excluded from government funding or participation in government-backed culture projects (Associated Press 2017). This officially confirmed that the Park government systematically, and unconstitutionally, controlled the cultural sector.

CHAPTER 3   SCREEN QUOTAS IN THE ERA OF THE U.S.-KOREA FTA

1. As of March 2017, the U.S. has FTAs with 20 countries; however, the majority of them are with economically small countries, such as Costa Rica, Guatemala, Morocco, and Singapore. Therefore, the Korea-U.S. FTA has become the largest of this kind after NAFTA, the North American Free Trade Agreement with Mexico and Canada (see USTR 2017).

2. The close relationship between the U.S. government and Hollywood is not new. It can be seen during the prelude to WWI. The U.S. government established the Committee of Public Information, which formulated guidelines for all media to promote domestic support for the war. The small but growing movie industry readily offered its support, with the *Motion Picture News* proclaiming in a 1917 editorial, 'Every individual at work in this industry' promised to provide "slides, film leaders and trailers, posters to spread that propaganda so necessary to the immediate mobilization of the country's great resources." Nevertheless, it was during the entry to World War II in which American prowar propaganda surged (Post 2014). The close relationship continues. According to MPAA Comments Regarding the 2016 National Trade Estimate Report on Foreign Trade Barriers (Motion Picture Association of America 2015, 1), for example, Joanna McIntosh, executive vice president of Global Policy and External Affairs at the MPAA states "on behalf of MPAA and its members, I want to express our appreciation for the critical assistance the U.S. government provides the industry's efforts to grow its foreign sales." It proves that, as long as Hollywood brings about great revenues from foreign film markets, the U.S. government and Hollywood will continue to develop their unique and close relationship. As Thomson (2005, 98) argues, "Hollywood is best understood as a business, and, at some point, the U.S. film industry has to make a deal with the big money." The U.S. simply cannot ignore this moneymaking business, and the U.S. government fully supports Hollywood because the U.S. film industry has achieved a huge success in making a current account surplus in global trade (Jin 2011a).

3. KOFIC is comparable to the French national center of cinematography (CNC), which was created in 1946, as it is a public administrative organization with legal entity status and financial autonomy. The CNC operates under the authority of the Ministry of Culture and Communication, and its principal responsibilities are regulation; support for the economy of the film, television video, multimedia, and technical industries; the promotion of films and television productions and their dissemination to all audiences; and the preservation and enhancement of cinema heritage (CNC 2017). As KOFIC is a special organization entrusted to the Ministry of Culture, Sports and Tourism of Korea and it aims to support and promote Korean films through various means, including public film funds, these two institutions pursue similar responsibilities. However, unlike the CNC, which has managed the state's financial support for the film and television industries, KOFIC only supports the film industry (KOFIC 2017a).

4. The labor costs support program is partially helps with labor costs for staff in the production of and accumulative support for Korean films released. It also that supports research and development for subsequent films as a result of box-office performance (KOFIC n.d.).

5. Commercial films in Korean cinema only includes films produced with more than ₩10 million and/or films shown on more than 100 screens when they are released. One of the major reasons for the growth in the number of films domestically produced in the 2010s has been the

introduction of several movie platforms, including IPTV, who want to label their programs as "movies screened in theaters," which might be attractive to their audiences (see KOFIC 2015a).

CHAPTER 4   CONGLOMERATION, SCREEN OLIGOPOLY, AND CULTURAL DIVERSITY

1. As explained in chapter 1, *screen monopoly and oligopoly* refers to a phenomenon in which a few powerful film distributors influence overall box-office outcomes. The Korean popular press uses the abbreviated term *screen monopoly*; however, English-speaking users may be confused as there is no actual monopoly. Therefore, in this chapter, I use *screen oligopoly* to describe the cartel-like control a few major distributors have over the distribution and exhibition sectors, which can occur as the result of vertical integration, and that therefore benefits commercial films either produced or exported by those distributors.

2. In the U.S., five major movie companies that produced, distributed, and exhibited films dominated the movie industry until the 1940s, when the U.S. Justice Department argued that this ownership structure gave the five majors inordinate control over the industry. It argued that the control of both production and exhibition allowed the majors to inflate prices for films, made it virtually impossible for independent producers to gain access to movie theaters, and gave the majors the power to force independently owned theaters to show smaller, less popular films along with the hits. In 1948, the U.S. Supreme Court (United States v. Paramount Pictures, Inc., 334 U.S. 131) ruled that the major movie companies were exercising illegal control over the industry, and the court agreed with the Justice Department's argument that the integrated ownership arrangement greatly reduced competition. The court ordered the majors to sell their theater chains and outlawed various trade practices that the studios had used to thwart independent producers (Croteau and Hoynes 2006, 67–68). Vertical integration came back during the Reagan era of deregulation as the studios were once again "allowed to become vertically integrated and swallow up the exhibition market" in the U.S. (Fox 1992, 517).

3. Chungmuro is located in central Seoul and is referred to as Korea's own Hollywood. Since the 1960s, Chungmuro has been known as the area of culture, artists, and the film industry, as Dansungsa—the first movie theater, established in 1907—is situated there. As several other old movie theaters, including Daehan and Myeongbo, were also around this neighborhood, moviegoers used to flock there to watch the latest films—before Megabox and other multiplex theaters multiplied in recent years (H. J. Lee 2009).

4. In Korean cinema, since the number of screens has continued to increase, the breaking point for determining screen oligopoly has changed as well. For example, in 2000, there were only 720 screens; therefore, 360 might be the standard to determine screen oligopoly. However, in 2015, there were 2,424, and so the standard would be 1,212. Nevertheless, in the 2010s, 1,000 screens have been symbolically used as an indicator of a screen oligopoly since the first movie (*Transformers: Revenge of the Fallen*) surpassed 1,000 screens in 2009.

5. In 2005, CJ CGV acquired Korea's fourth largest multiplex theater chain, Primus Cinema, which was established in 2002, and it totally integrated it in 2012, solidifying CJ CGV's presence as the leading exhibitor. Megabox was established in 2000 by Orion Confectionery, together with U.S.-based Loews Cineplex. It was later merged with Cinus, owned by the Joongang Media Network.

6. President Park Geun-hye's political scandal in 2016 was convoluted. She was impeached mainly because of her mishandling of several policy measures—mostly in the realm of the Ministry of Culture, Sports and Tourism—under the guidance of Choi Soon Sil (daughter of

former cult leader Choi Tae-min): "Choi is an old friend of Park and with no official position in the government and apparently without any qualifications that could have given her the sort of power she apparently wielded, she was involved in several issues in the realm of culture" (H. R. Kim 2016). Therefore, as of July 2019, no political decision, including the revision of this law, could be made.

CHAPTER 5   PUBLIC FILM FUNDING AND TRANSNATIONAL PRODUCTION

1. Although it is not a public fund, online marketing has taken an unusual turn in Korea's booming film industry. Film fans can turn to the web not only to read about their favorite films but to invest in them (Paquet 2001b). Referred to as netizen funds, these investment tools are the latest online developments among a populace that averages more time on the internet than any other nation on earth. The first netizen fund was conceived in 1999 at an industry meeting on internet marketing strategies for film. In dreaming up ways to boost their sites' interactivity, participants developed the idea of having online users invest directly in a film. Online startup Intz.com seized upon the idea and established the first netizen fund for Kim Jee-woon's wrestling comedy *The Foul King*. Such high, quick rates of return did not escape notice in an economy with a floundering stock market. Intz .com soon found itself the focus of widespread media attention, and a deal was sealed with local distributor CJ E&M for four more films (including record-breaker *Joint Security Area* [2000]). Other companies specializing in the funds quickly appeared and investor demand skyrocketed (Paquet 2001b).

2. Benefits range from covering fees for theater maintenance, helping produce marketing materials, programming films, and providing funds to go toward translations and subtitling for easier distribution. There is also a grant that is set aside for assisting the distribution of art, indie, and documentary films. KOFIC plans to allot $30,000 each to 15 films per year, which will go toward making prints, creating digital packaging, shipping and receiving, marketing, and advertising (KOFIC 2015b).

CHAPTER 6   COPRODUCTION AND TRANSNATIONALIZATION OF KOREAN CINEMA

1. By the late 1930s, "colonial Korea's filmmaking industry had been fully subsumed into the Japanese film industry, and regulations were established that required all films to assimilate imperial policies. The Korean Motion Picture Ordinance, passed in 1940 and implemented widely by 1941, was essentially a replica of the Japanese Motion Picture Law passed the previous year. The ordinance established the infrastructure for the complete subsumption of colonial Korean film into the imperial system. The new film law paved the way for the consolidation of film production under one production company, which was a de facto imperial organ" (Kwon 2012, 13). Therefore, several Korean films during the 1930s and the 1940s were coproductions, in the form of Japanese propaganda.

CHAPTER 7   TRANSNATIONALIZATION OF FILM GENRES

1. My previous works (2010, 2016) analyzed the genres and themes of local films in the contemporary era between 1988 and 2012. This chapter not only extends these previous works but

also emphasizes different aspects of the films discussed in terms of the periodization, interpretation, and subject matter.

2. A historical period drama (also known as a historical drama, period drama, or period piece) is a work of art set in, or reminiscent of, an earlier time period. While many film scholars exchange period drama and historical drama, the Korean Film Council used to differentiate them. "Period films of the 1960s more or less overlap with the genre known as the historical drama, but the events in those historical dramas do not necessarily correspond to real history. With little room for creativity, historical dramas were just cinematic renditions of what had been used and reused in other genres. In this respect, historical dramas were quite different from today's fusion period dramas that blend fact with fiction, wherein totally new ideas are combined with historical event" (Y. C. Lee 2014, 36). Since the introduction of the Motion Picture Promotion Law of 1995, there had been only two history movies (*King and the Crown*, 2005; *War of Arrows*, 2011) making it to the top of the box office. However, in the 2010s, history is the most welcome movie genre because film producers make similar movies that both theaters and audiences prefer. These history movies are connected to action, because several movie directors and corporations have strategically utilized Hollywood style action and special effects to create blockbuster-style movies. There is not enough room for film producers to create many other movie genres.

3. While there is some controversy, several films indeed portray some far-right-wing nationalism, including excessive anti-Japanese and anticommunist sentiments. These are known as *Guk-ppong*; the term's etymology comes from *gukga* (nation) and *hiroppong* (methamphetamine). Examples of such films include *D-War* (2007), *The Admiral: Roaring Currents* (2014), *Ode to My Father* (2014), *Northern Limit Line* (2015), *Operation Chromite* (2016), and *The Battleship Island* (2017).

CHAPTER 8   TRANSMEDIA STORYTELLING OF WEBTOONS IN FILMS IN THE DIGITAL ERA

1. For example, Hyung-Gu Lynn (2016) explains that the adaption of webtoons into other cultural forms, such as films and television programs is cross-media form based on the one source multiuse (OSMU) concept.

2. While Apple started to produce and sell its smartphones in 2007, it was in 2009 that Korean mobile makers, including Samsung and LG started to produce their own. Although there were some smartphones in Korea before this, they were not many; therefore, the smartphone age in Korea mainly started in 2009.

3. For example, as a reflection of webtoon's popularity, in 2016, MBC, one of the largest network broadcasters, developed a drama *W* portraying a famous webtoonist who disappeared mysteriously while writing the last chapter of his webtoon, also titled *W*. This was based on the true story of Yoon Tae-ho and his webtoon *Inside Men*, detailed later in this chapter.

4. Released in Korea in November 2015, *Inside Men* became a massive hit for distributor Showbox, garnering 7.07 million viewers ($48.43 million) during its initial run and another 2.08 million viewers ($14.52 million) when the director's cut version (*Inside Men: The Original*) was released at the end of 2015. *Inside Men* has been released in Australia and New Zealand and was shown in Japanese theaters in March 2016. What is interesting in the box office is that it is the highest-grossing movie among those rated for adults only (18 +). Previously, *Friend* (2001) held that spot, with 8.18 million viewers.

CHAPTER 9   CONCLUSION

1. While there are a few U.S. versions of Korean movies, China and India have recently increased their demand for these remakes. CJ E&M and NEW have worked with Chinese film corporations to remake Korean movies such as *A Wedding Invitation* (2013), *The Witness* (2015), and *Hide and Seek* (2013), in most cases as a form of coproduction. Some Indian production companies have also developed remakes of Korean films. For example, *Zinda* is a remake of *Oldboy*, and *Jazbaa* is the remake of *7 Days* (Korean Film Council 2017b).

2. VR refers to "the presentation of first-person experiences through the use of a head-mounted display and headphones that enable users to experience a synthetic environment as if they were physically there." Though a recent development, "with the emergence of inexpensive high-powered computer processing and display systems, VR has begun to become commercially viable and to be adopted by the public. Central to this take-up has been the development of so-called Cinematic Virtual Reality (CVR), referring to a type of immersive VR experience where individual users can look around synthetic worlds in 360°, often with stereoscopic views, and hear spatialized audio specifically designed to reinforce the veracity of the virtual environment (as a note, there are presently no initiating studies or foundational articles that can be seen as seminal at this point)" (Mateer 2017, 14–15).

3. In Hollywood, several films have been created based on Marvel comics, including *Iron Man 3* (2013); *Avengers: Age of Ultron* (2015), and *Logan* (2017). Several other movies, including *Betman vs. Superman: Dawn of Justice* (2016) and *Wonder Woman* (2017) are based on comics created by DC Comics.

REFERENCES

Abelmann, Nancy. 2003. *The Melodrama of Mobility: Women, Talk, and Class in Contemporary South Korea*. Honolulu: University of Hawaii Press.

Adler, Peter. 2002. "Beyond Cultural Identity: Reflections on Multiculturalism." In *Culture Learning: Concepts, Applications and Research*, edited by Richard Brislin, 24–41. Honolulu: East-West Center Press. http://www.mediate.com/articles/adler3.cfm.

Agence France-Presse. 2017. "Spectre of Censorship Haunts S. Korea Artists." 8 February.

Ahn, Sung Mi. 2014a. "Behind Korea's Film Renaissance Conglomerate-Controlled Scene Churns Out Megahits, but Stifles Diversity." *Korea Herald*, 12 October.

———. 2014b. "Rediscovering *Love with an Alien* on KOFA's 40th Anniversary." *Korea Herald*, 26 May. http://www.koreaherald.com/view.php?ud=20140526001417.

———. 2014c. "*Misaeng* Syndrome Grips the Nation." *Korea Herald*, 12 November. http://www.koreaherald.com/view.php?ud=20141112000845.

Aksoy, Asu, and Kevin Robins. 1992. "Hollywood for the Twenty-First Century: Global Competition for Critical Mass in Image Markets." *Cambridge Journal of Economics* 16:1–22.

Amelio, Ralph. 1976. "American Genre Film: Teaching Popular Movies." *English Journal* 65 (3): 47–50.

An, Jinsoo. 2018. *Parameters of Disavowal: Colonial Representation in South Korean Cinema*. Oakland, Calif.: University of California Press.

Appadurai, Arjun. 1996. *Modernity at Large: Cultural Dimensions of Globalization*. Minneapolis: University of Minnesota Press.

Aquilia, Pieter. 2006. "Westernizing Southeast Asian Cinema: Co-productions for 'Transnational' Markets." *Continuum: Journal of Media and Cultural Studies* 20 (4): 433–445.

Associated Press. 2017. "Ex-Park Aide, Culture Minister Guilty for Artist Blacklist." 27 July.

Baek, Byung-yeul. 2015a. "Film Completes Cartoon *Inside Men*." *Korea Times*, 14 October.

———. 2015b. "*Inside Men* Depicts World Controlled by Corrupt Power Elite." *Korea Times*, 4 November.

———. 2016. "Webtoons Emerge as Source for Dramas, Films." *Korea Times*, 27 January.

Bainbridge, Jane. 2012. "Sector Insights: Cinemas." *Marketing Magazine*, 18 September.

Baltruschat, Doris. 2002. "Globalization and International TV and Film Co-productions: In Search of New Narratives." Paper presented at MIT's "Media in Transition 2: Globalization and Convergence," Cambridge, Mass., May 10–12.

Barker, George. 2000. *Cultural Capital and Policy*. Wellington: Centre for Law and Economics, Australia National University.

Bechervaise, Jason. 2016. "*Inside Men* Review." Screen Daily, 4 January. http://www.screendaily.com/reviews/inside-men-review/5098469.article.

———. 2017. "Hollywood, Netflix Make Inroads into Korean Film Industry." *Korea Times*, 31 May. http://m.koreatimes.co.kr/phone/news/view.jsp?req_newsidx=230410.

Benshoff, Harry, and Sean Griffin. 2009. *America on Film: Representing Race, Class, Gender, and Sexuality at the Movies*. Malden, Mass.: Blackwell.

Bergfelder, Tim. 2005. "National, Transnational or Supranational Cinema: Rethinking European Film Studies." *Media, Culture & Society* 27 (3): 315–331.

Berliner, Todd. 2001. "The Genre Film as Booby Trap: 1970s Genre Bending and the French Connection." *Cinema Journal* 40 (3): 25–46.

Berry, Chris. 2010. "What Is Transnational Cinema? Thinking from the Chinese Situation." *Transnational Cinemas* 1 (2): 111–127.

BeSUCCESS. 2016. "Five of Kakao's Daum Webtoon Titles to Appear on Chinese Screens through Partnership with Huace Group." 14 March. http://besuccess.com/2016/03/five-of-kakaos-daum-webtoon-titles-to-appear-on-chinese-screens-through-partnership-with-huace-group/.

Bhabha, Homi. 1994. *The Localization of Culture.* New York: Routledge.

BIFF (Busan International Film Festival). 2017. "VR Cinema in BIFF." Accessed 22 July 2019. http://www.biff.kr/eng/artyboard/board.asp?act=bbs&subAct=view&bid=9611_05&page=3&order_index=regdate&order_type=desc&list_style=list&seq=162568.

Blomkamp, Emma. 2011. "Measuring 'Success' in Film Policy: Evaluating the New Zealand Film Commission's Short Film Fund." *International Journal of Cultural Policy* 17 (3): 341–355.

Bokova, Irina. 2014. *The Circular Letter,* 6 November. Paris: UNESCO.

Breen, Marcus. 2010. "Digital Determinism: Culture Industries in the USA–Australia Free Trade Agreement." *New Media and Society* 12 (4): 657–676.

Brook, Tom. 2014. "How the Global Box Office Is Changing Hollywood." *BBC News,* 20 June. http://www.bbc.com/culture/story/20130620-is-china-hollywoods-future.

Brown, Collin. 1995. "Seagram, Samsung Line up to Take Stakes in SKG." *Screen International,* 21 April, 4.

Burgi-Golub, N. 2000. "Cultural Identity and Political Responsibility," *Cultural Policy* 7 (2): 211–223.

Burns, Alex, and Ben Eltham. 2010. "Boom and Bust in Australian Screen Policy: 10BA, the Film Finance Corporation and Hollywood's Race to the Bottom." *Media International Australia* 136:103–118.

Busch, Anita. 2014. "*The Admiral: Roaring Currents* Becomes Top Grossing Korean Film in U.S." Deadline, 22 September. http://deadline.com/2014/09/the-admiral-roaring-currents-becomes-top-grossing-korean-film-in-u-s-838888/.

Byon, J. 2001. "Film." In *Korean Modern Art History III: 1960s,* edited by the Korean National Research Center for Arts, 187–244. Seoul: Sigongsa.

Castaneda, Liliana. 2009. "The Post-neoliberal Colombian Film Policy." *Revista de Estudios Colombianos,* 27–46. https://www.researchgate.net/publication/257528033.

Chadha, Kalyani, and Anandam Kavoori. 2000. "Media Imperialism Revisited: Some Findings from Asian Case." *Media, Culture & Society* 22 (4): 415–432.

Chan, Kenneth. 2009. *Remade in Hollywood: The Global Chinese Presence in Transnational Cinemas.* Hong Kong: Hong Kong University Press.

Chang, Ah Rum. 2014. "The Effect of Foreign Pressure on Liberal Policy Autonomy: The Case of South Korea's Screen Quota System." *International Review of Public Administration* 19 (1): 1–22.

Chang, Young-Hyun, and Sang Yeob Oh. 2015. "A Study on the Development of One Source Multi Use Cross-platform Based on Zero Coding." *Multimedia Tools and Applications* 74 (7): 2219–2235.

Channel CJ. 2016. "One Source Multi Territory Strategy, Korean Cinema's Global Project." 28 October. http://blog.cj.net/1912.

Cho, Soo Young. 2012. "Whom the Rule to Regulate Monopoly of Movie Screens For?" *Sookmyung Times,* 5 December.

Cho, Tae Sung. 2016. "Blacklist of 9,473 in the Culture World Revealed." *Hankook Ilbo,* 12 October.

Choe, Jun-hyung. 2014. "Systematic Beginning of Film Censorship: Film Law and Censorship between 5.16 Coup D'état and the Early 1960s." *People and Writing: Humanities* 43. http://rikszine.korea.ac.kr/front/article/humanList.minyeon?selectArticle_id=531.

Choe, Sang-Hun. 2016. "Choi Soon-sil, at Center of Political Scandal in South Korea, Is Jailed." *New York Times*, 31 October.

Choe, Youngmin. 2016. *Tourist Distractions: Traveling and Felling in Transnational Hallyu Cinema*. Durham, N.C.: Duke University Press.

Choi, Byung-il. 2002. "When Culture Meets Trade: Screen Quota in Korea." *Global Economic Review* 31 (4): 75–90.

Choi, Jinhee. 2010. *The South Korean Film Renaissance: Local Hitmakers, Global Provocateurs*. Middletown, Conn.: Wesleyan University Press.

———. 2017. "20 Once Again, or Forever Being a Mom: Regional Media Flows and Gender." Paper presented at the Chinese Film Market and Asian Cinema Conference, Nanyang Technological University, Singapore, 27–28 August.

Choi, Jung Bong. 2011. "National Cinema: An Anachronistic Delirium?" *Journal of Korean Studies* 16 (2): 173–191.

Choi, K. H. 2005. "Meet the Greatest Director." *Movie Magazine*, 5 September.

Choi, Won Mog. 2007. "Screen Quota and Cultural Diversity: Debates in Korea-U.S. FTA Talks and Convention on Cultural Diversity." *Asian Journal of WTO & International Health Law and Policy* 2 (2): 267–286.

Choi, Yu Sun. 2007. "Vertical Integration and Screening Period in Korean Film Industry." *International Business Review* 11 (1): 73–89.

Chung, Ah-young. 2013. "Webtoon Give Inspiration to Films." *Korea Times*, 5 June.

Chung, Hye Seung. 2005. "Toward a Strategic Korean Cinephilla: A Transnational Detournement of Hollywood Melodrama." In *South Korean Golden Age Melodrama: Gender, Genre, and National Cinema*, edited by Kathleen McHugh and Nancy Abelmann, 117–150. Detroit, Mich.: Wayne State University Press.

Chung, Hye Seung, and David Diffrient. 2015. *Movie Migrations: Transnational Genre Flows and South Korean Cinema*. New Brunswick, N.J.: Rutgers University Press.

CNC (French National Center of Cinematography). 2017. "The CNS's Responsibilities." Paris: CNC.

Conran, Pierce. 2015. "7 Korean Co-production Milestones." *Hankyoreh*, 30 August. http://english.hani.co.kr/arti/english_edition/e_entertainment/706547.html.

———. 2016. "What Happened in the Korean Film Industry in 2015." *Korean Cinema Today* 24:22–25.

Coonan, Clifford. 2014. "Co-productions Will Now Be Treated as Local Films Rather Than Imports, Avoiding China's Quota of 34 Films a Year on a Revenue-Share Basis." *Hollywood Reporter*, 3 July. http://www.hollywoodreporter.com/news/south-korea-china-sign-landmark-716743.

Co-operators. 2015. "The Co-operators Pledges $10 Million to Canadian Co-operative Investment Fund." Press release. 24 June.

Cowen, Tyler. 2002. "Why Hollywood Rules the World, and Whether We Should Care." In *Creative Destruction: How Globalization Is Changing the World's Cultures*, 73–101. Princeton, N.J.: Princeton University Press.

Crane, Diana. 2014. "Cultural Globalization and the Dominance of the American Film Industry: Cultural Policies, National Film Industries, and Transnational Film." *International Journal of Cultural Policy* 20 (4): 365–382.

Croteau, David, and William Hoynes. 2006. *The Business of Media*. 2nd ed. London: Pine Forge Press.

CRTC (Canadian Radio-Television and Telecommunications Commission). 2016. "Offering Cultural Diversity on TV and Radio." Accessed 25 May 2018. http://www.crtc.gc.ca/eng/info_sht/b308.htm.

Cunningham, Stuart. 2008. "Cultural Studies from the Viewpoint of Cultural Policy." In *Critical Cultural Policy Studies*, edited by J. Lewis and Toby Miller, 13–22. Hoboken, N.J.: Wiley.

DeBoer, Stephanie. 2014. *Coproducing Asia: Locating Japanese–Chinese Regional Film and Media*. Minneapolis: University of Minnesota Press.

Dena, Christy. 2009. *Transmedia Practice: Theorizing the Practice of Expressing a Fictional World across Distinct Media and Environments*. Thesis for Degree of Doctor of Philosophy, University of Sidney.

Derin, Seyhan. 2010. "No Money, No Movie." *Studies in European Cinema* 7 (1): 25–29.

Dong-A Ilbo. 1970. "Ekberg Arrived to Shot the Film Seoul Affair." 6 October, 5.

———. 2002. "Film Business against the Ministry of Finance and Economy." 22 January.

Export-Import Bank of Korea. 2014. *The Investment Structure, Profitability, and Future Direction of the Korean Film Industry*. Seoul: Export-Import Bank of Korea.

Falicov, Tamara L. 2000. "Argentina's Blockbuster Movies and the Politics of Culture under Neoliberalism, 1989–98." *Media, Culture & Society* 22 (3): 327–342.

Festival De Cannes. 2007. "Best Leading Actress: Jeon Do-yeon in Secret Sunshine." 27 May. http://www.festival-cannes.fr/en/theDailyArticle/55673.html.

Finn, Adam, Colin Hoskins, and Stuart McFadyen. 1996. "Telefilm Canada Investment in Feature Films: Empirical Foundations for Public Policy." *Canadian Public Policy* 22 (2): 151–161.

Flew, Terry, and Stuart Cunningham. 2010. "Creative Industries after the First Decade of Debate." *Information Society* 26:113–123.

Fox, Kraig G. 1992. "Paramount Revisited: The Resurgence of Vertical Integration in the Motion Picture Industry." *Hofstra Law Review* 21 (2): 505–536.

Frater, Patrick. 2000. "Korean Screen Quota Campaign Hits Venice." *Screen International*, 3 September.

———. 2014. "Politics Aside, S. Korea, China Find Plenty of Reasons to Work Together in Film Business." *Variety*, 1 October. http://variety.com/2014/film/asia/south-korea-china-work-together-in-film-1201318663/.

Freedman, Des. 2008. *The Politics of Media Policy*. Cambridge, U.K.: Polity Press.

Freeman, Matthew. 2015. "Up, Up and Across: Superman, the Second World War and the Historical Development of Transmedia Storytelling." *Historical Journal of Film, Radio and Television* 35 (2): 215–239.

———. 2017. *Historicizing Transmedia Storytelling: Early Twentieth-Century Transmedia Story Worlds*. London: Routledge.

Frey, Bruno. 2000. *Arts & Economics: Analysis and Cultural Policy*. Berlin: Springer.

Gao, Zhihong. 2009. "Serving a Stir-Fry of Market, Culture and Politics—on Globalization and Film Policy in Greater China." *Policy Studies* 30 (4): 423–438.

Garnham, Nicholas. 2005. "From Cultural to Creative Industries: An Analysis of the Implications of the 'Creative Industries' Approach to Arts and Media Policy Making in the United Kingdom." *International Journal of Cultural Policy* 11 (1): 15–29.

George, Sandy. 2000. "South Korea Keeps up Screen Quotas Fight." *Screen International*, 11 October.

Gerow, Aaron. 2015. "Japanese Film Industry Statistics for 2014." Tangemania, March 1. http://www.aarongerow.com/news/japanese-film-industry-2.html.

Giovagnoli, Max. 2011. *Transmedia Storytelling: Imagery, Shapes and Techniques*. Pittsburgh, Pa.: ETC Press.

Glancy, Mark. 2014. *Hollywood and the Americanization of Britain: From the 1920s to the Present*. London: I.B. Tauris.

Goodbrey, Daniel. 2015. "Distortions in Spacetime: Emergent Narrative Practices in Comics' Transition from Print to Screen." In *Storytelling in the Media Convergence Age*, edited by Roberta Pearson and Anthony Smith, 54–73. London: Palgrave.

Gordon, Ian, and Sun Lim. 2016. "Introduction to the Special Issue Cultural Industries and Transmedia in a Time of Convergence: Modes of Engagement and Participation." *The Information Society* 32 (5): 301–305.

Gross, Donald. 2006. "U.S.-Korea Relations: Forward on Trade as Nuclear Talks Sputter. Comparative Connections." *A Quarterly E-Journal on East Asian Bilateral Relations* 8 (1): 49–58.

Groves, Don. 1997. "S. Korea Snubs Hollywood's Woos." *Variety*, 22 September, 11.

Guback, Thomas. 1969. *The International Film Industry: Western Europe and America since 1945*. Bloomington: Indiana University Press.

Gunster, Shane. 2000. "Revisiting the Culture Industry Thesis: Mass Culture and the Commodity Form." *Cultural Critique* 45:40–70.

Ha, Jae Bong. 2003. "The Screen Quota System and the Korean Film Industry." *Journal of Culture and Art* 7:67–74.

Ha, Jung Min. 2016. "[Cine Feature] New Platforms and New Sources for New Korean Cinema: Webtoons." *Hankyoreh*, 20 May. http://www.hani.co.kr/arti/english_edition/e_entertainment/735818.html.

Hahn, Bae-Ho. 1978. *Communication Policies in the Republic of Korea*. Paris: UNESCO.

Hall, Stuart. 1990. "Cultural Identity and Diaspora." In *Identity: Community, Culture, Difference*, edited by Jonathan Rutherford, 222–237. London: Lawrence & Wishart.

Han, Gwang-jub. 1994. "Promises and Myths of Cable Television and Telecommunications Infrastructure in Korea." In *Media Elite Amidst Mass Culture: A Critical Look at Mass Communication in Korea*, edited by Chie-won Kim and Jae-won Lee, 156–157. Seoul: Nanam.

Han, Seung Joon. 2010. "A Study on the Role of Ideology in the Film Supporting Policy: The Case of the Korean Film Council." *Korean Journal of Public Administration* 48 (2): 309–337.

Han, Sunhee. 2007. "August Rush's Strikes Chord in Korea." *Variety*, 11 December. http://variety.com/2007/film/box-office/august-rush-strikes-chord-in-korea-1117977541/.

Harvey, David. 2005. *A Brief History of Neoliberalism*. New York: Oxford University Press.

Heo, Eun. 2011. "The Intervention of the United States in the Formation of the Nation-State and the Frontline in Terms of the Establishment of Hegemony during the Cold War Era: With a Special Focus on the Films Produced by the United States Information Service in Korea." *Journal of Korean History* 155:144.

Herman, Edward S., and Robert W. McChesney. 1997. *The Global Media: The New Missionaries of Corporate Capitalism*. London: Cassell.

Hesmondhalgh, David. 2013. *The Cultural Industries*. 3rd ed. London: Sage.

Hick, Jochen. 2010. "The Influence of TV and Film Funding on Current European (Low Budget) Art House Film." *Studies in European Cinema* 7 (1): 31–36.

Higbee, Will, and Song Hwee Lim. 2010. "Concepts of Transnational Cinema: Towards a Critical Transnationalism in Film Studies." *Transnational Cinemas* 1 (1): 7–21.

Ho, Hyun Chan. 2003. *Korean Cinema 100 Years*. Seoul: Munhwak Sasang Sa.

Hong, S. M. 2006. "Kim Says, 'The Reduction of the Screen Quota System Is to Help FTA Negotiation.'" *Dong-A Ilbo*, 10 July, 10.

Horkheimer, Max, and Theodor Adorno. 1969. *Dialectic of Enlightenment*. Translated by Edmund Jephcott. Stanford, Calif.: Stanford University Press.

————. 1972. *Dialectic of Enlightenment*. Translated by John Cumming. New York: Verso.

Hoskins, Colin, and Stuart McFadyen. 1993. "Canadian Participation in International Co-productions and Co-ventures in Television Programming." *Canadian Journal of Communication* 18 (2): 219–236.

Howlett, Michael, and M. Ramesh. 1995. *Studying Public Policy: Policy Cycles and Policy Subsystems*. Ontario: Oxford University Press.

Hwang, Dong Mi, ed. 2001. *An Analysis of the Structure of the Korean Film Industry*. Seoul: Munhwak Sasang Sa.

Hwang, Jang Jin. 1999. "Film Industry's Plea for Screen Quota Turns Emotional." *Korea Herald*, 18 June.

Iwabuchi, Koichi. 2002. *Recentering Globalization: Popular Culture and Japanese Transnationalism*. Durham, N.C.: Duke University Press.

————. 2010. "Globalization, East Asian Media Cultures and Their Publics." *Asian Journal of Communication* 20 (2): 197–212.

James, David. 2001. "Im Kwon-Taek: Korean National Cinema and Buddhism." *Film Quarterly* 54 (3): 14–31.

Jenkins, Henry. 2006. *Convergence Culture: Where Old and New Media Collide*. New York: New York University Press.

————. 2011. "Transmedia 202: Further Reflections." http://henryjenkins.org/2011/08/defining_transmedia_further_re.html.

Jeong, Seung-hoon. 2016. "The Seoul Film Collective: Leftist Strife, Open Cinema, and the Last Chapter of Korean Film Theory." *Quarterly Review of Film and Video* 34 (4): 1–15. Online first.

Jin, Dal Yong. 2006. "Cultural Politics in Korea's Contemporary Films under Neoliberal Globalization." *Media, Culture & Society* 28 (1): 6–23.

————. 2007. "Reinterpretation of Cultural Imperialism: Emerging Domestic Market vs. Continuing U.S. Dominance." *Media, Culture & Society* 29 (5): 753–771.

————. 2008. "Cultural Coup D'état: The Changing Roles of the UNESCO and the Local Government on Cultural Sovereignty." *Javnost—the Public* 15 (5): 5–22.

————. 2010. "Critical Interpretation of Hybridization in Korean Cinema: Does the Local Film Industry Create the Third Space?" *Javnost—the Public* 17 (1): 55–72.

————. 2011a. *Hands On / Hands Off: The Korean State and the Market Liberalization of the Communication Industry*. Cresskill, N.J.: Hampton Press.

————. 2011b. "A Critical Analysis of U.S. Cultural Policy in the Global Film Market: Nation-States and FTAs." *International Communication Gazette* 73 (8): 651–669.

————. 2012. "Transforming the Global Film Industries: Horizontal Integration and Vertical Concentration amid Neoliberal Globalization." *International Communication Gazette* 74 (5): 405–422.

————. 2015. "Digital Convergence of Korea's Webtoons: Transmedia Storytelling." *Communication Research and Practice* 1 (3): 193–209.

————. 2016. *New Korean Wave: Transnational Cultural Power in the Age of Social Media*. Urbana: University of Illinois Press.

————. 2019a. "Cultural Globalization through Film Co-productions in the Asia-Pacific Region." In *Asia-Pacific Film Coproduction: Theory, Industry and Aesthetics*, edited by Dal Yong Jin and Wendy Su, 133–154. London: Routledge.

————. 2019b. "Snack Culture's Dream of Big Screen Culture." *International Journal of Communication* 13:2094–2115.

Jin, Dal Yong, and Dong-Hoo Lee. 2007. "The Birth of East Asia: Cultural Regionalization through Co-productions Strategies." *Spectator* 27 (2): 31–45.

Jin, Eun Soo. 2014. "Smartphones Set off Webtoon Boom." *Korea JoongAng Daily*, 11 June. http://koreajoongangdaily.joins.com/news/article/article.aspx?aid=2990396.

———. 2015. "Issues of Monopoly in Film Market Re-emerge." *Korea JoongAng Daily*, 13 February. http://koreajoongangdaily.joins.com/news/article/article.aspx?aid=3000870.

Joo, Jeongsuk. 2007. "Beyond Binaries: Globalization, the Korean Film Industry, and Hollywood Hegemony." Dissertation, State University of New York at Buffalo.

———. 2010. "Setting the Scene for the Boom: The Korean Government's Policies and the Resurgence of the Korean Film Industry." *Asia Pacific Research* 17 (3): 151–167.

———. 2011. "Transnationalization of Korean Popular Culture and the Rise of Pop Nationalism in Korea." *Journal of Popular Culture* 44 (3): 489–504.

JoongAng Ilbo. 1993. "Conglomerates Actively Entered the Film Business-Samsung, Hyundai, SK, Daewoo, and Doosan." 7 December.

———. 2002. "Seoul Mulls Phased End to Film Quotas." 21 January.

———. 2006. "Screen Quota Reduction Erupts the Debates." 27 January. http://news.joins.com/article/2365652.

Jung, Ha Won. 2015. "Webtoon Craze Making Global Waves." *Taipei Times*, 30 November. http://www.taipeitimes.com/News/feat/print/2015/11/30/2003633650.

Jung, Sun. 2011. *Korean Masculinities and Transcultural Consumption: Yonsama, Rain, Oldboy, K-pop Idols*. Hong Kong: Hong Kong University Press.

Kaminsky, Stuart. 1985. *American Film Genres*. Chicago: Nelson Hall.

Kang, Aa-young. 2018. "Tom Cruise in Seoul: 'I Never Take Movies for Granted.'" *Korea Times*, 16 July. https://www.koreatimes.co.kr/www/art/2018/07/689_252367.html.

Kang, Han Sup. 2008. "Korean Cinema in Crisis: Who Is Responsible?" *JoongAng Ilbo*, 9 January. http://news.joins.com/article/3006081.

Kang, Jong Geun, and Won Yong Kim. 1994. "A Survey of Radio and Television: History, System and Programming." In *Media Elite Amidst Mass Culture: A Critical Look at Mass Communication in Korea*, edited by Chie-won Kim and Jae-won Lee, 109–136. Seoul: Nanam.

Kang, Ji-won. 2017. "Diversity Film? Resist the Word Itself." Ohmynews, 25 February. http://star.ohmynews.com/NWS_Web/OhmyStar/at_pg.aspx?CNTN_CD=A0002300625&CMPT_CD=TAG_PC.

Kao, Anthony. 2015. "Review: *Inside Men*." Cinema Escapist, 18 August. http://www.cinemaescapist.com/2016/08/review-inside-men-south-korea-2015/.

Kapur, Jyotsna, and Keith Wagner, eds. 2011. *Neoliberalism and Global Cinema: Capital, Culture, and Marxist Critique*. London: Routledge.

Kawashima, Nobuko. 2011. "Are the Global Media and Entertainment Conglomerates Having an Impact on Cultural Diversity? A Critical Assessment of the Argument in the Case of the Film Industry." *International Journal of Cultural Policy* 17 (5): 475–489.

KBS World Radio. 2017. "Artist Blacklist Also Existed during Lee Myung-bak Administration." 12 September. http://world.kbs.co.kr/service/news_view.htm?lang=e&Seq_Code=130099.

Keane, Michael. 2006. "Exporting Chinese Culture: Industry Financing Models in Film and Television." *Westminster Papers in Communication and Media* 3 (1): 11–27.

———. 2015. *The Chinese Television Industry*. New York: Palgrave.

Kil, Sonia. 2015. "Korean-Chinese Co-productions Boost Both Industries." *Variety*, 14 May. http://variety.com/2015/film/global/korean-chinese-co-productions-boost-both-industries-1201496270/.

———. 2016a. "Lotte, Busan City Launch $17.3 Million Film Fund." *Variety*, 4 March.

———. 2016b. "Busan: Crowfunding in the Korean Film Industry Slowly Catching On." *Variety*, 6 October.

————. 2016c. "Korea's Film Industry Struggles to Protect Freedom of Expression." *Variety*, 12 February.

————. 2017. "Busan: Korean President Moon Jae-in Takes Stand for Festival Independence." *Variety*, 14 October.

Kil, Sonia, and Patrick Frater. 2015. "Warner Bros. Sets Kim Jee-woon's 'Secret Agent' as Debut Korean Production." *Variety*, 3 August. http://variety.com/2015/film/asia/warner-bros-kim-jee-woon-secret-agent-1201555268/.

Kim, Carolyn Huyn-Kyung. 2000. "Building the Korean Film Industry's Competitiveness: Abolish the Screen Quota and Subsidize the Film Industry." *Pacific Rim Law & Policy Journal* 9 (2): 353–378.

Kim, Chung-kang. 2010. "South Korean Golden-Age Comedy Film: Industry, Genre, and Popular Culture (1973–1970)." Dissertation, University of Illinois.

Kim, Dongho. 2005. *The History of the Korean Film Policy*. Seoul: Nanam.

Kim, Dong Hoon. 2009. "Transnationalism and Film Genres in East Asian Cinema." *Spectator* 29 (2): 5–8.

Kim, Eun Mi. 2010. "Market Competition and Cultural Tensions between Hollywood and the Korean Film Industry." *International Journal on Media Management* 6 (3&4): 207–216.

Kim, Hoo Ran. 2016. "Troubling Revelations about Seoul's 'Shadow President': The Korea Herald Columnist." *Straits Times*, 27 October. http://www.straitstimes.com/asia/east-asia/troubling-revelations-about-seouls-shadow-president-the-korea-herald-columnist.

Kim, Hyae-joon. 2006. "A History of Korean Film Policies." In *Korean Cinema: From Origins to Renaissance*, edited by Kim Mee-Hyun and An Jae-seok, 351–355. Seoul: KOFIC.

Kim, Jung-ho. 2015. "Last Ten Years of Korean Movie Industry through the Analysis on the Concentrations of Film Admission and Screening." *Journal of the Korean Contents Association* 15 (5): 151–167.

Kim, Ju Oak. 2018. "Korea's Blacklist Scandal: Governmentality, Culture, and Creativity." *Culture, Theory, and Critique* 59 (2): 81–93.

Kim, Ju Young. 2007. "Rethinking Media Flow under Globalization: Rising Korean Wave and Korean TV and Film Policy Since 1980s." Dissertation, University of Warwick.

Kim, Kyu, Won-Yong Kim, and Jong-Geun Kang. 1994. *Broadcasting in Korea*. Seoul: Nanam.

Kim, Kyu Hyun. 2011. "2011 Korean Movies." Koreanfilm.org, http://koreanfilm.org/kfilm11.html.

Kim, Kyung Hyun. 2004. *Remasculinization of Korean Cinema*. Durham, N.C.: Duke University Press.

————. 2005. "Lethal Work: Domestic Space and Gender Troubles in Happy End and the Housemaid." In *South Korean Golden Age Melodrama: Gender, Genre, and National Cinema*, edited by Kathleen McHugh and Nancy Abelmann, 201–228. Detroit, Mich.: Wayne State University.

————. 2011. *Virtual Hallyu: Korean Cinema of the Global Era*. Durham, N.C.: Duke University Press.

————. 2012. "The Blockbuster Auteur in the Age of Hallyu: Bong Joon-ho." In *Hallyu: Influence of Korean Popular Culture in Asia and Beyond*, edited by D. K. Kim and Min Sun Kim, 181–201. Seoul: Seoul National University Press.

————. 2017. "South Korean Cinema Story in the Digital Age: 21st Century Success on a 20th Century Medium." In *Routledge Handbook of Korean Culture and Society*, edited by Youna Kim, 206–230. London: Routledge.

Kim, Mee Hyun. 2013. *Korean Film Policy and Industry*. Seoul: Communication Books.

————. 2014. *Korean Film History*. Seoul: Communication Books.

Kim, Mee Hyun, and Jae-seok An. 2010. *Korean Cinema: From Origins to Renaissance.* Seoul: KOFIC.

Kim, Mi Hui. 2001. "Film Funding Frenzy." *Variety,* 25 December.

———. 2002. "Korean Netizens Invest in Local Pix." *Variety,* 1 January, 19.

Kim, Myung-Hwan. 1995. "Samsung Launched Samsung Entertainment Group." *Chosun Ilbo,* 7 February, 21.

Kim, Neimo. 2014. "Can Distributors Compete without Theaters?" *Variety,* 6 October.

Kim, Soochul, and Jeong-soo Kang. 2013. "Digging Gangnam Style Transmedia Storytelling in K-pop." *Journal of Communication Research* 50 (1): 84–120.

Kim, So-ri. 2016. "Korea-China Co-production Failed, but Made Profits." *Ilyo Shinmun,* 29 February. http://ilyo.co.kr/?ac=article_view&entry_id=166207.

Kim, Yong Won. 2012. "Korean Governments' Cultural Policy." *JoongAng Ilbo,* 7 December. http://news.joins.com/article/10107383.

Kim, Young A. 2015. *Unexpected Alliances: The Post-authoritarian State, Independent Film Networks, and the Film Industry in South Korea.* Stanford, Calif.: Stanford University Press.

Kline, Steve, Nick Dyer-Witheford, and Greg de Peuter. 2003. *Digital Play: The Interaction of Technology, Culture and Marketing.* Montreal: McGill-Queen's University Press.

KMBD (Korean Movie Data Base). 2017. "Catherin's Escape." http://www.kmdb.or.kr/vod/vod_basic.asp?nation=K&p_dataid=02692&keyword=%EC%BA%90%EC%84%9C%EB%A6%B0%EC%9D%98%20%ED%83%88%EC%B6%9C&pgGubun=08.

KMPPC (Korea Motion Picture Promotion Corporation). 1977. *Korean Film Source Handbook: From Initial Stage to 1976.* Seoul: KMPPC.

Knorr, Andreas, and Christina Schulz. 2007. "Public Film Funding Schemes in Germany: A Critical Assessment." *Culture Economy Research* 10 (1): 51–79.

Knowledge@Wharton. 2012. "Transmedia Storytelling, Fan Culture and the Future of Marketing." http://knowledge.wharton.upenn.edu/article/transmedia-storytelling-fan-culture-and-the-future-of-marketing/.

Ko, Dong-hwan. 2015. "Korean Webtoons Turn to Technology, Genre-Based Stories." *Korea Times,* 2 November. http://www.koreatimes.co.kr/www/news/culture/2016/09/148_18 9995.html.

KoBiz. 2017. "Co-production Case Study." http://www.koreanfilm.or.kr/jsp/coProduction/productionCaseList.jsp?pageIndex=1.

KOCCA (Korea Creative Content Agency). 2015. *Webtoon Industry Status Survey.* Naju, Korea: KOCCA.

KOFIC (Korean Film Council). 2003. "KOFIC Sums up 2002 Korean Films." Press release. 20 January.

———. 2006. *Korean Movie Industry Report of 2005.* Seoul: KOFIC.

———. 2007a. *Film Development Fund Report.* Seoul: KOFIC.

———. 2007b. *Korean Film History: From Origins to Renaissance.* Seoul: KOFIC.

———. 2007c. *Korean Movie Industry Report of 2006.* Seoul: KOFIC.

———. 2008. *2007 Korean Film Industry's Yearbook.* Seoul: KOFIC.

———. 2009. *Korean Film Industry White Paper 2008.* Seoul: KOFIC.

———. 2011a. *Korean Movie Industry Report of 2010.* Seoul: KOFIC.

———. 2011b. *Korean Cinema Today.* Seoul: KOFIC.

———. 2012. *2011 Korean Film Industry Annual Report.* Seoul: KOFIC.

———. 2013. *Korean Movie Yearbook of 2012.* Seoul: KOFIC.

———. 2014a. *Korean Film Industry Report of 2013.* Busan: KOFIC.

———. 2014b. *Korean Film Yearbook 2014.* Busan: KOFIC.

————. 2015a. *2014 Korean Film Industry Report.* Busan: KOFIC.

————. 2015b. "2015 Global International Festival Support Result." Press release. April.

————. 2016a. *Korean Film Yearbook 2016.* Busan: Sanjini.

————. 2016b. *Korean Movie Theaters of 2016.* Busan: KOFIC.

————. 2016c. *All Time Box Office Ranking.* Busan: KOFIC.

————. 2016d. *Korean Cinema Today 26.* Busan: KOFIC.

————. 2017a. *2016 Korean Film Industry Report.* Busan: KOFIC.

————. 2017b. "Meet Korean Stories Again around the World: Global Remakes of Korean Films." *Korean Cinema Today* 27:66–67.

————. 2017c. *KOFIC Location Incentive—2017 Guidelines.* Busan: KOFIC.

————. 2018a. *Chronicle Box Office.* Busan: KOFIC.

————. 2018b. *2017 Korean Film Industry Closing.* Busan: KOFIC.

————. n.d. *Introduction to Korean Film Council.* Seoul: KOFIC.

Kokas, Aynne. 2017. *Hollywood Made in China.* Berkeley: University of California Press.

Korea Herald. 1999. "Gov't to Support Culture-Related Industries." 12 May.

————. 2004. "Screen Quota Hot Topic Again in U.S. Talks." 1 July.

————. 2012. "Crowdfunding Rescues Provocative S. Korean Film." 2 October.

Korea Media Rating Board. 2017. "Responsibilities." http://www.kmrb.or.kr/intro/orgintroBiz.do.

Korean Film Archive. 2017. "Fun Facts about Korean Cinema: What Is the First Korean Movie?" https://eng.koreafilm.or.kr/kmdb/trivia/funfacts/BC_0000005064?page=2.

Korean Film Commission Research Report. 2001. *Analysis of the Korean Film Industry Structure.* Seoul: Korean Film Commission.

Korean Film Council. 2016. "About KOFIC." http://www.koreanfilm.or.kr/jsp/kofic/intro.jsp.

————. 2017. "Yearly Box Office." http://www.kobis.or.kr/kobis/business/stat/boxs/findYearlyBoxOfficeList.do?loadEnd=0&searchType=search&sSearchYearFrom=2014&sMultiMovieYn=N&sRepNationCd=K&sWideAreaCd=.

Korea Statistical Information Service. 2018. "KOCIS National Statistics Portal." http://kosis.kr/search/search.do.

Korea Times. 2004. "Director Kim Calls for Screening of Low-Budget Films in Theaters." 16 February.

————. 2005. "New Finance Minister to Rekindle Debate over Screen Quota." 16 March.

Kraidy, Marwan. 2002. "Hybridity in Cultural Globalization." *Communication Theory* 12 (3): 316–339.

Kunz, William. 2007. *Culture Conglomerates.* Lanham, Md.: Rowman & Littlefield.

Kwack Jung-so. 2016. "Opposition Pushing New Legislation to Root Out Government-Business Collusion." *Hankyoreh*, 21 December. http://english.hani.co.kr/arti/english_edition/e_national/775555.html.

Kwon, Nayoung Aimme. 2012. "Collaboration, Coproduction, and Code-Switching: Colonial Cinema and Postcolonial Archaeology." *Cross-currents: East Asian History and Culture Review* 5:9–38.

Lange, Andre, and Tim Westcott. 2004. *Public Funding for Film and Audiovisual Works in Europe–a Comparative Approach.* Paris: European Investment Bank.

Lankov, Andrei. 2007. "Dictating Sex." *Korea Times*, 13 December. https://www.koreatimes.co.kr/www/common/printpreview.asp?categoryCode=165&newsIdx=15479.

Lee, Claire. 2012. "Movies Based on Webtoons Flourish." *Korea Herald*, 23 November. http://nwww.koreaherald.com/view.php?ud=20121123000597.

Lee, Dong yeun. 2011. "Monopoly in Korea's Culture Industry Monthly Art World." Korea Focus. http://www.koreafocus.or.kr/design2/layout/content_print.asp?group_id=103492.

Lee, Hailey. 2014. "East Meets East: China's Increasing Appetite for South Korean Entertainment." *CNBC*, 25 November. https://www.cnbc.com/2014/11/24/ades-south-korean-entertainment.html.

Lee, Hanna. 1998. "S. Korea Quotas Split Gov't, Pic Biz." *Variety*, 17 August, 16.

Lee, Ho-jeong. 2009. "A Street Where Film Cameras Thrive." *Korea JoongAng Daily*, 12 January. http://mengnews.joins.com/view.aspx?aId=2899711.

Lee, Hyangjin. 2000. *Contemporary Korean Cinema: Identity, Culture and Politics*. Manchester: Manchester University Press.

———. 2005. "Chunhyang: Marketing an Old Tradition in New Korean Cinema." In *New Korean Cinema*, edited by Chi-Yun Shin and Julian Stringer, 63–78. New York: New York University Press.

Lee, Hyo Won. 2015. "South Korea–Vietnam Coproduction Becomes Top Film of All Time in Vietnam." *Hollywood Reporter*, 6 June. http://www.hollywoodreporter.com/news/south-korea-vietnam-production-becomes-761312.

———. 2016. "South Korean Film 'Miss Granny' to Get English, Spanish Language Remakes." *Hollywood Reporter*, 6 November. http://www.hollywoodreporter.com/news/south-korean-film-miss-granny-get-english-spanish-language-remakes-944612.

Lee, Jae Hyun. 2006. "Digital Films and Realism as Digital Aesthetics." *Journal of Communication Research* 42 (2): 41–65.

Lee, Jeong Yeon. 2015. "Webtoon-Based Drama and Films Will Be Boom in the New Year." *Dong-A Ilbo*, 5 January. http://news.donga.com/List/3/all/20150105/68905908/4.

Lee, Jin-hyuk. 2006. "The Screen Quota, the Meaning and Future." *Korean Film Observatory* 18:9–11.

Lee, Kevin. 2008. "The Little State Department: Hollywood and the MPAA's Influence on U.S. Trade Relations." *Northwestern Journal of International Law and Business* 28 (2): 371–397.

Lee, Maggie. 2016. "Film Review: *Inside Men*." *Variety*, 30 April. http://variety.com/2016/film/reviews/inside-men-film-review-1201758418/.

Lee, Nikki J. 2012. "'Asianization' and Locally Customized 'Kor-Asian' Movies: *Goodbye, One Day* (2010) and *Sophie's Revenge* (2009)." *Transnational Cinemas* 3 (1): 82–92.

Lee, Sangjoon. 2017. "Creating an Anti-communist Motion Picture Producers' Network in Asia: The Asia Foundation, Asia Pictures, and the Korean Motion Picture Cultural Association." *Historical Journal of Film, Radio and Television* 37 (3): 517–538.

———. 2019. "Seoul–Hong Kong–Macau: *Love with an Alien* (1957) and Postwar Korea-Hong Kong Coproduction." In *Asia-Pacific Film Coproduction: Theory, Industry and Aesthetics*, edited by Dal Yong Jin and Wendy Su, 256–274. London: Routledge.

Lee, Sangjoon, and Abe M. Nornes, eds. 2015. *Hallyu 2.0: Korean Wave in the Age of Social Media*. Ann Arbor: University of Michigan Press.

Lee, Tae hoon, and Byun Heewon. 2014. "Korea-China Coproduction 2.0." *Chosun Ilbo*, 15 September. http://news.chosun.com/site/data/html_dir/2014/09/15/2014091500260.html?Depo=twitter&d=2014091500260.

Lee, Woo-young. 2016. "Korean Webtoons Make Big Strides in Global Comics Market." *Korea Herald*, 16 August. http://www.koreaherald.com/view.php?ud=20160816000430.

Lee, Yong-cheol. 2014. "The Secret of Period Drama." *Korean Cinema Today* 18:34–37.

Lee, Youkyung. 2017. "Director Turns to Virtual Reality to Tastefully Show Tragedy." Associated Press, 2 October.

Line Webtoon. 2016. "Line Webtoon Adapts Global Sensation Noblesse for First Animated Movie." Press release. 4 February.

Lionner, Francoise, and Shu-mei Shih. 2005. *Minor Transnationalism*. Durham, N.C.: Duke University Press.

Lopez, Daniel. 1993. *Films by Genre: 775 Categories, Styles, Trends, and Movements Defined, with a Filmography for Each*. Jefferson, N.C.: McFarland & Company.

Lynn, Hyung-Gu. 2016. "Korean Webtoons: Explaining Growth." *Research Center for Korean Studies Annual—Kyushu University* 16:1–13.

Ma, K. 2014. "South Korea's Film Development Fund Extended." Film Business Asia, 14 December. http://www.filmbiz.asia/news/south-koreas-film-development-fund-extended.

Magder, Ted. 2004. "Transnational Media, International Trade and the Ideal of Cultural Diversity." *Continuum: Journal of Media and Cultural Studies* 18 (3): 385–402.

Malik, Sarita, Caroline Chapain, and Roberta Comunian. 2017. "Rethinking Cultural Diversity in the UK Film Sector: Practices in Community Filmmaking." *Organization* 24 (3): 303–329.

Markey, Sanford. 1965. "Korean Television Relies on Its U.S. Telefilm: $65 an Hour Rate." *Variety*, 2 June, 39, 49.

Mateer, John. 2017. "Directing for Cinematic Virtual Reality: How the Traditional Film Director's Craft Applies to Immersive Environments and Notions of Presence." *Journal of Media Practice* 18 (1): 14–25.

Maxwell, Richard. 1995. *The Spectacle of Democracy: Spanish Television, Nationalism, and Political Transition*. Minneapolis: University of Minnesota Press.

McChesney, Robert. 1999. *Rich Media, Poor Democracy*. Urbana: University of Illinois Press.

———. 2000. "The Political Economy of Communication and the Future of the Field." *Media, Culture & Society* 22:109–116.

———. 2001. "Global Media, Neoliberalism, and Imperialism." *Monthly Review* 52 (10). Accessed 10 May 2017. https://monthlyreview.org/2001/03/01/global-media-neoliberalism-and-imperialism/.

———. 2008. *The Political Economy of Media: Enduring Issues, Emerging Dilemmas*. New York: Monthly Review Press.

McChesney, Robert, and Dan Schiller. 2002. "The Political Economy of International Communications: Foundations for the Emerging Global Debate over Media Ownership and Regulation." Paper prepared for the UNRISD Project on Information Technologies and Social Development, as part of UNRISD background work for the World summit on the Information Society, April 2002, 6.

McMillan. 2011. "Film and Television Production in Canada." http://www.mcmillan.ca/files/Overview_film_television_production_in_Canada_s3.pdf.

MCST (Ministry of Culture, Sports and Tourism). 2014a. *2013 Content Industry Final Statistics*. Seoul: MCST.

———. 2014b. *Planning on the Growth of Manhwa Industry 2014–2018*. Seoul: MCST.

———. 2015. *Contents Industries Statistics*. Seoul: MCST.

———. 2016. *Contents Industries Statistics*. Seoul: MCST.

Messerlin, Patrick, and Jimmyn Parc. 2017a. "Subsidies and the Film Industry: Lessons from France and South Korea." *Asia Pacific Memo*, Memo #390, 18 January.

———. 2017b. "The Real Impact of Subsidies on the Film Industry (1970s–Present): Lessons from France and Korea." *Pacific Affairs* 90 (1): 51–75.

Mikos, Lothar. 2016. "Television Drama Series and Transmedia Storytelling in an Era of Convergence." *Northern Lights* 14:47–64.

Miller, Toby, and Richard Maxwell. 2006. "Film and Globalization." In *Communications Media, Globalization and Empire*, edited by Oliver Boyd-Barrett, 33–52. Eastleigh, U.K.: John Libbey Publishing.

Miller, Toby, Nitin Govil, J. McMurria, and Richard Maxwell. 2001. *Global Hollywood*. Bloomington: Indiana University Press.

Miller, Toby, Nitin Govil, J. McMurria, Richard Maxwell, and T. Wang. 2005. *Global Holly-wood 2*. London: British Film Institute.

Min, Eunjung, Jinsook Joo, and Han Kwak. 2003. *Korean Film: History, Resistance, and Democratic Imagination*. London: Praeger.

Ministry of Culture and Information. 1979. *Culture and Communication for 30 Years, 1948–1978*. Seoul: Ministry of Culture and Information.

———. 1986. *Cultural Plan in Sixth Five-Year Plan for Economic and Social Development*. Seoul: Ministry of Culture and Information.

Ministry of Culture and Tourism. 2001. *Korean Film Export Statistics 1970–2001*. Seoul: Ministry of Culture and Tourism.

———. 2002. "Statistics of Film Business 2002." http://www.mct.go.kr/uw3/dispatcher/korea/sub56.html.

Mirrless, Tanner. 2013. *Global Entertainment Media: Between Cultural Imperialism and Cultural Globalization*. London: Routledge.

Modern Korean Cinema. 2011. "Jopok Week: Im Kwon-taek's the General's Son (Janggunui Adeul) 1990." http://www.modernkoreancinema.com/2011/12/jopok-week-generals-son-janggunui-adeul.html.

Mosco, Vincent. 1996. *The Political Economy of Communication: Rethinking and Renewal*. London: Sage.

MPAA (Motion Picture Association of America). 2007. *Entertainment Industry Market Statistics*. Los Angeles: MPAA.

———. 2009. *The Economic Impact of the Motion Picture and Television Industry on the U.S.* Los Angeles: MPAA.

———. 2012. *Theatrical Market Statistics*. Los Angeles: MPAA.

———. 2014. *Theatrical Market Statistics of 2014*. Los Angeles: MPAA.

———. 2015. *Theatrical Market Statistics of 2015*. Los Angeles: MPAA.

———. 2016. *MPAA Comments regarding the 2016 National Trade Estimate Report on Foreign Trade Barriers*. Los Angeles: MPAA.

———. 2017. *The 2017 Theatrical and Home Entertainment Market Environment Report*. Los Angeles: MPAA.

Mudge, James. 2006. "The General's Son 1–3: Trilogy (1990, 1991, 1992). Movie Review." Beyond Hollywood, 19 November. http://www.beyondhollywood.com/the-generals-son-1-3-trilogy-1990-1991-1992-movie-review/.

Nam, Sunwoo. 1978. "National Systems: Republic of Korea." In *Broadcasting in Asia and the Pacific*, edited by John A. Lent. 41–55. Philadelphia: Temple University Press.

National Archives of Korea. 2007. *The Abolishment of the Screen Quota*. Seoul: National Archives of Korea.

National Association of Theater Owners. 2014a. "Number of Screens." http://natoonline.org/data/us-movie-screens/.

———. 2014b. "Top 10 U.S. and Canadian Circuits." http://natoonline.org/data/top-10-circuits/.

Neale, Stephen. 2005. *Sightlines: Genre and Hollywood*. London: Routledge.

Netzer, Dick. 1978. *The Subsidized Muse: Public Support for the Arts in the United States*. London: Cambridge University Press.

Newman, David. 2008. "Australia and New Zealand: Expats in Hollywood and Hollywood South." In *The Contemporary Hollywood Film Industry*, edited by Paul McDonald and Janet Wasko, 295–305. Oxford: Blackwell.

———. 2009. "In the Shadow of the Empire: Domestic Feature Film Policy in New Zealand and Canada, 1999–2007." In *Small Nations, Big Neighbours: New Zealand & Canada*, edited by Ian Conrich, Dominic Alessio, and Itesh Sachdev, 57–82. New Zealand: Kakapo Books.

Noh, Jean. 2014. "Avengers 2 Pact Signed in Korea." Screen Daily, 29 March. http://www
.screendaily.com/news/avengers-2-pact-signed-in-korea/5069737.article.
———. 2015. "The Faces of Korean Cinema." Korea Prospects 11:50–61.
Noh, John. 2016. "The Korean Directors, Actors on Government Blacklist." Screen Daily,
14 October.
Noh, KwangWoo. 2009. "Compressed Transformation of Korean Film Industry from Old to
New Regime." Asian Cinema 20 (1): 137–154.
Nye, Joseph. 2004. Soft Power: The Means to Success in World Politics. New York: PublicAffairs.
Oh, Chang-Kyu. 2002. "Netizen Fund Is Shrinking." Munhwa Ilbo, 15 June, 16.
Oh, Eun Ju. 1998. "Screen Quota for 80 Days." JoongAng Ilbo, 8 September, 35.
Oh, John Kie-chiang. 1999. Korean Politics: The Quest of Democratization and Economic Devel-
opment. Ithaca, N.Y.: Cornell University Press.
Oh, Myung, and James Larson. 2011. Digital Development in Korea: Building an Information
Society. London: Routledge.
O'Regan, Tom. 2008. "The Political Economy of Film." In The Sage Handbook of Film Studies,
edited by James Donald and Michael Renov, 244–261. London: Sage.
Ouellette, Lauris, and Justin Lewis. 2004. "Moving beyond the Vast Wasteland: Cultural
Policy and Television in the United States." In The Television Studies Reader, edited by Robert Allen and Annette Hill, 52–65. London: Routledge.
Paquet, Darcy. 2000. "Genrebending in Contemporary Korean Cinema." Koreanfilm.org,
6 July. http://koreanfilm.org/genrebending.html.
———. 2001a. "Hana Bank Launches Korea's First Film Fund." Screen Daily, 28 November.
https://www.screendaily.com/hana-bank-launches-koreas-first-film-fund/407635.article.
———. 2001b. "Netizen Funds." Koreanfilm.org, November. http://koreanfilm.org/netizen
.html. Originally published in Screen International.
———. 2002. "Censorship Issues in Korean Cinema, 1995–2002." Koreanfilm.org, http://
koreanfilm.org/censorship.html.
———. 2005. "The Korean Film Industry: 1992 to the Present." In New Korean Cinema,
edited by Chi-Yun Shin and Julian Stringer, 32–50. New York: New York University Press.
———. 2007. "CJ in a Rush to Partner with WB." Variety, 22 January. http://variety.com/
2007/film/markets-festivals/cj-in-a-rush-to-partner-with-wb-1117957875/.
———. 2008. "Where the Money Comes From: An Overview of the Korean Film Business."
ASEF Culture 360, 18 April. http://culture360.asef.org/magazine/funding-the-korean
-film-business/.
———. 2009. New Korean Cinema: Breaking the Waves. London: Wallflower Press.
———. 2011. "An Insider's View of a Film Industry in Transition: Darcy Paquet's Mediations
on the Contemporary Korean Cinema." Acta Koreana 14 (1): 17–32.
Parc, Jimmyn. 2016. "The Effects of Protection in Cultural Industries: The Case of the Korean
Film Policies." International Journal of Cultural Policy, 1–17. Online first.
Park, Agenes. 2010. "Chungmuro Embraces 3d Technology." Korean Cinema Today 6:6–7.
Park, Chan-IK. 2016. "Study the Phenomenon of Cross-media between Video Media and
Webtoon." International Journal of Multimedia and Ubiquitous Engineering 11 (5): 245–252.
Park, Eun-jee. 2012. "Conglomerates Direct Korea's Film Industry." JoongAng Daily, 8 Decem-
ber. http://mengnews.joins.com/view.aspx?aId=2963465.
Park, Geun Seo. 2006. "Minority, Cultural Diversity and Korean Society." In Diversity in Media
Culture in the Global Era, edited by Kyu-chan Geun, Young Ju Lee, and Geun Seo Park, 21–
42. Seoul: Communication Books.

Park, Hyo Jae. 2014. "Webtoon Looks over Dramas after Movies." *Kyunghyang Shinmun*, 31 October. http://news.khan.co.kr/kh_news/khan_art_view.html?artid=201410132141575&code=960801.

Park, Hyung Ki. 2014. "Daum Webtoon Goes Global." *Korea Herald*, 17 December. http://www.koreaherald.com/view.php?ud=20141217000431.

———. 2016. "China's Increasing Presence in Korean Entertainment." *Korea Herald*, 21 February. http://www.koreaherald.com/view.php?ud=20160221000255.

Park, Jeong-ho. 2001. "Court Rejects Film Censorship: Another Ruling Upholds Ban on Political Blacklisting." *Korea JoongAng Daily*, 31 August.

Park, Ji Won. 2014. "Chinese Film Signs to Buy Megabox." *Korea Times*, 25 December. http://www.koreatimes.co.kr/www/news/biz/2016/07/123_170545.html.

Park, Ji Yeon. 2001. "Film Policy in Park Chung Hee's Modernization System: Revision of the Motion Picture Law and Industrialization Policy." In *Korean Film and Modernity*, edited by Yu Shin Chu, 171–212. Seoul: Sodo.

———. 2005. "From the Enactment of the Motion Picture Law to the 4th Revision." In *A History of Korean Film Policy*, edited by Dong Ho Kim, 189–267. Seoul: Nanam.

Park, Nohchool. 2009. "The New Waves at the Margin: An Historical Overview of South Korean Cinema Movements 1975–84." *Journal of Japanese and Korean Cinema* 1 (1): 45–63.

Park, Seo Kyung. 2013. "The Golden Days of Webtoon." *Postech Times*, 20 March. http://times.postech.ac.kr/news/articleView.html?idxno=6814.

Park, Seung Hyun. 2002. "Film Censorship and Political Legitimation in South Korea, 1987–1992." *Cinema Journal* 42 (1): 120–138.

———. 2012. "Establishing a National Identity from Above: Film Production and Wholesome Movies in South Korea, 1966–1979." *Journal of Japanese and Korean Cinema* 4 (1): 53–67.

Park, Soomee. 2012. "Busan 2012: Korean Film Report Stirs Debate." *Hollywood Reporter*, 7 October. http://www.hollywoodreporter.com/news/busan-2012-korean-film-council-report-democratic-party-chun-byung-hun-376942.

Park, Young A. 2014. *Unexpected Alliances: Independent Filmmakers, the State, and the Film Industry in Post-authoritarian South Korea*. Palo Alto, Calif.: Stanford University Press.

Pendakur, Manjunath. 1990. *Canadian Dreams and American Control: The Political Economy of the Canadian Film Industry*. Detroit, Mich.: Wayne State University Press.

———. 2013. "Twisting and Turning: India's Telecommunications and Media Industries under the Neo-liberal Regime." *International Journal of Media & Cultural Politics* 9 (2): 107–131.

Pfanner, Eric. 2009. "Foreign Films Get a Hand from Hollywood." *New York Times*, 17 May.

Post, Guest. 2014. "Hollywood and the Government: A Longtime Partnership." Valuewalk, 1 August. http://www.valuewalk.com/2014/08/hollywood-funding/?all=1.

Presidential Transition Team. 2013. *The 21st Century National Goals*. Seoul: Presidential Transition Team.

PricewaterhouseCoopers. 2006. *Global Entertainment and Media Outlook, 2006*. New York: PricewaterhouseCoopers.

Producers Guild of America. 2010. "PGA Board of Directors Approves Addition of Transmedia Producer to Guild's Producers Code of Credits." 6 April. http://www.producersguild.org/news/39637/PGA-Board-of-Directors-Approves-Addition-of-Transmedia-Producer-to-Guilds-Producers-Code-of-Credits.htm.

Rasul, Azmat, and Jennifer Proffitt. 2012. "An Irresistible Market: A Critical Analysis of Hollywood–Bollywood Coproductions." *Communication, Culture & Critique* 5 (4): 563–583.

Rist, Peter H. 2004. "Korean Cinema Now: Balancing Creativity and Commerce in an Emergent National Industry." *Cineaction* 64:37–45.

Rosenberg, Scott. 2000. "Koreans Push Quota Issue." *Variety*, 31 July, 49.

Rousse-Marquet, J. 2013. "The Unique Story of the South Korean Film Industry." Inaglobal, 30 September. http://www.inaglobal.fr/en/cinema/article/unique-story-south-korean -film-industry.

Russell, Mark. 2005. "Korea Faces Film Diversity Issue." *Hollywood Reporter*, 4 January.

———. 2008. "Eastern Promises: Korea." *Hollywood Reporter*, 26 September.

Russell, Mark, and George Wehrfritz. 2004. "Blockbuster Nation: How Seoul Beat Hollywood, Making Korea an Asian Star." *Newsweek*, 4 May.

Salmon, Andrew. 2004. "At the Movies: South Korea's Battle with Hollywood." *International New York Times*, 15 November. https://global-factiva-com.proxy.lib.sfu.ca/ha/default .aspx#./!?&_suid=14849377707970834442578938597 9.

Schiller, Dan. 1996. *Theorizing Communication: A History*. New York: Oxford University Press.

Schiller, Herbert. 1969. *Mass Communications and American Empire*. Boulder, Colo.: Westview Press.

Schilling, Mark. 2013. "Why Hollywood Movies Are Plummeting at Japan Box Office." *Variety*, 21 October. http://variety.com/2013/biz/global/japan-hollywood-no-longer -dominates-box-office-1200752940/.

Schirm, Stefan. 1996. "Transnational Globalization and Regional Governance: On the Reasons for Regional Cooperation in Europe and the Americas." *Program for the Study of Germany and Europe Working Paper Series* 6 (2): 1–42.

Schulz, Michael, Fredrik Soderbaum, and Joakim Ojendal, eds. 2001. *Regionalization in a Globalizing World: A Comparative Perspective on Forms, Actors and Processes*. London: Zed Books.

Schwarzacher, Lucas. 2002. "Korean Pix Lose Luster in Japan." *Variety*, 14 July. http://variety .com/2002/film/news/korean-pix-lose-luster-in-japan-1117869653/.

Selznick, Barbara. 2008. *Global Television: Co-producing Culture*. Philadelphia: Temple University Press.

Seo, Seung-eun. 2015. "Potentials & Limitations of *Misaeng* as Transmedia Storytelling." *Korean Language and Literature* 128:277–308.

Seo, Uk Jin. 2007. "Is Hallyu Already Ending?" *Korean Economic Daily*, 8 June.

Servaes, Jan. 1989. "Cultural Identity and Modes of Communication." *Annals of the International Communication Association* 12 (1): 383–416.

Shackleton, Liz. 2014. "Korean Producers Criticize Market Monopoly." *Screen Daily*, 8 October.

Shapiro, Andrew. 2011. "Small Cinema's Antitrust Win: Big Implications for Large Exhibitor Chains." Seeking Alpha, 29 September. http://seekingalpha.com/article/296691-small -cinemas-antitrust-win-big-implications-for-large-exhibitor-chains?page=2.

Shim, Sun-Ah. 2015. "Avengers Sequel Reignites Screen Monopoly Debate." *Yonhap News*, 30 April.

Shim, Sun-Ah, and Jae-Young Cho. 2016. "Hollywood Studios' Foray into Korean Market to Stir Up Catfish Effect." *Yonhap News*, 12 September. http://english.yonhapnews.co.kr/ news/2016/09/12/48/0200000000AEN20160912009600315F.html.

Shin, Chi-Yun, and Julian Stringer, eds. 2005. *New Korean Cinema*. Edinburgh: Edinburgh University Press.

Shin, Jee Young. 2005. "Globalization and New Korean Cinema." In *New Korean Cinema*, edited by Chi-Yun Shin and Julian Stringer, 51–62. Edinburgh: Edinburgh University Press.

———. 2008. "Negotiating Local, Regional, and Global Nationalism, Hybridity, and Transnationalism in New Korean Cinema." Dissertation, Indiana University.

Shin, Jin A. 2015. "Naver Daumkakao Webtoon, Second Creation of 200–300 Cases." *Newsis*, 2 August.

Shome, Raka, and Radha Hedge. 2002. "Culture, Communication, and the Challenge of Globalization." *Critical Studies in Media Communication* 19 (2): 172–189.

Siapera, Eugenia. 2010. *Cultural Diversity and Global Media*. Malden, Mass.: Wiley-Blackwell.

Sigismondi, Paolo. 2012. *The Digital Glocalization of Entertainment: New Paradigms in the 21st Century Global Mediascape*. New York: Springer.

Simons, Nele, Alexander Dhoest, and Steven Malliet. 2012. "Beyond the Text: Producing Cross- and Transmedia Fiction in Flanders." *Northern Lights* 10:25–40.

Sims, David. 2015. "Netflix's $50 Million Movie Gamble." *The Atlantic*, 10 November.

Smith, Anthony, and Roberta Pearson. 2015. "Introduction: The Contexts of Contemporary Screen Narratives: Medium, National, Institutional and Technological Specificities." In *Storytelling in the Media Convergence Age*, edited by Roberta Pearson and Anthony Smith, 1–17. London: Palgrave.

Soh, Kai, and Brian Yecies. 2017. "Korean–Chinese Film Remakes in a New Age of Cultural Globalisation: *Miss Granny* (2014) and *20 Once Again* (2015) along the Digital Road." *Global Media China* 2 (1): 74–89.

Sohn, B. K. 2003. "Does the Government Reduce the Screen Quota for the BIT?" Ohmynews, 29 October. http://m.ohmynews.com/NWS_Web/Mobile/at_pg.aspx?CNTN _CD=A0000150925.

Sohn, Ji-young. 2014. "Korean Webtoons Going Global." *Korea Herald*, 25 May. http://www .koreaherald.com/view.php?ud=20140525000452.

Song, Gwang-ho, and Mi-na Im. 2013. "Korean Film Industry Renaissance." *Korea Focus*, 28 August.

Song, Jung-a. 2016. "China Awash with Korean Waver Fever." *Financial Times*, 12 April. https://www.ft.com/content/167338ec-faob-11e5-8e04-8600cef2ca75.

Song, Jung-Eun, Kee-Bom Nahm, and Won-Ho Jang. 2014. "The Impact of Spread of Webtoon on the Development of Hallyu: The Case Study of Indonesia." *Kore Entertainment Industry Association Journal* 8 (2): 357–367.

Song, Soon-jin. 2014. "Can Crowdfunding Be the New Gateway for Film Diversity?" Korean Film Biz Zone. Accessed 23 July 2019. https://www.koreanfilm.or.kr/eng/news/ features.jsp?pageIndex=32&seq=257&mode=FEATURES_VIEW&pageRowSize=10& blbdComCd=601024.

———. 2017. "Dreaming of a Wider World." *Korean Cinema Today* 28:36–39.

Song, Yeongkwan. 2012. "Audiovisual Services in Korea: Market Development and Politics." *ADBI Working Paper Series* 354:1–22.

Song, Y. S. 2012. "Webtoons' Current Status and Features and Webtoons-Based OSMU Strategies." *Kocca Focus* 57 (23 August): 3–27.

Soompi. 2014. "[Movie Review] *Miss Granny* Learns about Love and the Value of Family." 4 February. https://www.soompi.com/2014/02/02/movie-review-miss-granny-learns -about-love-and-the-value-of-family/.

Spangler, Todd. 2016. "Korea's Line Webtoon Digital Comics Publisher Signs with CAA for TV and Film Projects." *Variety*, 31 August. http://variety.com/2016/digital/news/line -webtoon-comics-caa-tv-film-1201847907/.

Sreberny-Mohammadi, Annabelle. 1997. "The Many Cultural Faces of Imperialism." In *Beyond Cultural Imperialism*, edited by P. Golding and P. Harris, 49–68. London: Sage.

Staiger, Janet. 2003. "Hybrid or Inbred: The Purity Hypothesis and Hollywood Genre History." In *Film Genre Reader III*, edited by Barry Grant, 185–202. Austin: University of Texas Press.

Statista. 2016. "Most Popular Movie Genres in North America by Box Office Revenues, 1995–2016." https://www.statista.com/statistics/188658/movie-genres-in-north-america-by-box-office-revenue-since-1995/.

Stavroula, Kalogeras. 2014. *Transmedia Storytelling and the New Era of Media Convergence in Higher Education*. London: Palgrave.

Stevensen, Richard. 1989. "Japanese Put up $100 Million to Back Films in Hollywood." *New York Times*, 21 August. http://www.nytimes.com/1989/08/21/business/japanese-put-up-100-million-to-back-films-in-hollywood.html.

Stiglitz, Joseph. 2002. "Globalism's Discontents." *American Prospect* 13 (1): A16–A21.

Street, Sarah. 2014. "Film Finances and the British New Wave." *Historical Journal of Film, Radio and Television* 34 (1): 23–42.

Stringer, Julian. 2005. "Putting Korean Cinema in Its Place: Genre Classifications and the Contexts of Reception." In *New Korean Cinema*, edited by Chi-Yun Shin and Julian Stringer, 95–105. Edinburgh: Edinburgh University Press.

Su, Wendy. 2011. "Resisting Cultural Imperialism, or Welcoming Cultural Globalization? China's Extensive Debate on Hollywood Cinema from 1994 to 2007." *Asian Journal of Communication* 21 (2): 186–201.

———. 2016. *China's Encounter with Global Hollywood*. Lexington: University Press of Kentucky.

———. 2019. "Is the China Party Over? Global Integration, State Intervention, and Changing China-Hollywood Relations: 2014–2018." In *Asia-Pacific Film Coproduction: Theory, Industry and Aesthetics*, edited by Dal Yong Jin and Wendy Su, 133–154. London: Routledge.

Thomson, David. 2005. *The Whole Equation: A History of Hollywood*. New York: Alfred. A. Knopf.

Tiffany, Kaitlyn. 2017. "*Okja* Is the First Great Netflix Movie—Here's Why That Matters." *The Verge*, 26 June. https://www.theverge.com/2017/6/26/15747466/netflix-okja-bong-joon-ho-snowpiercer-cannes-hollywood.

Trumbore, Dave. 2015. "Netflix Backs Bong Joon-ho's *Okja* with $50 Million." *Collider*, November 10. http://collider.com/okja-bong-joon-ho-netflix-brad-pitt-plan-b/.

Tyrrell, Heather. 1999. "Bollywood versus Hollywood: Battle of the Dream Factories." In *Culture and Global Change*, edited by Tracy Skelton and Tim Allen, 260–266. London: Routledge.

UNESCO. 2017. *2017 Global Report on the Protection and Promotion of the Diversity of Cultural Expressions*. Paris: UNESCO.

Union Investment Partners. 2016. "Leading Contents Investor in Korea." http://www.unionip.net/home_e/.

U.S. Department of Commerce. 2016. *Survey of Current Business*. Washington, D.C.: U.S. Department of Commerce.

USTR (U.S. Trade Representative). 2009. *Summary of the U.S.-Korea FTA*. Washington, D.C.: USTR.

———. 2015a. "Free Trade Agreements." https://ustr.gov/trade-agreements/free-trade-agreements.

———. 2015b. "Statement by Ambassador Michael Froman on the Third Anniversary of KORUS." Press release. March.

————. 2017. "Free Trade Agreements." https://ustr.gov/trade-agreements/free-trade -agreements.

Utin, Pablo. 2016. "Sliding through Genres: The Slippery Structure in South Korean Films." *Journal of Japanese and Korean Cinema* 8 (1): 45–58.

Variety. 1997. "Samsung Entertainment Group." 12 May, 54.

Vaughn, Stephen. 2005. "The Devil's Advocate Will H. Hays and the Campaign to Make Movies Respectable." *Indiana Magazine of History* 101 (2): 125–152.

Veron, Luc. 1999. "The Competitive Advantage of Hollywood Industry." *Columbia International Affairs Online.* http://www.ciaonet.org/wps/velo1.

Wang, Wei-Ching. 2008. "A Critical Interrogation of Cultural Globalization and Hybridity." *Journal of International Communication* 14 (1): 46–64.

Wasko, Janet. 1981. "The Political Economy of the American Film Industry." *Media, Culture & Society* 3:135–153.

————. 1982. *Movies and Money: Financing the American Film Industry.* Norwood, N.J.: Ablex.

————. 2003. *How Hollywood Works.* London: Sage.

————. 2004. "Show Me the Money: Challenging Hollywood Economics." In *Towards a Political Economy of Culture: Capitalism and Communication in the Twenty-First Century,* edited by A. Calabrese and C. Sparks, 131–150. Boulder, Colo.: Rowman & Littlefield.

Wasko, Janet, and E. Meehan. 2013. "Critical Crossroads or Parallel Routes? Political Economy and New Approaches to Studying Media Industries and Cultural Products." *Cinema Journal* 52 (3): 150–156.

Wasko, Janet, Graham Murdock, and Helena Sousa, eds. 2011. *The Handbook of Political Economy of Communication.* Malden, Mass.: Wiley-Blackwell.

Watson, James, ed. 1997. *Golden Arches East: McDonald's in East Asia.* Stanford, Calif.: Stanford University Press.

Weekly Chosun. 2014. "The World of Movie Investment." 18 August.

Won, Ho-jung. 2015. "Inside Men Sees Darkness Everywhere." *Korea Herald,* 19 November. http://www.koreaherald.com/view.php?ud=20151119001101.

Yecies, Brian. 2007. "Parleying Culture against Trade: Hollywood's Affairs with Korea's Screen Quotas." *Korea Observer* 38 (1): 1–32.

————. 2016. "The Chinese–Korean Co-production Pact: Collaborative Encounters and the Accelerating Expansion of Chinese Cinema." *International Journal of Cultural Policy* 22 (5): 770–786.

Yecies, Brian, and Aegyung Shim. 2011. *Korea's Occupied Cinemas, 1983–1948.* London: Routledge.

————. 2016. *The Changing Face of Korean Cinema: 1960 to 2015.* London: Routledge.

Yecies, Brian, Aegyung Shim, and Ben Goldsmith. 2011. "Digital Intermediary: Korean Transnational Cinema." *Media International Australia* 141:137–145.

Yim, Hak Soon. 2002. "Cultural Identity and Cultural Policy in South Korea." *International Journal of Cultural Policy* 8 (1): 37–48.

Yonhap News. 2012. "Kim Ki-duk Back with New Film *Pieta.*" 20 July.

————. 2013. "Success of Spy Comedy Reignites Debate over Screen Monopoly." 14 June.

————. 2016. "Global Big Investors Jump into Korean Movie Production and Distribution." 10 April.

————. 2017. "CGV and Lotte Won the Legal Case of Screen Monopoly over the Free Trade Commission." 15 February.

Yoon, Tae-Jin, and Dal Yong Jin, eds. 2017. *The Korean Wave: Evolution, Fandom, and Transnationality.* Lanham, Md.: Lexington.

Yoo Sun-hee. 2017. "Two Wings in Film Censorship—Korean Film Council and the Korean Fund of Fund Should Be Reburned." *Hankyoreh*, 1 May.

You, Emily, and Chloe Kang. 2016. "Webtoons as the New Trend for Korean Dramas and Films." Korea.com, 18 January. http://www1.korea.com/bbs/board.php?bo_table=SHOW &wr_id=1501.

Zimmer, Annette, and Stefan Toepler. 1999. "The Subsidized Muse: Government and the Arts in Western Europe and the United States." *Journal of Cultural Economics* 23:33–49.

INDEX

ABOUT THE AUTHOR

DAL YONG JIN is a professor at Simon Fraser University. His major research and teaching interests are on Korean cinema, globalization and media, transnational cultural studies, and the political economy of media and culture. Jin has published several books, including *Korea's Online Gaming Empire* (2010), *New Korean Wave: Transnational Cultural Power in the Age of Social Media* (2016), and *Smartland Korea: Mobile Communication, Culture and Society* (2017).